mamas and papas

# mamas and papas

## On the sublime and Heartbreaking Art of parenting

EDITED BY

Alys Masek
&
Kelly Mayhew

SAN DIEGO
CITY WORKS
PRESS

ISBN 978-0-9816020-8-0
Library of Congress Control Number: 2010930422


San Diego City Works Press is a non-profit press, funded by local writers and friends of the arts, committed to the publication of fiction, poetry, creative nonfiction, and art by members of the San Diego City College community and the community at large. For more about San Diego City Works Press please visit our website at www.cityworkspress.org.

San Diego City Works Press is extremely indebted to the American Federation of Teachers, Local 1931, without whose generous contribution and commitment to the arts this book would not be possible.

Cover Design: Rondi Vasquez
Production Editor: Will Dalrymple | Layout & Editing | http://www.willdalrymple.com

Published in the United States by San Diego City Works Press, California
Printed in the United States of America

To Georgia and Walter

# Contents

## wanting (or NOT)

## Because Beginnings Are Beautiful and sometimes Brutal

## Make a Joyful Noise

## push me pull me

# taxi to the dark side

## who are you? what do you do?

## no sorrow like this sorrow

# Turning the Tables

# Introduction

## Kelly Mayhew

Both of us have a snapshot stashed somewhere in our houses. It's of the two of us—grinning girls in our twenties, lounging in front of a Pepto-Bismal pink wall atop a hideous brown plaid loveseat, and flanking my then-boy-friend (and eventual husband). We're flushed with the thrill of having met a fellow traveler, for this was our first weekend together. And twenty years later, we're still of a piece. This is why I love this picture: it captures that exquisite moment when people meet and completely click.

Flash forward: in our forties, now, we're married, working, writing, mothers, friends, and comrades. In those first few heady years we lived heedlessly and neither of us had a glimmer of what it would be to have a child, no less a stable household, job, and relationship. We were in graduate school and in love with literature and life. For us, the world was full of the possibility of becoming. Now, as we watch our children tumble through their early years (Alys's daughter is two; my son is six), we see their possibilities, their joy at what the universe holds in store for them, their disappointment when they don't get what they want—*their* becoming.

Alys and I both had circuitous journeys into and through motherhood. At 37, when my husband and I decided we could embark on parenthood, I assumed that once I dispensed with birth control, BANG!, I'd be pregnant. When fourteen months later I finally turned the pregnancy test pee stick blue, I was horrified when the Women's Health clinic folks had to categorize me on my medical chart as being of "Advanced Maternal Age" and then they proceeded to watch me like a hawk. I assumed—again erroneously—that I could simply sail through my pregnancy, working an overload and research-ing a book on Oakland Raiders football fans, which entailed spending a good

deal of the first three-quarters of my maternal life sitting amongst the rowdy
and profane silver-and-black faithful in Oakland Coliseum's famed "Black
Hole" that fall. Suffice it to say I was lucky that the worst thing that happened was that Walt was born only five weeks early, small but healthy and
fully developed. To say motherhood was an adjustment is quite an under-
statement.

I suppose to make up for our manic work-lives, my husband and I decided
to try attachment parenting. Walt slept with us, was perpetually glued to
us in some form of baby device, and nursed on demand until he was 2½
years old. We figured we could compensate for our busy-ness by Velcro-ing
ourselves together when we were home. This was both a sublimely delicious
time and completely, utterly hellish. To watch our son grow and develop and
to feel his every chortle, burp, fart, coo, yell, and squirm, was a far more
intimate experience than my parents had with me. On the other hand, I
was continually wracked with not only each illness Walt was exposed to and
deliriously sleep-deprived every moment of every day, but I couldn't shake the
guilt at not doing *enough*—mothering, partnering, work. It got so bad that
I ended up with pneumonia when my boy was one and a half, and I lost all
my hair—permanently, as it turns out—due to a rare reaction to the wicked
combination of a freaked out immune system, stress, and sleep deprivation.
When we found an ideal preschool (Walt started it at 19 months without
having to be potty trained and it was a co-op that functioned as a vast, joyful,
extended family), I finally came back to myself enough to see, to paraphrase
the Grateful Dead, what a long, strange trip parenting is. As I watch Alys now
go through those early years with her daughter—especially after her own
devastating road to get to motherhood—it's hard for me not to view these
experiences as epic dramas writ, admittedly, small, yet epic nevertheless. To
raise another human being with grace and good humor, while done everyday
across the globe, is still an amazing achievement.

Thus as Alys and I have witnessed our children's lives as they unfold, being
the inveterate questioners that we are, we've also been reading and writing
about "parenting." Yet often the books we read, while largely helpful, were
mostly just that: aids to childrearing. As two of the founders of City Works
Press and thus smitten with literature, we wanted to put together an anthology that doesn't aim to instruct so much as it zeroes in on feeding the mind

and soul. In both of our maternal paths, we've experienced the angst of feeling cut off from art, thinking, and life. Raising small children, as many have noted, can be mind-numbingly boring even as the time goes by so quickly. Hence, in *Mamas and Papas*, we selected authors that spoke of the truths of being parents artfully, deliciously, heartwrenchingly. For it is in the intense intersections of poetry and prose that we can get at the root of what it is to want (or not want), raise, and let go of children. As several in this anthology have noted in various ways, just as you get used to your child being one way they are replaced by someone new. Each moment of their lives is truly a moment of becoming, like the Taoist symbol of yin-yang.

*Mamas and Papas*, then, is arranged along the lines of a journey beginning with texts that articulate the poignancy of wanting—or choosing not—to have a child. We then take our readers through the first moments of parenthood, the joys of having small children and older ones, the harrowing times when one doubts one's sanity at ever starting a family, the crises of identity, the sorrow of losing a pregnancy or a child, and the complex relationships one develops with one's own parents in course of one's life. The pieces included here range from Wanda Coleman's stark poem about the brutality of want in " 'Tis Morning Makes Mother a Killer" and Richard Krawiec's "don't worry," which details a young mother's descent into mental illness, to Neal Pollack's laugh-out-loud description of a car trip with his young son in "This is What I've Become: Scenes from the Life of an American Parent" and Amy Yelin's recounting of her son's favorite plaything in "Once Upon a Penis." Our authors present a gloriously kaleidoscopic vision of parenthood that we hope will feed readers' minds and souls.

## Alys Masek

More than anything else, this book is the product of a decades-long friendship between my co-editor Kelly and myself. When we first met, we were in our twenties, both of us in school, and we bonded almost immediately over our shared idiosyncratic tastes in books, our passion for the Grateful Dead and obscure American roots music. Most importantly, we shared a fierce desire to squeeze every single bit of joy out of life.

Our friendship grew and deepened over the years. We took road trips together up and down the coast of California, went to countless Dead shows, and spent many a night at dive bars and all-night restaurants arguing passionately about everything from Henry Miller to whether Van Morrison or Jerry Garcia was the better singer. After I moved up to San Francisco, and Kelly and her boyfriend (and later husband) Jim decamped to Ohio for grad school, they came out every Christmas and spent at least a week sleeping on the hard wooden floor of my flat in the Haight. We spent our time hanging out at City Lights Books, drinking beer at Vesuvio's, and crossing the bay bridge for jazz shows at Yoshi's. This is all to say that becoming parents was the last thing on our minds. Like many middle-class Americans of a certain generation we were putting off many of the responsibilities of adulthood in favor of a protracted honeymoon of me time.

The mommy bug bit Kelly first. We were in our mid-thirties and Kelly and Jim were in San Francisco visiting when she told me that they were trying for a baby. I was absolutely thrilled for her. But even as I rejoiced, I was thinking inside, *no way, no way, no way*, did I want that for myself. Nearly a year and a half later, I flew down to San Diego for Kelly's shower. She was radiant and glowing with a perfect pregnancy bump. I tucked a Sharon Olds poem into the box with the baby clothes and the belly cream. Shortly thereafter, Kelly gave birth to a gorgeous baby boy named Walt.

It took another year for the mommy bug to bite me. But it bit hard. Suddenly, I was seized by a fierce and totally unexpected desire for a baby. Five long years of disappointment and heartbreak followed. Only those who have experienced infertility know what oceans of hurt, grief, bitterness and bile can be packed into the seemingly innocuous verb *trying*.

Finally, I was not only able to get pregnant but to stay pregnant. My baby was due at the end of August. I waded through the last months of my pregnancy breathless and huge, constantly stroking the hard ball of her head lodged under my ribcage. However, after all the heartbreak I had endured, I simply could not imagine what would come after she was born. In some strange, deep down place, I thought that if I started acting and planning as if I really was going to be a mom, then whatever sadistic god was in charge of my fertility would snatch my baby back, and I would once again be childless. I could not think past the day of her birth.

But as everyone who has been pregnant and had a baby, knows, as amazing and complicated as pregnancy is, it is only the beginning of the joyous and sometimes terrifying story of what it means to become a parent.

As a parent, you can only pray that the better angel of your nature will prevail, that you will summon up the patience, the wisdom, the love, and most of all the humor necessary to raise a child. And you must do this over and over again — when you are feeling your worst, strung out and exhausted from lack of sleep, after a long day with a cranky toddler who smacks you in the nose with a toy, while having to say no to a teen-ager who looks at you like you are some kind of crazy, clueless idiot. At its best, parenting is as natural and joyous as cubs wrestling in the grass. At its worst, you will find yourself wanting to hurl your child against a wall.

It is that depth and complexity of what it means to be a parent that we have tried to represent in this collection. As I read through the pieces for this book the line "I contain multitudes" from Walt Whitman's "Song of Myself" kept running through my head. Raising children is a universal rite of passage, yet each person's experience of parenthood is so different. Parenthood is a container for so many stories — stories of love, hope, despair, rage, and heartbreak.

We have dipped into that container to offer our readers a look at the entire spectrum of parenting from that first yearning for a child, to the wonder of touching the hot velvet of a newborn's head, through the storms and joys of adolescence. We also look at what it feels like not to have children. Thus we have Thea Sullivan's heart-wrenching account of her struggle with infertility and the lessons it taught her in accepting suffering as a fact of the human condition. Her piece ends, not with the birth of a child, but with the understanding that to be human is to suffer. I must also mention Dorianne Laux's gorgeously written poem about her daughter at twelve. Her poem perfectly captures the excitement of entering adolescence, while also suggesting the mother's loss as she moves into the background of her daughter's life. And then there is one of my personal favorites, Thomas Turman's "Gang of Eleven" in which he writes about his two daughters and their "gang" of nine friends. As he describes the breakfasts he cooks for them, the stories he hears, and the beautiful, self-confident young women they become, I wanted to bottle whatever parental magic he has, to save it for my own daughter's adolescence.

Tina Traster's "Love Learned" offers a very different perspective on what it means to be a parent. In this piece, she writes with painful honesty of her struggle to love her adopted daughter who suffers from attachment disorder as a result of the time she spent in an orphanage. Love does not come easily to either Traster or her daughter, but eventually they are able to create a fierce and loving mother-daughter bond. And lastly, I must mention Steve Kowit's long poem in celebration of his parents. He depicts his parents with such abounding love, with such clear-eyed affection, that he affirms that when you actually manage to be a good parent, the love you give comes back to you in ways and at times that you might never expect.

Above all else, this collection speaks of the powerful desire we all have to connect, to the resiliency of love, and to the fact that, at its best, parenting is a sublime and beautiful art.

# wanting
## (or Not)

*Bethellen Levitan*

# Cradle Space
## (On Wanting a Child)

Rings of a mobile circle in the swell
that seeps through the space
between window and sill.
Fog like milk
leans against the glass.

There's too much space in bed, the roof rises
on a room for voices
that accumulate as I sleep.
In the murmur
the meeting of unborn children.

I wake to a wind
in my heart, hope an umbrella
open against the wooly gale.
Intent to urge
one soul forward,
I curve my fingers, imagine
that I can deftly hook
and lift
one child
like a beet
from loose soil.

Sit back on my heels
adoring
in my dripping hand,
one child
washed by the rain,

one soul untangled,
a knot
worked free.

*Thea Sullivan*

# Trying

*Who can ever learn the will of God? Human reason is
not adequate for the task, and our philosophies tend to
mislead us... All we can do is make guesses about things
on earth*
—Wisdom 9:13–6
*The Good News Bible*

Recently, samples of baby products—diapers, formula, wipes—have begun
showing up in my mail. Packets of coupons with smiling infants on them
arrive in envelopes that say, "Congratulations!" in big red letters.

The first time the mail carrier rang my bell to deliver one of these packages,
I came down two flights of stairs, eager to find out what it was. Maybe a gift?
A catalogue order? The woman handed me a bright yellow box, which I soon
realized was a sample of Enfamil formula. I stood frozen in the doorway, my
mouth open as if to call out in protest. By the time I found my voice, she had
disappeared across the street.

Not so long ago, I would have pondered the hidden meaning of these
packages. I would have wondered if they were a good omen for my husband and me, a sign that our luck would soon change. And being a good
sport about the mix-up could only help our chances, demonstrate our cosmic
deservedness, our worthiness to have a child. (And what of the bitterness, the
rising bile of jealousy and anger? Better to push it down.)

Now I'm more likely to assume that some doctor or fertility lab simply
sold our address to the baby-product companies who, using a cruel calculus,

send promotional products to couples who are trying to conceive on the odds that some of them have gotten lucky. Clearly they're not worried about the ones like us, who haven't.

I implored the mail carrier to stop delivering these products, but still I couldn't figure out what to do with the formula that had already been delivered. Even if I didn't see its arrival as a sign, what I chose to do with it seemed fraught with symbolic meaning. Throwing it out seemed a bitter gesture that might cement our fate. Giving it to a pregnant friend, while sensible, felt like capitulation. Finally I tucked the box away in the back of our pantry, so it will be there if we ever need it—no, I correct myself, *when* we do.

From the start I was sure that Brian and I would conceive easily. I knew plenty of couples who'd had trouble, including my sister and her husband. But for years my intuition had told me: *You won't have trouble getting pregnant.* So waiting until my midthirties didn't worry me. Sure, I had read all the statistics—I just didn't believe they would apply to us. I thought that we would conceive easily because we deserved to. We were both teachers who loved kids, and we'd both spent a long time in therapy, which would only make us better parents. On top of that, our marriage was great—a true friendship, full of respect and honesty. Of course we would have kids.

We weren't oblivious to the passage of time—I was thirty when we married, Brian thirty-five—but we wanted a couple of years alone together. Admittedly, Brian was ready for children sooner than I was: I had a manuscript I wanted to finish, a project whose completion seemed crucial to my sense of self. Besides, I didn't want the low cloud cover of an unfulfilled dream darkening my parenting years. Both Brian and I had been raised by very young parents with troubled marriages. It seemed obvious that the more self-aware and fulfilled we were starting out, the better we'd do raising kids. Surely the universe would recognize that.

We started trying a month before my thirty-fourth birthday, giddy to be "playing without a goalie," finally free from birth control. After the first month, I was sure I was pregnant: my breasts felt different, my taste for food changed, and I sometimes got so dizzy I almost passed out. But then my period arrived more or less on schedule, and it did again the next month. That's when I got serious. I bought books, meticulously charted my temperature and cervical fluid, tracked ovulation patterns. We had sex on a schedule, in the missionary position, with me lying knees-up for twenty minutes after-ward. Once in a while, for good measure, we threw out the rule book and just had fun, figuring a child might prefer to enter the world as a result of some old-fashioned sexual abandon.

That first spring, a dove built her nest just outside the back door of our apartment in San Francisco and laid a perfect, pale egg in it. Brian brought me out to see it, and we stood there in silence, not needing to speak aloud the meaning it seemed to hold. For weeks we waited, careful not to disturb the nesting dove. But the egg never hatched. It just lay there, beautiful and inert.

Everybody's got a theory about why couples do or don't conceive. Friends and relatives shared stories about what they believed were the triggering events for them. "It was when my wife started taking prenatal vitamins," or "when we got a dog," or "when we cleared a space in the house for the baby." I had my own speculations: maybe the baby was choosing a particular astrological sign for herself. (I felt certain we'd have a girl.) Maybe she was waiting for me to finish my manuscript, or for Brian to complete his master's degree. I pictured her floating above us somewhere, amused by our worries.

As the months dragged on, a few friends asked if I'd examined any mixed feelings I might have about being a mother. This made me angry: were they blaming me for not getting pregnant? But secretly I wondered the same thing. Could I be unconsciously blocking conception in some way?

Like a lot of people I knew, I had gradually adopted the idea that we create our own reality, that our lives are a reflection of our thoughts, beliefs, and intentions. And just as we could create fortunate events in our lives, we could also bring misfortune or illness our way. When bad things happened, it meant we had fallen out of alignment with our divine origins or needed to learn a lesson. A book called *You Can Heal Your Life*, by Louise L. Hay, was the bible of such thinking. It featured a chart listing every imaginable physical malady and its corresponding emotional or mental cause. An ingrown toenail indi-cated "guilt about the right to move forward"; bleeding gums, "lack of joy in the decision made in life"; deafness, "rejection, stubbornness, loneliness."

I was a Louise Hay aficionado around the time my sister and her husband were going through their own infertility nightmare, which included multiple miscarriages. I felt terrible for them, but at the same time I nursed private thoughts about why this might be happening: her own unmet childhood needs and unacknowledged ambivalence toward parenthood. She had never been in therapy or done much spiritual work, and so, I believed, was more susceptible to such dramatic wake-up calls. Other family members whispered about my sister's stress level and possible depression, which "everyone knows hurts fertility."

Looking back, I think we were really protecting ourselves from the reality of my sister's raw suffering. Rather than feel the pain she and her husband were going through and acknowledge that we might one day suffer just as randomly and abjectly, we distanced ourselves with convenient theories. *Thank God*, I said to myself back then, *that I have the tools to work through my own issues before becoming a parent.*

At the six-month mark, on the book's recommendation, Brian gamely agreed to a sperm test. He told me later he'd had a feeling there'd be a problem. It was a November night, and darkness had fallen early. Brian and I sat quietly at the dining-room table, stunned by the test results: *Eleven million...low motility...might consider a donor.*

While 11 million sounded like a lot, it turned out to be only a fifth of normal. (Sperm counts have declined so dramatically in the developed world that the "normal" count keeps getting lower.) And "low motility" meant that, of the 11 million, only 10 percent were good swimmers. In follow-up tests, after Brian quit taking hot baths, the count more than doubled and the motility improved a bit, but both remained well below normal.

The only treatments for low sperm count are artificial insemination — injecting a specially treated sample of Brian's sperm into my uterus — and in-vitro fertilization, in which eggs would be removed from my body and joined with Brian's sperm in a lab; then the fertilized eggs would be implanted in my uterus. We could not yet imagine undergoing either treatment. And using a sperm donor felt out of the question; we wanted this baby to be both of ours. So we just kept trying ourselves. Out of all those sperm, we figured, we only needed *one.*

We were on vacation in Italy when we hit the one-year mark, an anniversary that, according to the books we'd read, signaled the need to see a fertility specialist. I had fantasized that a leisurely, romantic trip would do the trick: we could just relax and let it happen. After three weeks there, when my period arrived yet again, I was crushed. I emerged from the bathroom, sobbing inconsolably. There was no denying it anymore: we were in the infertility club, the one I had thought we would never join.

Then, just after we returned home, Brian was running by the Rose Garden in Golden Gate Park when he heard the words distinctly in his head: *Rosie's coming.* He heard the phrase again and again as he ran. It made no sense to him, until I told him that "Rose" was the name I had been leaning toward for a girl. *Rosie's coming.* Our spirits lifted, and I started to see roses everywhere I looked.

Still, I remembered the dove's egg that never hatched, and I didn't want to take chances. I made an appointment for my own fertility consultation. Though I was convinced that my reproductive system was in good working order, it seemed only fair to get checked out myself.

Then, before I had a chance to go to my first fertility appointment, my sense of smell went into overdrive and I found myself unable to eat a maple pecan muffin because it was too, well, *mapley*. The thin pink line on the drugstore test confirmed it: after more than a year of trying, I was finally pregnant.

Here's a partial list of the theories I had about why: 1. I had accepted that we were in the infertility club. 2. I had made the fertility appointment, letting go of my stubborn insistence that there was nothing wrong with me. 3. I had been brought down from my self-righteous spiritual pedestal.

Brian's and my reactions to conceiving were different. He was deliriously happy—for days he couldn't stop smiling—but also acutely nervous that something would go wrong. He arranged a little altar on his dresser for the safety of the baby: a stone placed in a tray of sand, surrounded by Buddhist prayer beads.

Though deeply relieved and pleased, I was suddenly plagued with fears about the downside of parenthood: the loss of time, the threat to my work, the potential for losing some of my hard-won sense of self. I felt profoundly guilty about this. How, after twelve months of longing, could I suddenly feel so afraid of having a child?

My therapist assured me that my fears were normal. Because I had felt subsumed by my mother's emotional needs growing up, she explained, I perceived any mother-child relationship as potentially suffocating. "The difference," she said, "is that you didn't want to take care of your mother. But you will want to take care of your child."

Unlike Brian, whose mother had suffered multiple miscarriages when he was a boy, I had few fears about pregnancy itself. I had always looked forward to being pregnant, despite the inevitable discomforts. I wanted to experience new life unfolding in my body. My best friend and I chatted excitedly about baby showers and maternity clothes. I was confident I would carry the baby to term.

"Wow, Thea, you're playing with fire," my brother said when I told him I was pregnant. Not, *Congratulations*. Not, *I know how much you've wanted this.*

I gripped the phone, my heart a hot stone in my chest. "Are you saying that my baby is going to die," I demanded in a shaky voice, "because I told you about it?" But I knew that was exactly what he was saying. He and his wife, who'd had two easy pregnancies resulting in two gorgeous children, had a superstition that sharing the news during the first trimester increased the risk of miscarriage—akin, I suppose, to baseball fans talking about a no-hitter in progress.

Two weeks later, I lay flat on my back in an examination room, Brian at my side, staring at the grainy gray shape of a tiny curled fetus on the ultra-sound screen. An agonizing silence filled the room. The doctor could find no heartbeat. I felt as if I were falling from a great height. The hard look on Brian's face told me that he wasn't surprised. Before we left the office, the doctor stretched out his arms and hugged us.

What they don't tell you about miscarriage is that, whether it starts with bleeding or not, you have to take drastic, painful measures to get the fetus out of your body. I knew I didn't want surgery, and so, with the support of my doctor, I decided to use herbs to stimulate contractions. For four hours I lay on the bathroom floor, Brian at my side, my pelvis exploding with pain. The bright red blood, the tiny fetus passing through me—I needed these things to know it had been real.

The next night, Brian and I climbed to the roof of our building to for a makeshift ritual of mourning. I hurled the white stick of our positive preg-nancy test off the roof. Brian tossed a handful of tiny plastic babies that had come tied to the ribbons of congratulatory balloons. One by one, we sent these frustratingly weightless objects flying and watched as they dropped into other peoples' backyards, three stories below.

My grief after the miscarriage was thick and gray. Besides the heartbreaking loss of the pregnancy itself, I felt guilty for having responded to impending motherhood with fear. (*Could it have been my fault?*) Worst of all, my unspoken assumption that my self-awareness kept me safe from harm was unveiled for what it had always been: an attempt to take credit for good fortune and keep fear at bay.

As a child, I'd often thought that if I was good, my parents would love me better, would even love each other more. By the time I began trying to get pregnant, I thought that I had given up this good-girl fantasy, but it turned out I had just transferred it from my parents to God: *If I am a good person, I will get pregnant.* Even though conceiving a child is a two-person act, even though Brian's sperm count was clearly an issue, even though I was thirty-five, I had somehow imagined it was all up to me and my goodness.

In the years since then, I've read countless books. I've tried cleanses, special diets, and an exercise video called *Yoga for Fertility.* I've taken licorice, red clover, and chaste tree root. I once drank, for fourteen days, a nauseating concoction of condensed milk and the water in which the heads of twelve light pink carnations had been soaked overnight—a Turkish home remedy that came with the promise, "Everyone I've ever prescribed this to has gotten pregnant."

Brian has eaten huge quantities of garlic (first thing in the morning, of course) and taken saw palmetto, devil's claw, and Swedish bee pollen. We have prayed to the Virgin of Guadalupe, Saint Anne (Mary's mother, who was barren for many years), and Saint Gerard (patron saint of pregnancy). We've created altars, displayed African fertility symbols, drunk Lourdes water, and eaten *vibuti*—healing holy ash manifested by the Indian guru Sathya Sai Baba. For a while, I knelt on the floor every morning and repeated Psalm 113 aloud: "To the childless wife he gives a home, and gladdens her heart with children."

We have worked with an acupuncturist, a homeopath, and an outrageously expensive, world-traveling naturopath from New Zealand. We have seen Western doctors, psychics, astrologers, medical intuitives, and a Christian healer who claimed to have once cured a woman's MS overnight. The acupuncturist said my spleen ch'i was too low. The naturopath claimed, after examining the irises of my eyes, that my intestine was resting on my uterus, changing its shape and decreasing the blood flow. One Western doctor diagnosed polycystic ovary syndrome, while the other assured me my ovaries looked great but that I had a "lazy" pituitary gland. (Both MDs checked the ultrasound and pronounced my uterus "gorgeous.")

One doctor said it had been a fluke that we conceived the first time, and that we shouldn't count on it happening again without in-vitro fertilization. The psychics mostly saw no reason why we shouldn't conceive naturally. The Christian healer swore it all hinged on the depth of our faith, our belief that it could happen. The astrologer said that invasive medical treatment was indicated in my chart—was, in fact, my karma. (Much later, after we tried in vitro and it failed, the Christian healer told us that had we *not* done it, I would have become pregnant.)

It might seem like masochism, going to so many different healers and doctors, seeking out countless opinions that are bound to contradict one another, but it's impossible to overstate the depth of the desire, once awakened, to have a child.

A friend once said to me, as I dissolved in tears across the table, "You just need to surrender." Her tone was matter-of-fact, distant. I wanted to pick up my chair and hit her with it.

Brian and I sat on the porch of my family's cabin in Vermont, watching the birch leaves shimmer in the breeze and the bumblebees tumble around the garden. Our dog settled into the warm grass and sighed. It was July, and we were by ourselves, taking the summer off: no remedies, no temperature charting. Our days were long and lazy, punctuated only by dips in the local pond and walks along the dirt roads around the cabin. We made love for pleasure, in a light-filled room with a view of the green hillsides. We needed, for a little while, to stop trying.

And yet, even as I sat on the porch letting everything go, I couldn't help harboring hopes of our very own "boom" story. You know, the ones where the infertile couple finally gives up trying and *boom*: they conceive. Or they file for adoption, and *boom*. Or they walk away from the fertility clinic, sell their house, start living on a boat, and *boom*. People love these stories. They can't help but enjoy the tidy ending: *All along they just needed to let go. How obvious!*

For those in the midst of infertility, however, these stories are infuriating. First of all, such cases are statistically uncommon. Most people who seek fertility treatment end up actually needing it, and you never hear about the couples who give up and *nothing* happens. Second, there is an unsettling glibness to the suggestion that infertile couples just need to relax. While stress surely hinders fertility, infertility also causes stress. Studies show that couples suffering infertility are as anxious and depressed as cancer patients. Would we tell someone with cancer to "just relax"?

Finally, as happy as the boom stories are, they offer no practical advice, because it's impossible to let go of the desire to conceive as a strategy for conceiving. Foregoing treatment in the hopes that giving up will result in a pregnancy is a recipe for regret. What these stories tell us, if they tell us anything, is that for the boom to happen — if, in fact, it is to happen — you have to get to a point where you've actually given up. And you can't get there until you get there.

Brian was ready to try medical intervention long before I was, but since I was the one who would have to undergo the invasive procedures, he deferred to me, and I dragged my feet as long as I could. It wasn't just that I found the Western approach alienating, a slippery slope of drugs and invasive procedures leading all too quickly, it seemed, to the high-stakes endgame of egg and sperm joined in a petri dish. It wasn't just the mind-boggling expense of it all, or the potential health risks. And it wasn't just that we had once conceived on our own. Most of all, I was plagued by the spiritual questions: What did it mean to use technology to create life? How did I reconcile my belief in God's will with the dry scientific approach of the fertility clinic? If everything we had tried thus far — all of it "natural" and therefore, I believed, more spiritual — had failed, was it plain bullheadedness to keep trying? Or was it only logical to try a more scientific route?

I longed to surrender to divine guidance: *Whatever you ask of me, I will do.* But what happens when you can't hear the voice of God, or even the voice of your own intuition? How do you surrender if you don't know what you're surrendering to? I didn't know whether surrender meant giving up my resistance to medical treatment, or giving up the timeline and letting it happen when it happened. Was continuing holistic treatment an example of being patient, or stubborn? Maybe surrender meant stopping altogether, just giving up. (*And then*, a small voice says, *maybe...boom.*)

What I knew was that I could no longer blame my mental state for what was happening to us. I had to accept the possibility that we might never know why, that there would be no magic solution, no "right thing" to do.

On my thirty-seventh birthday, which happened to fall on Easter, I went to Catholic mass for the first time since I was a child. There, amid the incense, the music, and the liturgy, I fell to my knees and wept. Listening to the kindly Jesuit priest's words, it came to me: we don't know why we suffer. Even Jesus wanted a reprieve from what he was asked to endure: "Father, take this cup from me." Inexplicable suffering, and being with others who are suffering, is part of what it means to be human.

I made an appointment at the fertility clinic. What had finally tipped it for me was when a dear friend fell in love with a woman he'd met on Match.com. Their wedding was a ridiculously joyful occasion. It seemed clear that God was working through the Internet. Why not the fertility clinic too?

"Your uterus looks good," Dr. Wong said, pointing to vague shapes on the ultrasound screen. "Your hormone tests are fine. And see here? You've already ovulated." He dictated a few numbers to the nurse next to him, then turned again to me. "Still, I recommend that you do in-vitro fertilization as soon as possible. Talk to your husband. See what he says."

It was just as I had feared: they were pushing us toward a treatment I still didn't feel ready for.

We finally settled on another clinic, where we tried artificial insemination first. One day we got stuck in traffic, along with our vial of sperm. In all the stress and excitement we had forgotten about morning rush hour, and at the appointed time we were only halfway to the clinic, the plastic jar stuck in Brian's pants for warmth. Brian cursed and ran a few lights, and we made it in time for the sperm to be cleaned and spun around in the centrifuge. Then we went out to breakfast, passing the time before the insemination by idly speculating on what "the boys" were doing now.

I was happily surprised by the new clinic we'd found. I had pictured dour, chilly, statistic-spewing doctors, not these compassionate, warm people who were helping us. And it was a relief, after years of going it alone, to finally have someone — or, more accurately, a whole team of someones — who would take the wheel. All we had to do was manage our emotional lives along the way (no small feat). They didn't promise success, just vowed to do the best they could. After all the false promises, this felt oddly refreshing, even comforting.

Once we'd begun medical treatment, we tore through our options with alarming speed. In preparation for artificial insemination, I took several cycles of Clomid, a pill that stimulates ovulation (and causes unbearably foul moods). But because of my "lazy" hormones, it wasn't enough. I needed the big guns of injectible drugs. And so we found ourselves in our kitchen every evening, mixing up powders and diluent and injecting me in the thigh with, among other things, a substance made from the urine of menopausal nuns. Though it was odd to be using a drug made from someone's urine, I liked knowing that it had come from women who'd spent their whole lives praying. (The other option was a drug made from hamster hormones.)

After our crosstown sperm adventure and a long breakfast, we returned to the clinic. As the doctor was preparing the catheter that would carry Brian's newly cleaned-and-spun sperm high into my uterus, he told us the sperm numbers had been bad, and not to expect too much.

His prediction of failure proved correct. After several days of sobbing, I decided I couldn't take waiting anymore. I was ready for in vitro fertilization.

"Now," the priest said, "we await with hopeful expectancy the coming of the child, and with him, a great light." I listened from the shadowy pews, full of hope and fear and inflamed hormones. After months of preparatory medicines and doctor visits, our in-vitro cycle was falling just before Christmas, during the church season of Advent, and the priests were constantly mentioning the "baby" and the "beloved child." I was alternately encouraged by the coincidence and wary of it. I kept tearing up, trying not to make it mean too much, praying this wasn't a cosmic setup.

Then the "transfer" — the procedure in which doctors would implant the fertilized eggs in my uterus — was scheduled for December 12, the Feast of Our Lady of Guadalupe. Even before my return to Catholicism, this particular vision of Mary, brown-skinned queen of the Americas, had been my patron saint. Her image was all over our house: on a wooden folk-art painting, a votive candle, even a switch plate. Having new life placed in my womb on her feast day, in the middle of Advent, was too much of a coincidence to dismiss. I allowed myself to swell with hope.

Once the eggs were removed from my body—an outpatient surgery called "retrieval"—they were fertilized by an embryologist, who handpicked the best of Brian's sperm and inserted one into each of my eggs, thus, however blindly, determining the gender and genetic makeup of our potential children. Finally, a few days later, we returned for the quick-and-painless transfer to complete the process.

"She's up, and she's pregnant!" one of the doctors called out, smiling, when I passed him in the clinic hallway with three fertilized embryos newly implanted. I wanted to hug him. Right away, I did feel acutely pregnant, with extremely sore breasts and heat coursing through my body. Doing my Christmas shopping, I walked with one hand on my belly, as if I could hold them all in. We were hoping for at least one to survive, but for a short time, I felt like the mother of three.

A week later, I woke up feeling nothing—no symptoms at all—and somehow I knew. A leaden curtain came down inside, protecting me from the flood of grief that would come. I told Brian, "I don't think it worked."

Just two days before Christmas, we got confirmation. I was pregnant, but it wasn't viable. It was an ectopic pregnancy, in which a fertilized embryo inexplicably gets drawn into a fallopian tube and stuck there. A rare occurrence, said the doctor. Just bad luck. They gave me twin injections of a low-dose chemotherapy drug to attack the embryo's DNA so that it wouldn't grow and cause me to hemorrhage. *Kill or be killed,* I thought darkly.

On Valentine's Day, after weeks of blood tests, I was once again pronounced not pregnant.

In his book *Grace and Grit,* philosopher Ken Wilber writes about the problem of looking for meaning in physical maladies. He describes his wife Treya's struggle with cancer, her bouts of self-blame, and the hurtful comments she endured from spiritually-minded friends about the likely emotional causes of her disease.

There are three states of awareness, Wilber writes: prerational, rational, and transrational. Prerational awareness relies on "magical" cause-and-effect interpretations to understand suffering: cancer is caused by buried resentment, or infertility is due to ambivalence about parenthood. Rational awareness uses observable scientific evidence: disease is caused, and healed, on the physical plane alone. Both ways of thinking confer a comforting sense of knowing how life works, of having some control over suffering.

Transrational awareness acknowledges and includes reason, but also transcends it. In a transrational state of awareness we do our best to act on what we know, but we also allow for the possibility of not knowing, of not having control, of being part of a larger reality. Of the three ways of thinking, only the last helps us overcome our need for a narrative, usually a much too simple one, to tell us why things happen the way they do.

At the end of Wilber's book, his wife, who has tried treatments from East and West, who has looked deeply into herself, who has inspired others with her courage and equanimity, dies at forty-one. The "problem" of her cancer is never solved. And he writes about her tragic death not as a failure but as a part of the mystery.

After the in-vitro didn't work, people pretty much stopped offering us theories and advice. The sheer longevity of our suffering seemed to shut them up. Even better, it quieted the incessant voice in my head that was hellbent on trying to explain or control what was happening. Now I spend more time in the mystery, in the place of not knowing, without falling into the dispiriting belief that life is simply random or cruel.

None of us really knows why we suffer. I don't know why, after almost five years, Brian and I are still childless. I don't know if in vitro will work the next time, if I will become pregnant naturally again, or if we will adopt. But I nurture the belief that we will create a family.

I won't go so far as to say I think our infertility has been a good thing. It's been horribly difficult and painful, and I wouldn't wish it on anyone. But I'm grateful for some of the changes it's wrought. I've given up trying to protect myself from the fear that bad things will happen. (They already are happening.) I've grown in compassion, and I'm much less apt to distance myself from other people's suffering. And Brian and I have learned to do what he calls "leaning in," drawing as close to each other as we can in the face of hardship.

Most of all, I'm not as desperate to understand *why* as I used to be. I'm less afraid of "getting it wrong," of failing to discern God's will. When I try too hard to figure it out, to do it right, to be "good," I only cause myself more suffering.

Baby products continue to arrive in the mail, but I try not to attribute meaning to their arrival, or my disposal of them. The other day I hauled out the box of baby formula from the back of the cupboard and gave it away to my church for its food drive. This wasn't a symbolic gesture; it was a practical acknowledgment that someone else—someone who is suffering in an altogether different way than I am—might get some use out of it.

And yet there are still moments I can't shake off easily, details that seemed charged with significance—like the dove's nest, that spring of roses, the Virgin of Guadalupe. I cannot interpret these events, but they linger the way images from dreams do: palpable, enigmatic, insistent.

This, I have come to believe, is where real magic resides: not in facile equations—psoriasis equals "the fear of being hurt," or surrender begets conception—but in those luminous moments that hint at patterns and connections running through our lives; those subtle glimpses that suggest we are continually being led somewhere, even if the path takes us through pain and suffering, even if we don't know where we are going, or why.

*Tracy Wall*

# In Vitro

On the first day
of the new year
we walk to the fisheries
and sit on a bench
beside a lake

half-frozen —
the trees reflect
incomplete:
a gap in the water
like the space

between our fingers.
In the corner
of the lake
an up-turned boat
is cradled blue

into the bank.
Suspended,
its spine
curves
foetus-like

into ice.
We promise
to return
later in the year
to see if the lake

has thawed
and search for
newly-hatched fish
swimming
in spring waters.

*Mary Anne Maier*

# A Life Complete

My dear friend Sarah has decided that she must, must have a baby. When she does, I will be among the very last of my closest friends and family to remain childless. This leaves me with a frightening pile of emotions to sort. Which are too delicate? Which are permanently pressed into my heart of hearts? Is there a danger that my fears could run and end up staining my purest wishes for a friend's well-being?

After years of hope-dashing fertility treatments, Sarah and her husband have decided to adopt. All these years of their working toward a baby follow even more years of my husband and me working toward the same goal, once upon a time, so it's not as if we haven't had time to talk about the issue. But this isn't something one can be talked into (don't we know it) or out of. This baby means Sarah and I, who have lived thousands of miles apart while remaining inseparable emotionally for more than twenty years, are just now reaching a point of major divergence in the general directions our lives will take. When the baby comes, whether in two weeks or a year, my friend will from then on be a Mother, and I won't.

Sarah, who is more fearful of fleshing out dreams on the strength of a maybe than anyone I've ever known, is even beginning to talk of names.

What do I think of Nina? Caroline? Susanna?

I think I will love her dearly, marveling at her perfection as few parents seem to remember to do with their own children after the first year or so. I think I will ache for her as I reminisce already about the scrapes, the uncertainties and scars that have to come in her life. I think I will delight in buying her outlandishly adorable baby outfits, and later, I'll wish her friendships as full of love and sustenance as her mother's and mine when she asks me to call back later because she has a friend on call-waiting. I think I will be a stranger to her, too far away to be more than Mommy's friend. And that makes me start to imagine, before she's even born, her memories of me forty years from now: will she recall a stale, closed-in odor, like an airless closet, and too much lipstick, crooked on my shriveled lips, as come to my mind when I think of my Aunt Tillie and the other childless old women who inhabited my young years?

Why does childlessness bring these images to mind? Does a woman without a child age faster than her maternal peers? Is she bound to be known as just a little off—sweet but slightly pathetic, lonely with a twist of the eccentric—whatever the state of her other relationships or achievements, just as my own childless and batty Aunt Tillie was always thought of?

These days, I suppose we need to add a whole new batch of labels relying on more up-to-date stereotypes than we had for Aunt Tillie's generation: driven, ambitious, career-centered—maybe even child-hating or self-obsessed, as two fathers whom I was unfortunate enough to be sandwiched between on a plane once labeled me when they got the "zero" answer to that inevitable first question about number of kids. "So," they laughed, "you're a DINK: Double Income, No Kids. Must be nice to have all that money." I won't bore you with the creatively obscene acronyms I came up with for labeling *them* in my mind as I sat through that endless flight, refusing to let surface the none-of-their-business feelings that come with infertility, as they talked around me and about people "like me" as if being childless were equivalent to choosing not to work for a certain corporation or never owning a certain kind of car.

Before my husband and I were stunned by the realization that all our careful birth control had been for naught, we had spent our early married years being childless by choice, and I knew as I sat stinging between those insensitive clods that I no more needed to explain *that* choice to them than I needed to apologize now for the physical inability to bear young.

My own experience teaches me that childless women have no other reason to be lumped together than their lack of children, so that talking about them as a group is about as easy as talking about women without lofts in the city or women without laptop computers as unified groups. And yet we do it all the time, assuming we know the motivations and meanings of childlessness. I ought to know: before I thought of myself as childless, I used to do it as well. I remember laughing at couples who had so much more money than time that they had to pay somebody to teach them how to have a baby. Now, of course, it singes the edges of my heart to hear my twenty-something friend sneer at women obsessed with their biological clocks, especially since she knows I'm one of them.

My husband gets as sick as I do of people explaining to him that he can't really understand life without having children, that he is in fact not fully an adult himself if he's not a parent. We both know that sinking feeling in the gut, the one we all used to get as children when we weren't picked till last on the playground, each time people make special arrangements to keep their kids away from us, just assuming we would never understand or appreciate that kids are noisy and messy and lots and lots of trouble and fun. And we're both enraged (at the same time that we grow a little smaller inside) when the stray word or gesture or look says perhaps we can't be trusted with children, perhaps we're strange or even dangerous since we have no children of our own.

But I think for a woman there's another dimension, as well, to facing the world without a child by her side. Childlessness has been viewed quite differently by diverse cultures and at various periods in history. Yet Woman has been the universal symbol of fertility since fruit first sprang from Mother Earth and babies fell from between women's legs. And I know that in the history of our species, Woman was long believed to be the sole creator of new life, so that men feared and respected her for this ultimate of mysterious powers. All of this means that today, whether the maternal instinct that has most recently claimed my Sarah is biological or the creation of a people's shared imagination, it is a concept with such strength in our society that women without children can't help but feel their power is diminished.

The most devastating moment in my husband's and my infertility came the day he said what felt at the time like the cruelest words I'd ever heard: "I can't live with your sadness any longer." What was I to do if I couldn't fill this empty pit with tears? How could I buy another baby shower gift, walk through the children's section of a department store, watch my little niece cross her fingers behind her back as she and my husband tell each other taller and taller tales, and accept the notion that I'd never cradle the soft fur of my own baby's head in the hollow of my neck one day?

We came to a point, eventually, of understanding that our years of longing for a new life to the exclusion of all else were also years of throwing away life—our own. We vowed, finally, to celebrate the precious life we have together rather than giving it over to the overpowering vortex of mourning what is not. And so when Sarah's baby comes, I've begun to think of the joy that will come of being able to fly out to be with her without the restraints of small children at home. In our own life, my husband can work the odd schedules of his journalism career without worrying about missing a child's all-consuming job of growing into an individual being. We can continue to hike and snowshoe together, and though I'm sure we'll always think of what it would have been like to carry a backpack with a squirming baby or pull a sled with a child along the sparkling snow trail, we will enjoy talking of music or mountains instead of orthodontia appointments or swimming lessons.

And so we go along today, as excited to get our nephews' school magazine in the mail as we might be about a surprise gift arriving, as exuberant over our brother and sister-in-law's upcoming twins as they are overwhelmed. I believe I'm ready, as well, to relish Susanna or Caroline or Nina. Yet I can't help feeling the loss of Sarah as my childless friend, my mirror of a life complete in itself, distinctly devoid of that stale closet smell or crooked lipstick caked on withering lips—full, instead, of love and strength and achievements all her own.

*Mary Christine Delea*

# How to Have an Abortion

It is summer. You are nineteen. You are living in a place surrounded by rivers, and you will need to cross some on the two-hour drive to the clinic. The car has air conditioning, and under its spell you fall asleep; the boy who is driving is thankful for that. You dream of roaches—you'd had no experience with them where you grew up, surrounded by ocean, and, since not much makes you squeamish, the fact that roaches do worries you. You sit in a white room for four hours, have the abortion in another white room, lie on a cot in still another white room until they kick you out. They want to go home. So do you, but what would you say to your father, as Catholic as a priest. You find a motel and get Chinese food. You wonder if you will marry the boy who's paying for all of this. You will. You watch him clean up your blood from the motel's bathroom floor, this being the first boy you ever spent a night with in a motel. You know other girls have different experiences in motel rooms with boys. You wonder what your mother will say. Years later, when you tell her, she will hug you and demand that you don't tell your father. You won't. And you will never know—always too afraid to ask anyone—what your hometown gynecologist meant when, 6 months later during an exam, he muttered, "Jesus, they really did a job on you down there."

*Sara Lippmann*

# Girl

Here is where she waits to get one. It is a particular place—this waiting room—for particular services although there are no visible markers. No activity clogging the sidewalk, gruesome posters slung from anyone's neck. Instead there is an elevator and a hallway and a door that opens onto the predictable hum of fluorescence, a waiting room like any other. Absent only are Matchbox cars careening along the rim of the coffee table, the clumsy presence of strollers. A ground-in trail of snack puffs.

The twins she has left at home.

The wallpaper is floral pastel, like what one might expect in a suburban family's powder room. Once she locked herself in Stephanie Quinn's down-stairs powder room. She was 16 and high on mushrooms but sitting here now she remembers how the petals wove and sparkled, that night, how she lay there on the floor, holding on to it all for a while before twisting the knob to show Stephanie Quinn: how beautiful.

There was no sex at 16 and while there were other things, she was con-sidered a good girl for this reason. The room is filled with girls, slouched in chairs, their heads resting on the shoulders of mothers, aunts, older sisters. Girls sucking the strings of their hooded sweatshirts, sucking until the wet cotton squeaks in their mouths, hoods pulled tight, compressing their skulls. They are not like her and yet she is one of them.

"Hang on Sloopy" comes on the oldies station and two girls in full wigs spin heels straight from the club.

It is eleven o'clock in the morning. Her husband has taken off work. He is reading the newspaper on his handheld device. The radio plays. Heat spreads from her ears, stamping down her throat, like how she used to get while giving an oral presentation when no one was paying attention. She squeezes her husband's arm but he has a call and stands up to take it outside. Lowering her eyes, she scans the waists in the waiting room: a tight peach t-shirt, a midriff baring a belly ring, a cheap blazer stretched over a bulge.

There are fathers here, too.

A vase rests on the windowsill full of cloudy water. Lilies. Their scent could nauseate her even when fresh, but these flowers have started to turn, stamens spilling rust along the ledge. Bile rises but then her name is called and she reports for the transaction, her credit card swiped through a machine. There are receipts and consent forms and handouts, poorly copied, detailing risks and side effects, a slip with prescriptions to fill.

She signs off on everything.

The office assistant asks if there is anything else.

She shakes her head. The doctor had ordered a twelve-hour fast and now she feels like she does on Yom Kippur. Her nose tingles. She fights it as she's been fighting for weeks but she is failing. A nurse with a cross pendant appears at her side.

"Something wrong, sugar?"

"It's only," she says, halting. "I am a mother."

The nurse tells her try not to think of it like that.

Her voice breaks, "you don't understand," but before she can whisper "already" there is her husband, kissing her forehead and saying, "What did I miss?" She looks at him through smeary eyes and he says, "Remember, this is your decision." Just like that he's excused himself as if to clarify: this is her problem. She could stop it but where would that leave them? The nurse with the crucifix balls up a wad of tissues and offers them up as a bouquet. Her husband invites her to blow.

"Isn't that sweet," the nurse speaks in a tone used on small children. Rubs her back and it is embarrassing. "You two are a breath of fresh air."

A door opens and her husband turns. The nurse throws out her hand like a crossing guard. "The girls in there are half-naked." His protest is thin but at least there is a protest and at least he is here, she reminds herself, as her husband retreats to the waiting room and she follows the nurse down the corridor labeled "no men allowed."

The changing area feels like the dressing room of a discount women's department store. Vainly she'd fretted over what to wear this morning, not wanting to look too prim or too casual. Too much like a mommy. The twins had clomped around the closet in her shoes, draping rejected pieces around them like boas. Squealing: "look at me." Once the disposable gown is tied, she gathers her belongings into a pile. It is freezing. There are paper bags on her feet. One girl—no, a woman—looks at her nipples begging through and indicates a row of lockers, their keys attached to springy neon rings.

"Girl," the woman says. "Just wait for that tea." The air conditioner grunts and she shivers, shuffling to her locker, sliding the key chain over her wrist.

A new waiting room. More girls. Fidgeting in their chairs, thumbing outdated issues of *Prevention* and *Country Home*. One speaks into a smuggled cell phone, loudly, so it is impossible to mishear the words "dilation" and "sticks." Another picks a scab on her arm. It's taking forever and the light screams down at her. The gown provides insufficient coverage. Tugging at it, she has begun to feel dizzy so when a girl asks, "what time is it?" she almost says, "naptime."

Inside she does as she's told: dangles her ass off the table, presses her feet into stirrups. The doctor enters. His nose and mouth are masked but she recognizes his eyes from his website. This man could sell her a bridge. He stands at her feet, waving a wand, and says with an accent:

"First we need to confirm what is there."

She is grateful for the nurse anesthetist. It will not take much. Only yesterday the twins had crashed toy carriages, dolls expunged in a lifeless heap, and begged her for a real baby brother. They are not quite three, her girls, but she's settled on a tea set and pair of wings for them each as consolation. The anesthetist rolls out his questions of consciousness. Her teeth clatter.

"Relax," the anesthetist says.

The gas hisses and she breathes; "that a girl," she hears as the cup closes down on her face.

Again with the flowers, faded border. Drop ceiling. A room lined like a convent with beds; still, more are needed. The nurse rushes to move her. To accommodate the ones who must wait. The girl beside her is sobbing; the girl across rises and spills. Now that it is over she is ravenous—sucked and pink and scraped clean—and the only thing she can think is what to eat.

The girls spoke of abortion tea for good reason. Blend of Lipton, chamomile flower, peppermint; whatever bags are left over. Brewed in a samovar and served thick with honey in a Styrofoam cup. The nurse brings it to her chair in recovery, along with two pills to help out the cramping. Her crucifix winks and here comes a pad used for housebreaking puppies. The nurse coos: "slide this under your bum." She is so hungry the hot tea is heaven going down, fills her right up, as if it were all she could want.

*Kristy Athens*

# Think of the Children

"Thanks so much for being here—you are building a future for our students! Please give generously!"

Alicia had been a little bit afraid to bring Jake to this auction; he hadn't been himself lately. But maybe getting out of the house would do him good.

"Why are we going to a fundraiser?" said Jake on the way over, sulking in his green rain parka. "We can't afford it right now."

"I know," said Alicia, "but I promised Elaine that we'd go before you got fired."

"I was laid off," said Jake.

"And we skipped last year's," continued Alicia, "so I feel guilty."

The fundraiser—a silent auction—was being held in the gymnasium of the George Washington High School. Alicia's friend Elaine had organized it for the last three years. It was her "job"—her husband supported the family as a corporate attorney, so Elaine volunteered for their children's school.

The gymnasium looked a little like prom: pink crêpe paper and student-made signs announcing the upcoming school musical. Along one wall, between the doors to the girls and boys locker rooms, was a table supplying the usual red punch, tea and coffee. Cookies that come in packages of one hundred. A couple of bouquets of carnations, dyed to match the school colors. White vinyl tablecloths covered this and three lines of tables in the center of the room, around which people were considering complex, Mylar-wrapped gift baskets; colorful handmade platters donated by a local artisan; a trip to Cancun.

"Should we bid on this lamp?" said Alicia.

"We already have lamps," said Jake. "Why don't we get something we don't already have?"

Alicia was unsure if Jake was Making a Comment. Had there been an edge in his voice? She hadn't been able to hear it over Elaine: "Be generous! It's so great to see the community coming together for the sake of the children." Jake had recently begun lobbying to have a baby, after they had already spent years traversing the decision-making process, concluding that they would not have children, and breaking the news to the Stakeholders.

"Why this?" Alicia had asked him while they were in the bathroom the other night, she brushing her hair and he flossing his teeth. "You've never wanted kids before."

"Maybe it's the thing we're missing," Jake said.

"We're not missing anything," Alicia twisted the cap from the toothpaste tube. "You're panicking. Don't worry, you'll find a new job."

They had generally received support for their decision over the years; some confusion, but Alicia understood that not procreating seemed to the average person anathema to human existence—what else *was* there? Some framed this as concern for their future wellbeing: "Aren't you worried you'll get breast cancer? Who will take care of you when you're old?"

The argument that Alicia failed to understand was the "selfish" one: what was selfish about not throwing another person out into the world? Was the pain of childbirth a necessary human experience? She found it ironic that even her most hyper-environmentalist friends had over the past few years integrated into their lives copious non-recyclable plastic toys, car seats and feeding implements, and discarded thousands of gel-filled diapers into local landfills or gallons of bleach water into their neighboring rivers.

Over the loudspeaker, Elaine kept her guests on task: "I see a few items out there that have low bids—remember, this is a fundraiser, not a trip to the outlet mall. We're not here to get bargains, people. Think of the children."

Alicia was amazed at the naïveté of her friends as well—they all envisioned a challenging yet successful upbringing. No one was going to have a drug problem, unplanned pregnancy or falling-out that lasted thirty years. Apparently, all of her friends' progeny were going to be inquisitive yet reasonable as children, and social and respectful as teenagers. They would continue to make good decisions throughout college, enjoy successful and fulfilling careers, and nurture fun-loving, mature and mutually beneficial relationships with their parents until the tearful "and yet beautiful" end.

Most of Alicia and Jake's friends had preschoolers, time-consuming yet adorable. Elaine, who was ten years older, had two teenaged daughters who called her a bitch to her face, stole money from her purse and sometimes stayed out all weekend without calling home. If Elaine dressed up to go out for dinner, they snarled, "Why do you bother?" and then wore her Prada shoes without permission.

The pressure to "produce" had eased off over the last few years; Jake's parents had begun to realize that this was not a phase they were going through. But Alicia remembered the worst of it: endless inquiries, allusions. Her mother showing her the booties she was knitting, "just in case." The "So, when are you gonna have kids?" from neighbors; cousins; even their mechanic. Once during a phone conversation, a friend interrupted: "Alicia, are you pregnant?"

"What? No."

"Oh."

"Why?"

"I don't know. You sounded happy."

Jake, the product of a bitter divorce, had always doubted his ability to parent. Alicia simply lacked conviction. It was like the semester in college that she'd signed up for the History of African Pottery—she was interested in the topic, but when she projected its reality: memorizing names, dates and places; writing research papers; taking tests about the subject; and that it would affect her grade point average, she dropped out of the class and picked up another biology course.

If parenting had been her Number One priority, she would have pursued it. But it wasn't. She and Jake had decided they'd rather invest their time in their own relationship, and their money—when they had it—in organizations that were doing good in the world. Filling a hand rather than creating another empty one.

Alicia put her name on the bidding sheet for a free oil change at a garage that wasn't too far from their house. So far, no one had bothered with it, and the opening bid was just $10. An oil change cost $25 anyway, so she might as well offer that much. They would have to get the oil changed eventually.

Every time she thought that her mother had finally accepted her and Jake's decision, she was proven wrong. Usually it had to do with Alicia's brother's four boys. Never mind that her brother was separated and constantly battling with his ex-wife over who would get the kids over Easter and who was going to pay for Colin's braces: Her brother had delivered.

"I sure would love to have a little granddaughter to dote over," said her mother. "I'd sure love to go dress-shopping!"

*Take Colin*, Alicia thought. *He loves to wear dresses.*

"You could get a sperm donor," said her mother. Alicia had once old her that Jake was sterile. "Or adopt. Those little Chinese babies are adorable."

But now, even her co-conspirator was crumbling under the pressure. The other night, Jake faced her, floss hanging down from either side of a bicuspid: "I know, and those things are important, and I still respect those ideas and other people who don't have kids. But I don't know. I've been thinking about teaching a kid stuff. Like that hike we were on last Sunday. There was that big slug, and you've seen a slug, and I've seen a slug, but a little kid would get all excited about a slug. And that would be fun!"

Alicia rinsed out her toothbrush. "And then ten minutes later he'd get tired and want you to carry him, and start crying and coughing snot bubbles into your ear."

"That might be fun, Alicia," said Jake. "Just think about it, okay?"

Alicia had cycled around the tables and returned to the oil change. Someone had raised it to $30. She searched for Jake, but he was across the gymnasium, talking to Elaine. He looked to be in a better mood. *It takes a village*, thought Alicia, and counter-bid $100.

Because Beginnings Are Beautiful
and sometimes Brutal

*Brent Newsom*
# Strawberries
*Ten Weeks*


You cannot come soon enough
for your mother, vomiting
strawberries in the bathroom, the strawberries
I bought for her because they are rich
in folic acid, and folic acid is good,
the nurse says, for your brain;
so I bought them for your brain,
put the plastic carton in the cart myself
since I now shop for groceries
so your mother can rest and eat
crackers every so often,
something to settle her stomach
so she will not throw up the folic acid
—but there, suspended in toilet water,
half-digested strawberries
looking like some awful afterbirth,
and your mother spits,
then rinses her mouth,
trudges back to our bed
pledging to be done with strawberries,
and I am caught between
*please be normal* and
*we will love you if you aren't*
as I hold down the lever, watch
the deep red swirl of bile and berries.

*Jim Miller*
# Moloki

I wake after a nightmare
and lay in the darkness
with my hand on her belly
as she tosses and turns
struggling with the new life
within her—
one tiny speck of big being—
like the barely discernable light
of a single star
lost in the immensity of night sky.
The sound of the ocean lull
in the near distance
does not bring me sleep.
Instead, I think of the infant's grave
outside the spare white chapel
by the seaside
and the priest's words on the sign
at the cusp of the cliff overlooking
the colony where so many died—
"One's Moloki can be anywhere."
Some of the lepers were cast off ships
into shark-filled waters,
others were rudely abandoned
on the barren black lava.

How cruel the azure blue Pacific.
How mean the dense, shaded green of the tumid shore.

I stare at nothing,
unable to yield
as I listen to the ceiling fan whirl

frantically
and think,
"We crucify each other."

She moans in her sleep,
rolls over and leaves me
her behind.
Before dawn comes the birds' song
and I lose myself
as she and I
and the world
keep breathing.

*Lori Miller Barrett*

# A Brussels Sprout:
## My Nine-Month Course in Foreign Relations

My husband and I had been living in Brussels for a year when I began to suspect I was pregnant with our second child. I felt confident ordering food in French. I could greet my neighbors in the hallway. Ordering a nursing bra was another matter. I feared my condition would compound the confusion and frustration I felt as a foreigner.

My fears were realized when I failed the language part of my home pregnancy test. The instructions were in French and Dutch, the two languages spoken in Belgium, a country with a population in the north closely linked to France and a population in the south closely tied to the Netherlands. I couldn't understand either set of instructions, so I simply held the plastic wand where it would get wet. Then I set it aside for the allotted time, waiting for a + or − sign to show up. After the allotted time had passed, plus a few hours, and I'd achieved neither a + nor a −, my husband looked at the instructions. Turns out I hadn't properly opened the dipstick, and my urine never even made it to the test.

I decided to let a professional handle the situation. Brussels is an international city, so it didn't take long to find a doctor who spoke English. The office visit was very different from those I'd had when I was pregnant in New York. The doctor himself showed me to his examining room, and then told me to take off my clothes and wait on the examining table. Take off everything? "Oui," he said. Where was my paper robe? Where was the friendly assistant to check my weight? Apparently neither is necessary in this part of the world.

After a few visits, I became comfortable being nude, and even found it liberating to sit with nothing on and chat about whether my son was prepared for a sibling. After he examined me, the doctor would ask me to weigh myself and get dressed, and then he would walk behind a fabric screen to his desk. I would report my weight once I reached his desk, and he'd write it down in my chart without looking up. Then, five or six months along, he looked up after I'd told him my weight. "You'd better be careful," he warned. "You're gaining too much weight."

I mentioned this exchange the next time I was at my son's English-speaking play group. Many of the mothers there were recent veterans of the Brussels birthing scene. "Lie!" they all immediately said. Belgian doctors are strict about weight gain, they told me, but none of them watch as you weigh yourself. So from then on, I had a proud spring in my step as I walked over to the doctor's desk and reported my weight gain. Who needs personal trainers and personal chefs? Not only was I convincing my doctor I was fit and pregnant, I managed to convince myself as well.

I became close friends with two British women with "bumps." The night they discovered I was pregnant we were at dinner, and I had declined a cocktail and then wine. I was American and my condition was obvious. I found out a few months later that not only were they pregnant as well, they had been that night, when they'd each had an aperitif and a couple of glasses of wine. I found this revolutionary. I went the next day to the bookstore. And there it was in print, in Sheila Kitzinger's "The New Pregnancy and Childbirth," a handbook for English mums-to-be. Alcohol use during pregnancy should be restricted: no more than ten units a week. She defines a unit as half a pint or a small glass of wine.

I started asking other women about drinking while pregnant. A Belgian friend said that if my body is used to a drink with dinner then it wouldn't hurt to continue during pregnancy. And an Irish friend recommended Guinness—for the iron. Too much alcohol can hurt a fetus. Everyone understands this. But the American medical community doesn't trust women to use their own discretion, so it warns against any alcohol at all. The American Academy of Pediatricians says, "Because there is no known safe amount of alcohol consumption during pregnancy, the Academy recommends abstinence from alcohol for women who are pregnant or who are planning a pregnancy."

When my friends and I were huge and clumsy, and close to birth, we were gathered at another dinner party. This time I accepted wine with my dinner. My friends, meanwhile, each complained of feeling slightly hungover from the wine they'd had the night before. Their babies were born healthy and both crawled well before my chubby girl could make a move.

In the weeks before birth, pregnant women in Belgium are prescribed a physical therapist. The therapist holds exercise classes to help strengthen the pelvic muscles. This, too, was revolutionary. Near the end of my New York pregnancy I was shuffled off to breathing classes. Unless midwives or a progressive doctor cares for an American woman, her pelvic muscles are rarely considered. Not coincidentally, Caesarean births are more prevalent in the U.S.

In class the physical therapist, Winnie, told us to imagine that our hips were spoons stirring a cup of coffee. We'd spend class time gyrating, while standing up and while sitting on giant rubber balls. And she repeatedly told us never to arch our backs: the baby needs a straight path to make it out quickly. This sometimes goes against what feels natural during pregnancy, when the weight (you might have pretended you didn't gain) pulls your belly forward. Winnie, in her broken English for the class full of expatriates, would say, "rock well back," meaning rock my hips forward and pull my belly in.

Because it was about a third less expensive to give birth in Belgium, our American insurance allowed me to have a room to myself in a private hospital — and to have Winnie with me throughout my labor, making sure I rocked well back. There are no nurseries in the hospitals; the babies sleep in the room with their mothers and eat when they are hungry. When I gave birth in New York, my son had to sleep in a nursery and was wheeled in every four hours so he could eat, then wheeled right back out — except in the daytime, when I could sign him out like a library book and take him to my room.

The food in the hospital consisted of dishes such as Lapin a la Gueuze (rabbit stewed in beer) or Pain de Veau (meatloaf made with veal). But I wasn't allowed to lounge around and eat. Winnie marched in the second day to teach me exercises to get my pelvic wall back in shape. Once home, I rarely did the exercises, and I now catch myself standing like a fertility statue, with a deep arch in my lower back and my belly protruding.

I returned to New York with a drooling souvenir of my time in Belgium. We tried to preserve some of our daughter, Stella's, Belgian heritage by putting her in a French preschool. But because we never spoke French at home, she didn't make much of an attempt to speak French at school. All I can do for her now is make sure she rocks well back.

*Judith Sanders*

# Eating While Pregnant

### I.

I am a lumbering brontosaurus:

My busy gullet swivels
on a cement-mixer belly.

Settling on my stump legs,
I chew and chew.

My walnut brain
dozes over Shakespeare

but my jaws never tire.
I masticate whole forests.

My nostrils flare:
I raise my dripping muzzle.

Coffee and bacon reek
of extinction.

### II.

I am a white-robed priest
raising the chalice of flat coke,
the saltine host.

I am a black-caped magician
slipping greens to a rabbit
hidden in my hat.

I am a tattered witch
stoking my cauldron.
I brew dead earth and rotted leaves
salted with rain.

I am a foolish sparrow
who nipped the wrong red berry.
Now I'm perched atop
an ostrich egg
wrung somehow
from my narrow entrails.
I try not to skid off.
I try to warm it
with my puny wings.

### III.

A seed turns into a tree
into an apple into me.

Like Eve, I sank my teeth
into sweet flesh

and presto!

I turn into a boy
who won't get into bed
but runs around instead
with his p.j.'s on his head,
dancing in Mommy's shoes.

*Greg Schreur*

# Waiting for Charlie

*ESTRAGON: Nothing to be done.*
*VLADIMIR: I'm beginning to come round to that opinion.*
—Samuel Beckett

The birth of our second child, three hot summer days after his due date, was finally induced by the admittedly unorthodox combination of sex and baked beans. This is, at least, what we will continue to claim even when he is finally old enough to be appropriately apprised of and embarrassed by such details, perhaps, for example, when I am called upon to give his high school commencement address or the toast at his wedding. The truth of this fact is indisputable, and I defy anyone to challenge its logic. We had baked beans for supper and sex later that night (with no baked beans directly involved, of course), and early the next morning my wife went into labor. Later, as we reviewed what we did to affect this outcome, it was obvious, and nothing and no one will ever be able to convince us otherwise, because the alternative—our being powerless even against this puny unborn child—is simply too frightening to face.

Three days sound inconsequential when taken out of context and when compared to the nine months of gestation. Our first child, though, was born two weeks early, establishing a precedent we had no reason to believe would not continue, so when we passed the t-minus-two-weeks-and-counting point, we eagerly expected the onset of labor and interpreted the slightest contraction or vaginal leaking as a sign to begin packing. So when put into perspective, our second child was *seventeen days* overdue—or roughly 86,400 minutes, which is really a number that more accurately reflects how exhausting such periods of heightened anticipation can be.

Our first child came like a thief in the night, poking through the membrane of my wife's amniotic sac at three in the morning. My wife then woke me and we each separately took care of our business: she, concerned with the number of strangers who would soon be inspecting her vagina, took a shower while I, a first-year teacher sincerely troubled by the thought of what would happen to my students without me, typed up some plans for the substitute teacher.

Of course there is only so much preparing that can be done, and let's face it, *nothing* can prepare you for that first baby, certainly not the surprisingly graphic videos shown at birthing classes nor the somewhat morbid infant CPR classes where you are taught how hard is too hard to strike a choking baby (and are scolded by an unsympathetic instructor for your naïve zealousness). These no more prepare you for the arrival of this first child than watching *Close Encounters of the Third Kind* prepares you for the actual appearance of extraterrestrial beings in your back yard.

The shock and awe of this first child passed and we conceived a little more than a year later, foolishly thinking we knew what to expect this next time, that it was simply a matter of addition: three plus one equaling four. But that simple arithmetic does not adequately represent the effect of a second child, not when you consider the fact that the new one divides up a night's sleep into parts that never seem to equal the whole and multiplies the stress by a factor totally incommensurate with his size. We had wrongly imagined that this new child would come at some conveniently arranged and expected time, something maybe like the ball dropping on New Year's Eve, and then be smoothly assimilated into our sweet little nuclear family. He wouldn't come three days past his due date, wouldn't ever cause us to rethink bringing him in to the world, and certainly wouldn't bite his sister and me until we were covered in O-shaped bruises the size of silver dollars. Alas, thinking we had any idea was such folly.

About a year later again we conceived, my wife and I treating family-raising the same way we treat road trips: the destination is the goal and stopping to pee or stretch your legs is for the weak. By this point, however, we knew all we needed to know; that is, we knew only that we knew nothing. By accepting this reality and by anticipating surprise, we could avoid being surprised. This smug conviction bolstered us through the first nine months and assuaged us as Flag Day (the official due date) passed with all the usual Flag Day festivities (nothing). But *touché!* We had expected this—or at least by rejecting all expectations this development could not technically be called unexpected. I felt vindicated and triumphantly went about my business. Meanwhile, my wife peed a lot.

Then three more days passed and suddenly we were waiting even longer than before. Against my will and better judgment I became hopeful with each Braxton Hicks contraction, but honestly I could have gone on waiting, knowing as I did the effect this new child was soon going to have. I could have, that is, except waiting has a way of intensifying every little thing while at the same time overshadowing those same things. We did everything with the thought of imminent birth on our minds, which meant that everything from raising the other children to driving and shaving was done with less attention than they deserved. This kid was making the world a less safe place.

Then an entire week passed. I considered serving baked beans and a bottle of wine for a romantic supper each evening but rejected the idea not because pregnant women shouldn't have alcohol but out of fear that it wouldn't result in labor, thus invalidating all prior claims and depriving me of future opportunities to speak of baked beans and sex in the same context.

Fortunately, there was no shortage of alternatives. Methods for inducing labor abound in the worlds of both medicine and superstition. Nowhere in either medical research or the annals of old wives' tales is the specific combination of baked beans and sex mentioned, although orgasms are reputed to have some effect, by reliable doctors and apparently satisfied women alike. Some of the more common methods include walking, drinking raspberry tea, eating eggplant, drinking castor oil—which my wife tried, failing to send her into labor but succeeding in making her hate being pregnant even more—and nipple stimulation, which helped me feel useful. There is, or at least was, even some belief among Iraqi Arab women that getting a tattoo just below your belly button would work. It's clear that humans inherently desire control, especially when confronted with our own natural futility and feebleness, which is why, I suppose, certain Native American tribes perform rain dances and why a woman would fondle her breasts while choking down castor oil.

With no disgusting liquids to take and little more than the occasional nipple tweaking to keep me occupied, I took a more abstract approach, which at the time I thought was quite crafty: I figured that leaving things undone and by remaining brazenly unprepared for a few days at the hospital, I could trick the God of Labor of Delivery into punishing my obstinacy by parting my wife's waters. So I let the grass grow too long, took meat out of the freezer to defrost, and held on to library books right up to their due date, smugly believing that just when my life was in a sufficient state of disarray, God would chasten my irresponsibility and declare, "Let there be labor," in a voice like Charlton Heston's, because there's nothing like a pound of spoiled ground beef and forty-five cents in overdue library fines to teach you a lesson.

But still no baby.

We took our impatience out on each other. At times it seemed my wife wanted to push *me* through any opening slightly narrower than my skull. While her frustration was expressed more overtly, I resorted to subtler stages of grief, including denial and acceptance—both of which were understandably made easier by the fact that I didn't have another human being inside me as a constant and particularly nocturnal reminder. Much more than she, I was able to go on with my life, which I tried doing discreetly so as to not incur her jealous, hormonal wrath.

For one, I could still run; she couldn't—something about mucus membranes and engorged breasts making it dangerous, uncomfortable, and probably unsightly. For the most part I strongly dislike running, seeing as it primarily serves to remind me of my physical shortcomings. But there is at least one thing I really do like and that is making it back home, of forcing by sheer will one foot in front of the other until I make it back where there is television, couch, and beer.

My usual route is roughly a three-mile long figure eight. At the intersection of these two loops I can decide to take the easy way or the hard way. If I turn right, the hard way, I run up the steeper side of the hill—although using words like *steeper* and *hill* makes it sound more substantial than it really is. All I know is that whenever I'm climbing it I invariably slow to something that is more of a bouncy walk and suddenly become insecurely aware of people watching me and thinking things like, "I really *should* exercise more, but I just don't want to look like *him*."

Most often I turn left, taking the easy way which amazingly never seems to go uphill, just an easy jog along flat ground with a nice downhill stretch to make me feel, at least for a short while, like an Olympian. For years I accepted this impossible reality: that the universe would bend its immutable laws and allow me to run a continuously downhill loop that leads magically to where I began. The fact is that any rise in elevation within a circular path must be exactly equivalent to the total decline. Left or right, there is no difference, and even where it seems like there is, it is usually only a trick of perception. One way the incline is crammed into a narrow stretch; the other way it is spread out but still there. Inclines and declines, grades and slopes, all of it is relative. In the end, the decision—and this is probably true of most our decisions—doesn't amount to much if anything, except to further foster our deep-seated delusions that we are in control of our lives.

But like most delusions, it gets us through our days. We believe our practices and rituals will ensure a happy and successful life, that we can make it rain or help our favorite sports teams win or bring about the birth of our perfect child at a time of our choosing. Except then it *still* doesn't rain and our team loses and the baby is overdue and, if we are lucid and brave enough, we confront the illusion of our control, which is a surprisingly hard reality to face. In the meantime all we can do is go on making decisions—tackling the hill, going the easy way, taking meat out of the freezer for tomorrow night's supper—pretending we have control when all we are really doing is setting ourselves on a path and subjecting ourselves to whatever may come.

Charlie, our third and final child (provided my vas deferens does not heal itself), was eventually born, right about the time we started figuring he was taking up permanent residence in utero. He was nine days overdue. This is no record. A Mrs. Beulah Johnson was reportedly ninety-five days overdue. But still, come on, nine days. Of course, this new development simply reset the slate: a time for waiting became a time for labor that became a time for waking up in the middle of the night to feed the baby and pretend to hear a burp so you can hurry and get back to bed. Ironically, the very event whose time we sought to influence became the very event that consumed the rest of our summer.

Ultimately, it was not baked beans but endless drips of pitocin that brought about the miracle of childbirth, and with it the astonishment of bringing another human being into the world and seeing the knees and elbows that had been contorting my wife's stomach for months, and with that the feedings every few hours and those icky, seedy baby poops and the congratulations and the *My God, what have we done?* and the sometimes wonderful, sometimes excruciating adjustments in family dynamics. And no choices can ultimately or fundamentally change any of it except one: the decision to will one foot in front of the other and to continue doing so until you've reached the end of the loop, wherever that is, and you're able to finally collapse, the new life you brought into this world now sleeping peacefully in your arms and, at least for the moment, there is nothing in the world you are waiting for.

*Malaika King Albrecht*

# On Your Birth Day

I ride the steady refrain
of your heart beat, its simple
dance on the screen, a comfort
when contractions begin.
The song changes to a rap, a
beat, a pause, a
beat
and silence. The room
becomes a beehive
of nurses, doctors, equipment.
                          A mask
on my face, I'm adrift, bobbing
on a huge bed in a sea
of activity. *Push.* I can't
remember what the word
means. I think *push, gush*
*rush* — the sounds of water.
I hear a gurgle
and then a wet cry. This is how
it feels to spill the whole of you —
an ocean wave —
that knocks me back to shore.

*Karen K. Lewis*

# Modern Miracle

If you're going to beat the odds of birthing a dead baby, you arrive to the medical center before you give birth. The transport team wheels you into an elevator. You're strapped down and drugged so you cannot even lift a finger to scratch the place that tickles on your neck. You send silent messages to your unborn infant not to struggle, not to seek the light at the end of the birth canal.

You find yourself in a lonely room overlooking the bay and you try to roll over for a better view of the Golden Gate Bridge. You wonder whether the next time you cross that bridge you will be nursing an infant or carrying an urn of her remains. Somewhere out there, cypress trees sway in a salty breeze that you wish you could still smell.

The duty nurse assures you that you are considered low risk. The monitor shows a strong heart beat. Newborns have survived at 24 weeks gestation while yours is already 29. Another mother just delivered quintuplets, all less than 3 pounds and all stable. You hope for more than *stable*. You want your baby to wail into the night and crawl into mischief. You want her to run the Bay-to-Breakers like her daddy did last year. You worry about your toddler at home who wonders where the ambulance took his mommy.

You spend the next four days immobilized. The IV drip dings periodically. The nurse assures you it won't be long. You want it to be long. You want eight more weeks of umbilical insurance that your baby will survive. You make silent bargains with a god you are not sure you believe in. Six more weeks? Five? The doctor insists that this is not what you want, because your water has broken. Soon, the demons of infection stalking the polished hospital cor-ridors will find your baby and harm her.

You yearn to ditch the apparatus of the monitors, and the disinfectant stink, and the pain of cervix examination, and the chill of jelly on your belly when the ultrasonographer manipulates the fetus for a better view. You dream to walk a hundred miles home and hide in the forest where you will build a nest of ferns and birth your baby alone, the way the ancestors knew how to do. Forget technology. Let nature take her course.

The attending physician explains every detail of fetal lung development to eight very serious interns. When you look at the monitor, you realize that your daughter's arms and legs are smaller than the thinnest twigs on last sum-mer's cherry tree. She swims, suspended in amniotic oblivion, connected to every tide, to every moon, to a universe where she knows everything and you know nothing.

A very small voice calls to you from a far away place. The voice says *mommy*. The staff suddenly promises: *your daughter will now be able to breathe on her own*. They wheel you down the corridor to the operating room, *just in case*. You are beyond fear. She is calling. This is the moment. She slips into her father's hands for just a touch before they wheel her away in an isolette.

The next day, you are free to leave, anytime before noon. But your daugh-ter must stay. Two months, maybe three. The intensive care nurse takes your soft, musical lamb toy and promises to play the wind-up lullaby every so often. You do not want to leave your baby here, but you must. *Get some rest. Come back in six hours. She will be fine*, they promise. You want to believe them, as you walk out the front door of the hospital, alone.

*Jyotsna Sreenivasan*

# The Mirror

I'm lying on this hard hospital delivery bed with only a small thin robe over my body. My legs, even my knees, are all uncovered and my bare feet are in these stirrups, they call them. It's indecent, how you must be to give birth. In India do they cover the women more? I don't know, but here in America, no one cares, they go about in shorts and swimming suits anyway, even the old fat ladies do it, exposing all their white wrinkled flesh just like that.

My hands and arms are cold. My stomach is a big mountain. Every so often it gets hard and I know I'm having a contraction. It doesn't hurt at all. They gave me a shot in my back, an epidural they call it. I'm glad. I was afraid I would scream and embarrass myself.

The American nurse comes in. She's thin and tall. She wears a short white skirt and white stockings and white shoes and a white cap. She smiles. I have gotten used to these Americans smiling all the time. When I first came here in April of 1963, almost two years ago, I thought, why are they always laughing at me? At first I thought, it's my sari and my kumkum. They have never seen someone wearing a sari and kumkum before. Then, after I took off the kumkum and began wearing skirts and shaving my legs and everything, still they laughed. I thought, what's wrong with me, that they should be showing their teeth every time I appear? Maybe it's because I'm brown, I thought. But they have seen brown people before. There are plenty of these Africans everywhere, Negroes they call them, and they would also laugh at me. I could not understand it. Finally I asked my friend Mary Pryor. She's my closest friend in America. She is a single lady and she owns a house and we stay in the apartment in the basement. Imagine, a single lady owning her own house and even renting it to strangers!

Mary told me, Prema, they are not laughing at you. They are just being friendly. You must also smile when you meet someone.

My husband isn't here yet. He's a resident doctor at this hospital and that's why he will be allowed to be with me at the birth. He's just finishing up some work and he'll be here soon. Otherwise, I would have to be all alone. I'm glad I will not be all alone.

In India, I would have my baby in the "nursing home" near my mother's house. That's what they call the places where ladies go to have babies — "nursing homes." The place is just two streets from my mother's house. It's in the home of a doctor — a lady doctor, of course. In India, they don't have men doctors for ladies. But here they think nothing of having a man look at that part of a lady and put his fingers in and everything. Thoo! It's disgusting. But what to do? Here I am in America.

My elder sister went to this nursing home last year to have her baby and I still have not seen my first niece. I don't know when we will go back home. Sometimes I wonder, why did I agree to marry a man who wanted to study in America? I thought it would be fun to come here. I saw pictures of American homes in magazines, and everything looked so nice, so clean. When I was a little girl I thought, people in America must not ever use the toilet. I could not imagine such large white people ever needing to do something dirty like that. It's funny what children think about.

"How're we doing, Mrs. — " The nurse looks at a piece of paper on a clipboard. "How d'you say your name?"

"Mrs. Venkatesh," I say. "I am fine, thank you." I smile a little bit. I am too cold to smile very much.

The nurse pushes up my robe and puts her fingers in down there. This is the part I hate about having a baby, having everyone feeling around down there. "Good," she says. "Eight centimeters. When you start pushing, I can adjust this mirror so you can see." She points to a round mirror above the bed.

"See what?"

"So you can see the baby coming out!" she exclaims.

"Oh. No. No." Then I remember my manners. "No, thank you." Only in America would they have something so the woman can see! What is there to see? It's bad enough to have all this happening down there, in that part of my body. But what can I do? God made us give birth from there. Don't ask me why. Seeing isn't going to help anything.

The nurse leaves the room. I don't know where my husband is. At the time I agreed to come to America, I had no idea what it would really be like. When I first arrived here in Akron, Ohio, there were no leaves at all on the trees. I thought, so America is like this, with no leaves on the trees, no flowers. I have come from India, which is full of flowers, to this God-forsaken place. I was so unhappy. Before I arrived I thought, my husband is a doctor, and we will be going to the richest country in the world. I will live like a queen. I didn't know the hospital did not pay residents well. I didn't know we would have to live in a basement apartment with paint and everything falling off the ceiling. I didn't know we would not be able to find basic Indian groceries, not even dal or ghee or yogurt. At home we have a cook and I never learned to make my own ghee or yogurt. Here I somehow make something or other using split peas and corn oil and sour cream. My mother sends me spices every so often, sambar powder and rasam powder, but I cannot find fresh chillies or coriander leaves. The only coconut in the store here is dried and sweetened, so I cannot use it. Imagine, eating South Indian food without coriander leaves or coconut!

But it's not so bad. I am used to it now. The main thing was, I was bored. My husband was at the hospital all day and even at night sometimes. I don't drive and anyway, where would I go? There is only one other Indian couple near us, and both of them, husband and wife, are doctors, so they are both just as busy. How to spend my time? Besides cooking and cleaning, I did some knitting and I went upstairs to watch TV with Mary. Finally one day I said to my husband, let's have a baby. My mother is writing asking why we are not expecting yet. I need some way to spend my time. Let's have a baby.

So here I am in the hospital. The nurse comes in again and checks me. "Ten centimeters," she says. "You're ready." The doctor is here now, a man doctor. He's wearing a mask and is pulling on some rubber gloves.

The nurse puts her hand on my stomach. "OK, push now," she says. So every time I feel my stomach tighten, I push as hard as I can.

"Good!" the nurse says. "I can see the head. Are you sure you don't want to see?"

I put my elbows on the bed and try to sit up. I want to see my baby.

"Lie down," she says. "You can't see that way. You need to use the mirror."

"Yes," I say. "Yes, I want to see." My heart is going thump-thump-thump so fast.

The nurse pulls the mirror down and I can see something, a shiny black-haired head. I can see what the man doctor is seeing. I don't care that he is seeing that part of me. I want to see my baby's face.

"Push," the nurse says.

I hold my breath and push. I can see the head come out. The face is turned the other way.

"Good," says the doctor. "Push again."

I see the rest of the body slide out, and the doctor catches it. "It's a girl!" he says.

A girl. I had wanted a boy first, and then a girl next. I wanted a big brother who would protect his younger sister. But I have a girl! I thank God. Anyway, my older brother never protected me. A girl is good. I hold out my arms and try to sit up. "Let me see her."

The nurse laughs. "So you wanted to see after all. I'll clean her off."

I don't want to wait. Just then my husband arrives. I had forgotten about him. "A girl!" I shout to him. "There she is."

He peeks over the nurse's shoulder. I'm jealous that he gets to see her first, when I'm the one who's been carrying her. "Bring her here," I say.

He brings her to me all wrapped up tight in a white blanket. Only her face shows. I try to sit up and take her, but the doctor, who's still doing something down there, says, "Lie still!"

So I can only look. Her black eyes look at me. "She's so white!" I exclaim. "Why is she so white?" I wonder if this is one more thing I didn't know about America—that babies born here turn white.

"It's OK," my husband says. "Even Indian babies are white when they're first born."

I look at her dark eyes and dark hair. I touch her cheek with one finger and she turns her mouth towards my finger. "She thinks it is food!" I say. "What, are you my American baby?" I ask. "I saw you come out in that round mirror," I tell her. "Here in America, they have things like that, so Amma can see you right away."

*Teresa Breeden*

# The Good Book

## 1. Bonding

The Book discusses Bonding:
the methods, the timing, the
importance of.
Even before birth, in-utero, that special connection
between mother and child, father and child, siblings and child
worlds, and universes, and worm-holes and child. The lovely
nirvanic state of familial
Bonding.

Bondage, though apropos,
is not a term found in the Book.
The fact that you will not sleep, or leave your home, or
even depart your stained and rank chair for several weeks.
That you will spend 16 hours a day with a
turbine powered, supercharged, fuel injected, V8
suction assaulting some of you more tender parts —
also not mentioned.

## 2. The First Month

The book describes the pain
of not knowing if that wavery keening
is a hunger cry or a tired cry.
The pain of worrying about your child's percentages
head-size-wise and weight and length.
It doesn't spend text
on chapped nipples, cracked nipples, bleeding
nipples, medicated breast pads, doesn't

mention at all that special sort of ripping pain
when it's time to remove
the breast pad your nipple has scabbed to,
the tenderized flesh collecting, connecting
with any form more solid than its
broken-throated self.


## 3. Getting to Know Your Child

The Book uses euphemisms that sound
like something you will pay at the dentist's for later:
sweetheart, precious, muffin, munchkin, darling girl, dear boy.
or like something you spend twenty minutes with a pair
of pliers and a wire cutter to remove the packaging from:
brand new, newborn, newest addition.
And a prize, a trophy, that engraved plaque or at least
the gauche-3-cent-shiny-yellow-science-fair ribbon
is awarded to…
New Arrival—
like she just came in on a plane, taxied
her way into our well-ordered lives from
New York or Belize with maybe a short
stopover in Detroit.
Arrived.
No nine months, no Braxton Hicks
contractions, no
maternity clothes, back spasms, incontinence. No KY.
No ultrasounds or stirrups, no probes.
Arrived.
Just Like That.


Other, more practical names
are not mentioned, at least,
not by the Book. Not in the table of contents, the section titles. Not even
in the reference tables or glossary—
As though never spoken by other parents, who must think
all babies are always precious
all of the time—
Yoda, Wrinkled Old Man (for a girl), Scowlface,
Wiggle Worm, Human Pacifier, Baby Mole,

Snapping Turtle, Little
Piranha Girl, Parasite
Leech.

## 4. Acknowledgements

The Book.
Accepted as one of the best
sources for new parents. Referenced by other,
thinner books, recommended
by 9 out of 10 pediatricians
but maybe, I think,
not primarily for accuracy.

Although, we do like our little Snapping Turtle
a little bit more
than a little bit, so maybe they weren't
entirely wrong. Not entirely.
And maybe
we weren't either.

*Curtis Smith*

# Vision

There's a spot on your child's heart.

As a ten-year-old boy, I had entered a phase of gullible fascination. I believed in the Bermuda Triangle, ESP, Bigfoot, satanic possession and any other variable of chance that could be categorized as paranormal. Of course ancient astronauts had visited the Aztecs. Of course the dead stranded between heaven and hell walked among us. What further proof did a boy need beyond the night shivers of an old house, the creaking steps and wheezing pipes? The gust-rattling windowpanes? The curtains' billowing dance?

The ultrasound—what a glorious machine! The hidden exposed! The inner revealed! Now if only we could look inside and retrieve the disjointed images of our dreams. The ten-year-old perks up at the notion, but would the present-tense me really want to revisit such pictures, scenes unfiltered by the defenses and stances it's taken me all these years to develop? I think not.

The summer of my wife's pregnancy, I was haunted by petite baby hearts. The nicked golf balls I kicked back into my neighbor's yard would be the size of his heart. In the supermarket produce aisle I became transfixed by grapes and plums. In the detachment of idle moments, I would cup my hand and study the empty air cradled in my palm, gradually drawing my fingers in, then out, trying to approximate the dimensions of that briefly glimpsed organ.

Repeating nightmares from my childhood: wandering room to room in a stripped bare house where all the windows were sealed and no door led outside; my teeth turning to candy corn and crumbling in my mouth; flames shooting out of electric outlets. The ten-year-old's gothic imagination leaves him trembling beneath his covers, and he is certain the nooks of his room are inhabited by missing children and headless soldiers. Some nights I became so convinced of their presence I would lapse into paralysis, my stricken throat unable to mutter a syllable…yet I never shut my eyes for I secretly yearned to witness the breach that surely waited between my world and theirs.

Amazing, the amplified *swoosh-swoosh* of my wife's womb. Amazing, the wonders buried beneath her skin. The curve of the spine. The hands' tiny yet complete bones. The skull's network of thread-like fissures. The boy's package of turtle-shaped genitalia. Amazing!

The ten-year-old boy keeps his eyes opened in hopes of glimpsing the other side. The forty-year-old man, having finally realized his desire, wishes he'd blinked.

*There's a spot on your child's heart.* The image froze on the monitor, and the doctor pushed a button. The machine purred, and when a linked series of pictures shimmied out, I thought of a boardwalk photo booth my wife and I had crammed into years before, our skin sunburned and smelling of ocean salt.

A hot, dry summer, my wife and I sharing a lap lane at the local pool after she got off work. She shoved off first with an effortless backstroke, and I struggled in her wake with a splashing freestyle, my years of jogging and biking not translating to the demands of the water. Each night the moment came where the low sun set the surface ripples ablaze, a scintillating display that, for a few passing minutes, obscured what lay beneath. The lifeguards leaned forward in their perches, their lazy, day-long vision now tested. The children's cries feathered over the open water — *Marco? Polo!* — and the daredevils yelped as they leapt from the spring-twanging boards. And in our lane, the childish antics continued for our unborn son loved the water. I finished each lap with a submerged kick, my hands outstretched and my heartbeat thudding in my ears, my chlorine-stung eyes opened wide in this hidden world. My fingers touched down on the stretched fabric of my wife's suit where my arrival was greeted by joyous kicks and punches.

The ten-year-old, fearful of the nebulous evil lurking in his room, can't fall asleep, his consciousness gripped like a raft in a tempest sea. The forty-year-old rockets from fitful dreams into an even more fitful reality in the small hours after midnight. Playing in my head — a continuous loop of the ultrasound's show, the mesmerizing four-chambered mechanics, the cadenced squish of contracted muscles, a tiny, white-cloud spot which now burned neon-bright.

In a sun-baked parking lot after our third-trimester ultrasound, my wife and I cried, a clinging pose easily mistaken for grief by passers-by. The spot had vanished, our doctor shrugging and saying these things happened...but in this world where matter can neither be created nor destroyed, what had become of the spot? Did it still exist in my child's body, a free-floating particle of malice? Had it escaped the trappings of my wife's belly and tumbled off on the wind like a dandelion seed? Did it follow me around, brushing against my world, showing itself as the tickle that preceded a sneeze, an irritation begging to be scratched?

Six weeks later, our son came forth in a fury of blood and pain, and within twenty-four hours of his arrival, another wondrous machine had detected the pinprick hole between the lower chambers of his heart, a murmur so benign yet distinct the staff's pediatric cardiologist smiled as he handed us his stethoscope. *Flub-a-dub* sang our boy's imperfect heart.

Images from my post-birth dreams — books with print that turned liquid, black streams running off the page and puddling in my lap; a bathroom renovation project which exposed a secret lair behind the shower's tiled wall; a shared cup of coffee with a long-dead friend, his face obscured by the rising steam, his words instantly forgotten but the sound of his voice so unmistakable that I woke feeling reassured about life and death and my position on its heartbreaking continuum.

By six months, our boy rolled across the floor to snag the blocks and stuffed animals we were too oblivious to fetch for him. By seven months, he'd already dismantled our alphabetized collection of CDs. At eight months, he was cruising around our living room, a path of surprising ingenuity, the sofa and chairs and coffee table latched onto with the tenacity of a sailor clutching the rails of a storm-tossed ship. At ten months, he walked, four shaky steps before thumping onto his diaper-cushioned rump, and once this bit of self-propelled magic was discovered, there was no turning back, my wife and I laughing at his relentless forward-focus, the unblinking intensity of his steely blue eyes, the quivering momentum of his jowls. With each visit to the pediatrician, his murmur grew fainter.

Our one-year checkup with the pediatric cardiologist, another dimly lit room, our boy stripped to his diaper and stretched across a dwarfing examination table. He smiled at the nurse's antics as she slathered gel on his naked belly, laughed at the slippery contact made when his fingers poked his navel, stared solemnly as the doctor lowered the ultrasound's paddle.

A rapid *flub-flub* played over the speakers, and on the monitor, a red and blue tide flowed through the chalky maze. The doctor pointed to the hole's spritzing leak, a miniscule spray of mixed colors. The doctor was pleased, the gap now almost closed, and he predicted by next year it would be gone. For a moment, even our son seemed rapt by the monitor's show. Amazing.

The image blurred as our boy began to struggle. My wife and I whispered the words that normally soothed him. The nurse cooed and jangled a set of plastic keys, but our boy responded to each consoling effort with increased agitation. Deafening, his cries of displeasure and confusion. *Hush, baby, please hush*, yet soon our calming attempts gave way to the necessity of restraint, the nurse and my wife and I pinning his limbs as the doctor attempted one final look. Our son's pulse quickened, a dizzying frantic sound that reminded me of the time a frightened sparrow had been trapped in my grandmother's garage. My boy writhed against my grip, tears streaking his cheeks, his throat choked with anger. On the monitor, blips of static knifed into the image of his distressed heart.

*Wendy Wisner*

# His First Week

I feared the blood on the sheet,
the knifey zap of letdown,
the choking spray of milk.
Each time he fell asleep, his death.
And when he wouldn't sleep,
his gray, feral eyes.
My face: puffy, swollen,
as though I'd suckled at the amnion,
drowned in the birth pool.
And what if I did die,
what if he had no mother, no milk.
What if we never slept again,
and the world became dream
and the dream became world.
I feared the world,
the polar ice caps melting,
my son never knowing
winter, his life an endless summer,
his lungs, his skin, the boy
who had grown in my body
black and burning.
It was winter and the bedroom
was shot with bourbon light.
I folded him up in a blanket
and carried him through the apartment.
*This is it*, I told him,
the sink gleaming with dishes,
my old clothes in twisted heaps on the floor.

*Juliet Eastland*

# Night and Day

Several months ago, I gave birth to my first child, a baby girl. At the same time, a strange thing happened: I began dreaming of Paris. Not, helas, the City of Light. Rather, I was spending my nights with Paris Hilton. Paris and I lolling on a yacht; Paris and I glittering in gowns; Paris and I cantering on thoroughbreds, our long, bleached hair fluttering like the silk from genetically-modified corn.

I have short, dark hair, and I don't even like horses. What is this meshugas? How is it that now, at the rawest, most deeply emotional time of my life, I am spending my evenings with a shiksa sexpot? My feelings are not amorous—I prefer brunettes—and I'm not exactly envious, although I do covet her body mass index and her bank balance. I do not seek to emulate her contributions to society (her contributions to "Society" are another story). As far as I can tell, Paris espouses no cause larger than Paris.

And that is the point: she embodies, to the nth degree, gleeful, shameless self-absorption. She is id incarnate, a sort of ur-child jetting between fetes and fiancés. And as she appears in my dreams, dancing me through the high life, I too get to play at being a glamorous, gallivanting kid.

This escapism makes sense. My current life, after all, is anything but high. I forego showers; I forget to eat; I have left home sporting mismatched shoes and a fuzzy pacifier-holder clipped to my lapel like a corsage. I worry constantly: will my daughter find happiness? Will she vote green? And what's that spot on her face? It's exhausting, parenthood. No wonder I need a break.

But this is not the full story. The real transformation is taking place below the surface, as every cell stretches and shifts to accommodate this new feeling — a visceral, ferocious love unfurling like a vine, winding its tendrils around my organs and wrapping its roots around my bones. This is not the placid adoration of Mother for Child; there is nothing ethereal or holy about my feelings for my baby. My passion is so vehement that my stomach tightens when she holds my gaze and I want to enfold her in my arms and absorb her back into my body. When she falls asleep, her fingers curled in mine like tiny sea creatures, her trust moves me to tears. I think about my role as protector, and for the first time, I am certain I could kill another human being. It's an unsettling feeling.

I am her guide, and what a privilege it is to be present at her first encounters with the universe. Today, I bring her to the florist and watch as she stares, taking in the saffron gerberas and the velvety purple of the tulips. She is seeing these colors for the first time, and she is mesmerized. Her concentration is contagious, and I feel myself grow still, breathing with her. Watching her pulse beat under her scalp, I imagine her neurons popping and firing. I think of the carpet of electric-blue ajuga I stumbled on deep in the woods at summer camp, and the log coated with scarlet fungus that I tripped over on my post-college hiking trip out west. I am overjoyed beyond reason to think of her similarly hijacked by moments of jubilant, colorful surprise. At the same time, I know that part of the thrill of discovery is the joy of possession, of secrecy. After a certain point, the colors that surprise her will be hers, not ours. They will be added, like a tile, to the mosaic that is her life — a life separate from mine. Even though she is snuggled against me, the chill of bereavement spreads through my chest, and for one dark, rageful moment I wish I did not love her.

Then the door to that unlit space closes and I am back, holding her to me, and I understand Paris' presence in my life. This glossy-lipped Barbie is my escape, not from the daily frazzle of parenthood, but from this unseen, buffeting passion. I frolic with Paris at night, and awake ready to wrestle anew with the unsettling and exhilarating feelings. For a double life, it's not half bad.

*Davi Walders*

# It's So Different Now

As soon as our daughter, Anna, returned home with her first baby, Jacob, breastfeeding became the main issue. She had had a great pregnancy, relatively easy birth, and both mother and son had done wonderfully in the hospital while Jacob slept a lot and fed occasionally with the nurses standing by to help.

But at home, Jacob didn't nurse well. He would fall asleep just after latching on or not latch on well and cry for long periods. Anna, growing more worried with each try, asked how breastfeeding had gone when she was an infant. I had to tell her I didn't remember much about those days. Which was true, although I kept to myself dim memories of winter hours that passed in the peace of a daughter sucking happily away as I dreamed my dreams, read my books, or even cooked with her in a sling. That's what memory does—erases the struggles, the sleepless nights, the frantic calls to the doctor, all those long-ago winter worries.

As she holds Jacob in her arms, trying again and again to feed him, I can only clean the house, change diapers, cook for her, and champion her efforts. And quickly learn how ignorant I am. It's not just a matter of poor memory—I am ignorant. The world has changed. When she was a baby, we only had Lamaze and La Leche League to help. Now there are is a whole allied health field of lactation consultants. There are breastfeeding classes, thousands of different style breast pumps, back supports for feeding, boppy pillows of myriad colors and shapes. As well as teas, herbs, and pills to increase milk supply.

My heart breaks for her when I hear Jacob's cries as she tries to feed him. We pack him in the car seat and go to consultant after consultant. He's not a "natural latcher," says one. Another says our daughter has an infection, wants her on antibiotics. Another says she has a fungus and should puncture her nipples. Determined, she keeps trying, nursing and pumping, day and night. Her husband begins to give him a supplement after her breast feedings. Even the supplement takes hours.

"Jacob is beautiful," I say. "He's healthy. He's just not a big eater yet. It will work out. You're doing great," I tell her over and over, but, of course, she doesn't believe me. After all, what do I know? I'm just her mother.

Jacob's feeding problems continue and the nights without sleep take their toll. "How long did it take for your milk to really come in?" she asks groggily one morning on the verge of tears. "I don't remember. Maybe a couple of days…maybe longer," is all I can say, failing her again. "It will work out." I sound like an ignorant robot.

Her nipples crack and bleed, her breasts become engorged. We go to the pediatrician. The baby has gained only a few ounces. The pediatrician says it will happen, her milk supply will kick in. Her husband says it will happen. I say it will happen. "But how do you know?" she asks disbelieving, tearing up again.

We are following them in our own car on the way to the *bris*, the Jewish ritual circumcision which takes place on the eighth day after birth. We are driving to their synagogue where the service will take place. The pediatric surgeon and rabbi are waiting as are friends and sweets for the reception. It is a sunny fall afternoon and we are all looking forward to getting this milestone behind us and him. Suddenly our son-in-law pulls off on a side street and motions to us to pull up beside them.

"Quick," Anna says, leaning over. "Can you run back to the house? Look in the second drawer of the dresser. You'll find my breast pads there. I didn't think I'd need them, but look," she says with a smile. And there is her beautiful rich milk from her beautiful full breasts leaking all over her red silk blouse.

"Oh, and bring me the black sweater hanging in my closet," she says. "I need to cover the stains up."

We turn around, rush back to the house. We pick up the pads and sweater and head to the synagogue. The *bris* is beautiful. Jacob receives his name. Anna's husband, Ben, speaks about the grandfather he is named for. Anna speaks of the joy of giving birth to this little boy; the rabbi, the surgeon, and others in the family say blessings. The circumcision is over in a second. Jacob doesn't cry at all.

Afterwards, while friends stand around talking, drinking coffee, and eating sweets at the reception, our daughter and grandson leave the crowd and relax in the mommy and baby room. Jacob is blissfully breastfeeding in the quiet room. No one says I told you so. We just watch her beam looking down at her son in her arms.

A few days later, after loads of laundry, freezing meals for the week ahead, and one final vacuum and sweep, we fly home. Several days later, Anna calls barely able to contain herself. She has just been to the pediatrician for a weigh-in. Our grandson has gained two pounds. She and he are doing great. Her milk supply is growing daily. He's sleeping three to four hours between feedings. The pediatrician says he's become a "good latcher."

"Mom," she says, "can you believe how well he's doing!" I smile, congratulating her on how well they're both doing.

We're heading into winter. Someday, I think, Anna, too, will have memories of quiet hours breastfeeding Jacob, reading her novels, dreaming her dreams. On second thought, maybe it's not so different now.

*Jenny Kurzweil*

# Weaning

Sasha is eating rice cereal now. At six months old, he looks tiny in his over-sized white high chair—yet another hand-me-down from his big brother Jacob. He sits upright in a wobbly, intent way and reaches vainly for the spoon as my partner Andrea aims, dodging and weaving, for his mouth. The baby books suggest that he should sit in one of our laps to provide intimacy and promote comfort with mealtimes. But the feeding process is still in the interactive sport stage and I can't handle rice cereal smeared all over my body. The baby knocks the spoon out of Andrea's hand and the sweet smelling, pasty cereal goes flying—splattering Jackson Pollack like across the wall. Sooner or later, he'll join the rest of us solid food eaters and leave me and my breasts far behind.

I didn't think I'd love breastfeeding so much. I had no firsthand experience since Andrea birthed Jacob and was not able to nurse him due to a supply and demand issue (voracious newborn appetite, not enough milk). Now that it was my turn to give birth, I began an intense observation period of all things breasty.

After visiting a friend and her six month old son, I wasn't so sure I was ready for the nipple calisthenics of nursing. My friend and I sat on the couch talking while she fed the baby. Then he turned his head to look at me with my friend's nipple still in his mouth. Her nipples were cartoonish, stretching like silly putty. It seemed inconceivable that my sensitive little nipples could transform into this flexible, udder-like phenomenon.

My friend laughed at the expression of terror on my face and she gently focused her baby back on his meal. "I know," she said breezily, "breastfeeding seemed so weird to me when I was pregnant. Now it feels like the most natural thing."

"It just looks like it hurts so much," I whined.

"You have to get used to it. In your last trimester, massage, pull, pinch your nipples to condition them for breastfeeding. It worked for me."

I smiled and nodded and thought to myself, "Yeah…that's one piece of pregnancy advice that I am going to leave in the dust."

But a couple months later, there I was, squeezing into the bathtub, my huge belly knocking my knees against the side of the tub. I dutifully grasped each of my nipples between my thumbs and forefingers. Nothing. I couldn't muster what it would take to really rough myself up.

As it turns out, I had longer than anticipated to get ready for breastfeeding. Sasha was hospitalized for a month after he was born due to meconium aspiration syndrome (poop in the lungs). By the time he was two weeks old and I got to hold him for the first time, I would have gladly cut off one of my nipples if it would have enabled him to breastfeed. Rather, I would have given any one of my limbs, organs, anything to have him get better. A little nipple discomfort seemed laughable now.

I was astounded by the strength of my post partum animal instinct and I felt like a tormented beast in the neonatal intensive care unit (NICU) when I went to visit Sasha. My heart pounded as I entered, my breath becoming fast and shallow in my chest. The unit was blaring white and noisy with the beeping of machines, the comings and goings of doctors, and the steady chatter of nurses who had the amazing ability to converse pleasantly about real estate, movies, and their husbands, while concentrating on the painstaking and intricate work of keeping critically ill infants alive. Their white gloved hands delicately monitored blood oxygenation levels, dispensed medicine in IVs as thin as veins, and bathed preemies not much larger than my outstretched hand.

Sasha was tucked in a quiet corner of the unit, right by the heart and lung bypass machine—just in case he needed it. His bed, more like a cushioned platform with a heat lamp over it, was waist high to allow for easy access by doctors and nurses. The heat lamp was kept warm enough so that Sasha, who lay splayed on his back, arms out to his side, was able to be kept only in a diaper. This enabled all of the tubes, wires and IVs to be constantly checked and adjusted.

I would lean as far over his bed as possible so that he might get a whiff of me, as though catching my scent might re-establish the mother/child bond I feared had been broken since I was not able to hold or nurse him. When I couldn't stand it anymore, I would leave his crib and go pump milk like a maniac—which I was supposed to do every three hours. It was the only tangible thing I could do to help Sasha. The nurses kept cheerily encouraging me, "This is your job! Your milk is going to be so good for the baby."

"Isn't this milk all going to go to waste?" I growled to the nurses, since for the first couple of weeks, pumping seemed more like an exercise in futility as Sasha was only able to take a thimble full at a time through the feeding tube which traveled down to his belly through his nose.

Sasha's primary nurse, a young wispy woman with an air of elegant efficiency and rock solid competence, smiled knowingly. "Jenny, before you know it, Sasha will be sucking so much milk down, you'll barely be able to keep up with it."

Despite all evidence to the contrary, I held on to the nurse's words and with this glimmer of hope in my heart, I would trundle off to the whitewashed walls of the pumping room in the parent's "lounge." The lounge was an area with a couple of hospital issued couches, a bathroom, two bare bedrooms for families to crash in temporarily, and a kitchenette area with a sink, a dirty crusty microwave and a small refrigerator stuffed with forgotten leftovers.

The pumping room was sparse, sanitary, and smelled of disinfectant and rubber shoes. There were four pumping stations sectioned off with privacy curtains, each with a small low table, a standard hospital armchair of brown vinyl, and a super sonic breast pump. The short squat pumps were a cheery yellow and made an efficient swishing sound when working. We mothers supplied the rest of the needed equipment—air tubes that connected the pump to suction-like cups that we held to our breasts, and bottles that the milk dripped and then streamed into. We schlepped all of the pumping paraphernalia around in bright pink hospital tubs from baby's bedside to pumping room and back again. We never talked to one another while we were pumping.

The room was always strangely silent except for the rhythmic hum of the machines. It was not the comfortable and hushed warmth of an old-fashioned barn at dawn, where cows chew their sweet grain together while being milked, tails gently swishing against one another's bodies. This was a strained silence, a deep silence, as if talking would take too much effort, or be much too painful.

A couple of times I spoke to the other women while we were in the lounge, waiting for a pumping spot, or washing our equipment. The conversations were formulaic. A weary exchange of "hi's."

Then, "What is your baby here for?"

The ailments described would be worse than the last, "Organ transplant." Or "heart surgery." Or "brain surgery."

Then, "How long have you been here?" Sometimes the answer would be just a couple of days, often, for the critically ill preemies, a couple of months.

Then, "I'm so sorry."

"Yeah, I'm sorry for you too."

Then there would be a wan smile and nod, and we would slowly trudge in opposite directions.

After about two weeks, Sasha turned a corner and began to officially recover. A condition of his leaving the hospital, however, was teaching him how to eat. Period. Although the nurses were philosophically supportive of breastfeeding, their main concern was that he take the milk, in whichever vehicle he responded to most readily—boob or bottle, they didn't care. The nurses had to measure his intake of breast milk (my frozen hard work now coming in handy) to make sure he was getting enough to gain weight. It was easiest for the nurses and for Sasha to just take a bottle, since after such a battle for his life, he was still too weak to exert the effort to nurse despite my continued efforts and the help of the lactation consultant.

I suppose it helped that the last four days we were at the hospital, I got a bad cold and had to stay away. Andrea would call me after every time Sasha ate to report how much milk he had taken. I was filled with gratitude that he was recovering, but would cry after we got off the phone, terrified that he would become too conditioned to bottle feeding to take to the breast.

I had become so fiercely attached to the idea of breastfeeding that I was losing sight of the miracle of his complete and full recovery. Breastfeeding was my last hold out in the fantasy I had concocted for my "perfect birth." I didn't have the vaginal delivery I imagined, where they haul the baby out of me and place his bloody slimy body on my chest while I cry tears of joy and the morning sun streams golden into the hospital room. Instead I had four days of protracted labor that ended with the doctors rolling me (on all fours and ass-backward to halt the contractions) into a c-section because the baby was in severe distress. I didn't have the baby a week, two weeks, three weeks later. I was panic stricken that he wouldn't know me, that we wouldn't have a physical bond.

When we got home he was still too weak and tired to breastfeed and I sullenly felt like I spent more time pumping than I did holding him. I imagined a distance growing between us. I couldn't stand to feed him by bottle myself, so would watch miserably as Andrea cuddled him, cooing, as he sucked down breast milk from a plastic nipple.

Despite my deep desire to breastfeed, we introduced it slowly as Sasha regained energy, on the verge of panic that he wasn't taking enough. My breasts were so round and full that they ached and I could see from my pumping, that the output of milk had increased exponentially since we had gotten home. But to make sure that he was eating sufficiently from the breast, Andrea and I visited our local lactation center with Sasha so they could weigh the baby before and after a feeding.

Lili, the head lactation consultant welcomed us into the office with warm hugs. She had been bedrock for us after the births of both boys, coaching Andrea through the process of providing what she could for Jacob, and coming to the house with different models of pumps for me to experiment with after Sasha was born. Almost in tears, I spilled out all of my fears that had built up over the last month.

Lili talked me down, sat me in an armchair while she weighed Sasha, then placed him gently in my arms and coached me into a comfortable position and good latch. She carefully watched Sasha suck, breathe, and swallow, and then she weighed him again when he was done eating.

Lili smiled as she lifted Sasha off the scale and handed him back to me. "You have nothing to worry about," she laughed. "He just took over four ounces in the feeding, nearly twice as much as normal for babies his size."

That moment, when Lili pulled him off the scale and announced how much he had eaten, that was my birth. That was my moment of pride, of joy, relief, and triumph. There was no sunshine or blood or birthing placenta, just the creak of the teal faux leather armchair, the stuffy warm air of a hospital, and a five week old baby with sweet milky breath and a full belly.

I breastfed Sasha exclusively for the rest of my maternity leave. He and I ate voraciously; I walked about with my nursing pillow still Velcroed around my waist like a plush hula-hoop, and happily heaved my huge breasts in and out of my nursing bra when Sasha made even the slightest peep. It seemed as though the world fell away when I was flooded with the tingle of my milk letting down, and I would settle with a sigh onto the couch or the rocker or the bed and nurse Sasha as though my life depended on it.

One night, a couple of months after bringing Sasha home, my parents were over and we were all in the living room talking. At least, they were talking. I was gazing adoringly at Sasha across the room in Andrea's arms. I couldn't take my eyes off him. It was though I had tunnel vision and the rest of the room, my partner, parents and my older child, were a blur in the periphery. Someone had to call my name repeatedly to get my attention, and for a moment, the world sharply came into focus again.

Later that night, Andrea and I lay with Sasha bundled between us and Jacob was asleep in his "big boy" bed across the hall. As I snuggled as close as I could to Sasha without waking him, my heart pounding with his every stirring, I could see that I was obsessed. When I wasn't nursing the baby I was holding him, and if I wasn't holding him, then I wanted to hold him. It was though I was a bottomless pit of need, hungrily trying to satiate the weeks of longing I had felt when he was hospitalized.

It is hard to shake this feeling, and I wonder, if I'm not careful, if an obsession can turn into a habit. In my fleeting moments of clarity I can see that this is not such a good idea. So perhaps this rice cereal is an important first step in regaining some balance and learning how to be a mother to two children instead of a fanatical nurser of one. I have to start weaning myself from Sasha, even though he is not ready to wean from me. Because despite the newfound thrill of rice cereal, he still loves his breast milk, for now. He still approaches me with that urgent voraciousness that I could only dream of when he was sick. He breathes and gulps and drinks, his belly against mine, his hands dancing, reaching for the air.

And this too shall pass.

*Rosalie Sanara Petrouske*

# My Daughter's Births

*I begin to love this little creature, and to anticipate his birth as a fresh twist to a knot, which I do not wish to untie.*
                                        — Mary Wollstonecraft

The first time I held my daughter was four days after her birth. Senara's father, Christopher, pushed me in a wheelchair to the second floor Neonatal Intensive Care Unit where my three-pound baby slept under the glass roof of her incubator. Her skin was dusky pink and wrinkled like a withered rose petal, the soles of her feet scarred and bleeding from being pierced every day to check the levels of her blood gasses. Two small oxygen tubes, called C-paps, were pushed into her nostrils, and an intravenous tube was taped to her right arm. The nurse wrapped her in blankets and pulled a pink knitted cap over the swathe of dark hair that framed her face and swooped down into a miniature widow's peak above her eyebrows. Hands trembling, I reached to take her into my arms. Senara opened her eyes and pursed her lips, then settled back into sleep, not even noticing the tubes and monitors sustaining her life.

"Let's sing to her," Chris said.

So we sang, "Hush little baby, don't say a word," and Senara opened her eyes again and smiled, but the nurse told us it was just a reflex because newborn babies couldn't smile yet. Chris and I exchanged knowing looks.

As I sat watching Senara's curled fists, her eyes closed once more as she slept, I wondered what it was like for her to be pulled into the light two months early when she was used to the dark in my belly, that small cave where she floated and sucked her thumb. I did not expect the incision releasing her into life so soon. It didn't seem fair my body grew sick and rejected her presence the way one might reject an unwanted gift. I missed the warm kicking of her foot above my bellybutton.

Senara and I were just beginning to know each other. I was getting used to the thrumming of her heel or palm, to her being more than the image I saw on the sonogram, to thinking of her as the daughter I would soon hold in my arms and rock to sleep. I waited for that unexplainable feeling of motherhood to encompass me, but I didn't feel any different. What was a mother supposed to feel like anyway? I only felt empty and cold inside as I watched her small chest move up and down erratically, her tiny ribs almost pushing through the thin skin covering them.

Senara was doing well for a premature baby. Her lungs almost fully developed, and her heart was strong. "But her first night was terrible," Chris told me. "All night long she held my thumb and grunted air in and out of her lungs. She struggled so hard to breathe. I never felt so afraid in my life. I was so worried about the two of you," he said.

Five days after Senara's birth, on Tuesday, January 12, I was discharged from the hospital. As I waited in the hallway for Chris to bring the car around, another mother, holding onto an "It's a boy" balloon, waited in a wheelchair. In her arms she held her red-faced infant swaddled in a blue bunting. In my arms, I rocked a purple flowering cyclamen. As we drove away from the hospital, I remember looking up at the second floor windows, trying to find the one square of yellow light from the window of the NICU. I felt small and lost as I did on my first day at the Lincoln Elementary School when I stood clasping my fingers around the chain links of the fence, watching my father walk away.

Chris and I pulled on yellow gowns, scrubbed our hands, and entered Senara's world of beeping monitors, fluorescent lights, and Beatrix Potter wallpaper. I didn't feel like a mother then, only a visitor viewing the procedures, the bustle of the nurses, the muffled wails of babies in their glass houses, and the endless beeping and buzzing as one monitor went off and then another. I was afraid to pick Senara up, afraid of the feeding tube going down her throat, the way her head lolled like a china doll's with a broken neck.

On the evenings when Chris was at work, I visited Senara and just sat watching her sleep — this was my daughter, this creature wrinkling her forehead as if she was full of wisdom and making some great decision. There was loose skin on her arms and neck, and in her face I could see the eighty-year-old grandmother she might be someday.

The monitors above her incubator sent wavering lines in slow motion across the screen. The lines peaked until the screen looked like mountain ranges. Suddenly, the mountains became a straight line, a rolling plain — then the lights blinked, the beepers resounded, and for a second, a space, an instant in time, my daughter stopped breathing. For that moment, her heart paused, her breath looped out into the universe, into the space of the winter night. And I felt as if my heart had stopped also. I held my breath and thought of a childhood game, *I can hold my breath longer than you can. One second, two, three...* I felt as if my chest would explode, my heart catapult through the air.

The lines on the monitors began jumping and peaking. My daughter was breathing again. *She's okay, she's still breathing*, I'd tell myself. *She'll be fine.*

When I sat alone watching Senara sleeping inside her glass box, the brittle bones in her ribs caving in and out, her small fists suddenly jerking at some loud noise in the room, I would imagine her at seven years-old in a red velveteen jumper, her dark hair falling in two long braids, and while snow fell outside the window, I would read *The Snow Goose* to her, our heads bent together over the book's pages as time stopped, the only way it can for a moment that captures both mother and daughter.

A faint anticipation began building somewhere inside me when I thought of Senara's first word, her first step, and her first pair of patent leather Mary Janes. I saw her, a shy, doe-eyed little girl skipping rope, making snow-angels, reading *The Secret Garden* under the flowering dogwood tree. I pictured the first day I'd walk her to school, kicking through leaves, or pulling her in a red sled to the top of a hill, or tucking her into bed, telling her the story of *Rapunzel*, the way my mother used to recite it to me until I knew every word, until I dreamed radishes and towers, and woke up frightened because I dreamt I saw old Gothel in her garden.

I'd look up at the green mountains peaking on Senara's monitor, and I'd tell myself over and over, *She's fine.*

When I thought of Senara's homecoming, of her feedings at 3:00 a.m., I had planned to tuck her into bed with me, pull her against my breast, as we dozed wrapped in the quilt while the wind tugged at the eaves of the roof above us. Instead, I had to sit in an old wood rocker in the NICU and feed

Senara less than an ounce of formula through a gavage tube inserted through her mouth and into her stomach. It took over forty-five minutes for the formula in the tube to drain. My back ached from being pressed into the stiff rocker slats. Chris and I often took turns holding and feeding her.

"I'll never forget the way she held my thumb that first night," Chris said over and over.

When Senara slept and I watched her, I could feel her growing stronger. She was like a small snake expanding into her skin—her wrinkles stretched and smoothed into delicate pink flesh, the membranes in her ears took on a definite shape—no longer did they stick flat and useless to the sides of her head, but now became curved and smooth as the inside of a seashell. My daughter's life had begun in a world of needles, noises, lights, strange faces, and pain. I wondered what she would remember from her experience.

My earliest memory goes back to the age of two when my father held me over my grandpa's coffin. My mother told me I touched "da, da's" face and asked why it was so cold. I'm not sure I recall this exactly, but there are vague impressions of being carried past rows of headstones, of people moving in dark clothes, and my mother crying softly in a pitiful voice, half-sob, half-moan. This was the first memory I can name, but I think, perhaps, even though we can't conjure earlier memories and put complete thoughts to them, they are still with us, those impressions of fear and pain that later shape our adult lives.

When Senara grasped at my finger, or opened her eyes—eyes I knew would be brown, eyes that reminded me of my father's eyes since that's whose eyes I inherited—I would be overwhelmed at the miraculous idea Chris and I had created this new life. A feeling of peace, of marvel, stole through me like a halcyon wind. *Is this it? What it feels like to be a mother?* I felt then I had found it, the first incredible moment of motherhood I had been waiting to experience, but the uncertainty inside of me was stronger, and I knew it was not so simple. Perhaps, motherhood was something I would never be able to define.

Three weeks passed slowly in the NICU. Chris and I checked the chart above Senara's incubator during every visit. The first week in the NICU she lost six ounces, and we were told babies usually lose weight first before they gain it back. The graph on her chart leaped upward during the second week and, from that time on, Senara gained a few ounces each day at a steady pace.

By the end of her second week, she was weaned from the gavage tube to a nursing bottle that still looked to us like a laboratory test tube. On Sunday evening, January 31, Chris and I arrived at the NICU to discover Senara had been removed from the monitors and was now sleeping in an open crib. She weighed 4 lbs. 6 ozs., and we were also told she would be able to go home the following Saturday.

We spent the Friday night before Senara's homecoming in a hospital room adjoining the NICU. This was our trial period in learning how to be her full-time parents. The next morning, after our good-byes to the staff, we carried Senara wrapped in blankets and a pink moon print quilt, made by a hospital volunteer, through the hallways. Patients and visitors smiled at us as we walked by, trying to peer under the blankets at our new baby girl. I felt like a mother now, full of plans and expectations for my child. I felt like I had just given birth.

When we got home, Chris and I opened a bottle of champagne and sat quietly next to Senara's bassinet alongside our bed, watching her sleep. I placed my cheek near her mouth and felt the warmth of her breathing against my skin. In the months following her birth, I'd often wake up during the night if I did not hear her stir for a long time, and watch for the movement of her breath, feel for the air whooshing softly against my hand.

When Senara was nine months old, Chris and I were driving home from the store one October afternoon. We saw a little boy playing in a pile of leaves at the curb. Suddenly, he jumped out in front of our car. Chris slammed on the brakes. The little boy was fine, and his mother soon came running out of her house to scoop up her sobbing child. Later in the evening, as we sat watching television, Chris turned to me.

"I didn't see him there, and all of a sudden he was right in front of the car. I just can't forget it. What if it was Senara? I keep thinking about all the things she's going to have to face, all the times she might be in danger and we won't be there."

I nodded. I think I felt this when she was born, even before, but I just didn't know how to put it into words. Senara was napping on the floor between us covered up with her Mickey Mouse quilt. Chris and I turned the television off and sat in the dark, feeling the soft wisps of Senara's breath brushing the backs of our hands.

*Charlie Rossiter*

# Comforting Jack When He Wakes Coughing and Crying with a Cold

cheek to beard we sway
our breathing slow

slower…
I tell him about the day

the moon, anything
it's not the words

it's our shadow on the wall
night whispers around us,

he is old enough to hold me
as I hold him, close

we grow heavy together,
almost asleep, I put him down

pull the cover up around him.

*Carol Gremli*

# Sizing a Child

"Is there anything I can do for you, dear?" The saleslady leaned over the counter, smiled, then sighed in the silence that followed. I couldn't answer. I stood in the center of Macy's children's shoe department, a box of baby sandals in my hand, struck still by indecision and self-doubt. Minutes were skittering by. In a few hours, my husband Jack and I were set to fly halfway around the world to Chisinau, Moldova, the former Soviet Socialist Republic, where our newly adopted two year old daughter, Ana Christine, waited in a state orphanage. I still had so much to do to bring her home. Besides more forms and documents, medication, baby cereal, and juice, Ana needed clothes. Every sweater and sock she'd worn in her life would be left behind, property of the Botanica Children's Home. And for me, her "almost mother" back in Macy's, the small matter of buying her a pair of shoes had suddenly become large and overwhelming.

I confess. On most days, shopping is one of my favorite forms of stress management. Narrowing my attention to the search for an exact purchase, no matter how trivial or unnecessary, helps direct some of that extra nervous energy that tags along with high anxiety. Until I'd reached the shoe department, I'd been having a wonderful time choosing sundresses and rompers for Ana. But when I came to face the baby sneakers and patent leathers, I froze. The new clothes were of the loose, "one-size fits just about all" variety. But shoes—shoes should fit. How was I supposed to buy a pair for a walking, skipping, jumping child I barely knew?

I thought I'd come prepared. In my right hand, I clutched a sheet of notebook paper on which, three weeks earlier, I'd traced the outline of Ana's foot during our "Get Acquainted and Get Approved" trip to Moldova. In my left hand, I held the pretty little box of toddler-sized summer sandals. The usual details—the quality, the style, the price—were not the concern. Instead, I had discovered the size chart on the back panel of the box, and was reading it with an intensity more suited to the study of Scripture.

I soon realized that the tiny foot drawn on the paper did not correspond with any of the information on the size chart. According to the pink and blue graph, Ana, at almost twenty-four months, should be wearing a size five. My sketch matched up against a size fit for a twelve month old. Though we'd only spent a few hours together, I didn't remember her as being undersized. She was beautiful. Her deep brown eyes were huge, and her hair, when allowed to grow in, would probably be a rich, chestnut brown. Her skin was one of the paler shades of pink—but that would be true of any child who spent most of her time indoors. There was nothing alarming in her appearance that I remembered. All she needed was some vitamins and fresh fruit and continuous servings of family love. But then, could her foot really be this small? The foot I'd traced belonged, according to the chart, to a much younger child. Ana was almost two.

Adding to my confusion was the fact that this was not my first experience in buying children's shoes. Fitting my son, Jordan, now a pre-teenager, had long ago demonstrated the unreliability of size charts. With over ten years of parenting behind me, I should have been able to simply pick a pair and be done with it.

But I knew Jordan. I knew all his sizes as well as his very particular tastes in color and fashion. Everything connected to Ana was still a mystery. Already, even in something as basic as choosing a pair of shoes, I was grasping for guidance, reaching for anything, any standardized structure that would help me begin to organize the sweet chaos of this new relationship. At the same time, I decided to deny what I had seen and experienced for myself. With only a pencil sketch for support, how could I trust the truth?

The saleslady tapped her fingers on the register keys, in rhythm, it seemed, to the throbbing in my head. Both she, and the time, demanded a decision. Casually, or so I thought, I tossed her my selection. The box hit the countertop with a thud that betrayed my true frame of mind and heart. I bought the bigger sandals. I left a bit of my sanity in Macy's that day when I chose the generic expectations of the size chart over the unique reality of my own sketch of my soon-to-be daughter's foot. And as a result, three days later, Ana tripped through the airport in Chisinau with tissues stuffed in her toes.

We survived. I endured the puzzled stares of the orphanage staff as "Anushka" shuffled out of their lives in her spacious new American sandals. And my daughter handled the result of her new mother's first stupid decision by kicking them off with two flips of those tiny feet. The fit was wrong, but we made the best of it. By that time, I'd already moved on to the next chapter of our adoption story, a chapter begun in Macy's. While bureaucrats on both sides of the Atlantic were still processing, stamping, and stapling reams of official documents, I'd faced the frightening fact that there was a lot about Ana, this child who I'd claimed as "mine," that I didn't know. And there would be more: secrets and mysteries about her early life in Moldova that she and I would never resolve. But I was the "mother" now, the one who is supposed to know what's for lunch and where to find the missing sneaker. As for the questions, especially the ones that had no answers, I'd just figure that out later. The time had come to grab my boarding pass and prepare for flight. Ana was waiting. She was no longer the barely discernible face in the adoption agency's referral Polaroid, or even the guarded little girl I'd met a few weeks ago. She was my child, complete with a specific shoe size, a unique temperament, an unknown genetic history, and two year's developmental experience in a place no one I knew had ever heard of. And I've yet to find a chart, graph, or reference table designed to measure or predict all the possibilities presented by that exquisite little miracle.

*Lucille Lang Day*
# Birth Mothers

They are blond or brunette,
look younger than their years.
Their names are as foreign-
sounding as Edeltraut
or familiar as Sue.

They laugh at the cat
that plays "go fetch" like a dog,
but then their gaze turns on
a faraway place where they watch
something unspeakable.

As decades pass, they clink
wine glasses each night
with the husband who knows
or doesn't know, and they carry
their sorrow like a small stone

hanging from the heart,
until one day the phone rings
and a young woman says,
very softly, "Does July 28th
mean anything to you?"

Or a wedding picture drops
from an envelope, and before
reading the letter, the woman
marvels that the bride
looks just like she did at twenty.

Or she answers the doorbell
one morning, and the young man
standing awkwardly on the porch
has the same green eyes
and smile as her first love.

And when I meet these women,
I always remember green
hospital gowns, an awful sound
and the rings that opened
my cervix wider and wider,

and I whisper names
as offerings to the nameless
child who will never find me.

*Stephanie Silvia*

# A Rose, A Name

Like most little girls I had a baby name, a boy and a girl name, for most every letter of the alphabet. J was a good letter. Jews name for their dead. My grandfather's name was John. So was my dad's. Although I didn't even know he was dead until I was 38 years old and he'd been gone for over a year and a half, by then it was obvious, even without a doctor's say so, that there was some sort of fertility problem. I was going to have to adopt. J. Jade or Jacob.

By 38 it didn't even seem possible that I would adopt a baby. R. Rosie or Rueben. I was a dancer. I was a choreographer. I had a dance company. I supported it by working in restaurants and offices and classrooms. How would I be able to take care of a baby? And you know? Babies were kind of overrated anyway. Yeah, they smell like brand new pale pink petals and they squeeze your finger tight making you feel loved and important, and birthing my own would have been beyond joy and I'm sure if someone handed me a baby whose parents had just died in a car wreck I would love her to pieces, but single momming a baby? I had to go to work every day. Babies were exhausting.

Ah…but a kid, a kid went to school. And I loved kids. As the reaction a friend from high school I hadn't seen in twenty years when I told her I was childless can attest. Her mouth dropped open as she stammered: "I thought for sure, you'd have five kids by now! Five boys."

I made dances. Dances were my children. Everlasting love and babies hadn't come, actually with any kind of love babies hadn't come. There was no reason to stop making dances, except that it was inconceivably hard to make dances. Aha! I had held out to forty in the unforgiving dance world of an unforgiving city. Trees, tall trees haunted my dreams. Not to mention that sleeping on a futon on the floor was getting…er…old. It was time to fall back on my degree. (No, not the MFA that still costs me dearly every month in student loan payments.) (The ed degree from twenty years ago that my aunt had encouraged me to get if my then-current dream of becoming a stage actress didn't pan out). Well, fall I would, as segueing into full-time teaching sat, fortuitously, on the near-horizon.

If I was a teacher I could adopt a little girl, A. Annie. Annie could go to school with me. We'd walk or take the subway. I could drop her off at creative movement class or basketball practice or swimming lessons after school, while I went to dance class. (Only twice a week, the other days we'd play together.) (Oh, how I longed to make sacrifices and clothing for my children.)

A teacher's salary could support a little girl. We'd have health insurance, although paying the rent on my apartment would be a problem for L. Lily. (I'd had a Great Aunt Lily.) And I. At the foster parent orientation meeting we were told there was a monthly stipend of about $500.00…even after adoption. That would cover my roommate's rent, the roommate who would graciously move out of my apartment to make room for K. Kitty. (Name of my mother's mother.) Kitty, my precious girl child to be.

My family was not too keen on this foster-adopt thing. I was the wild one. I never had any money. I had bad relationships. I was an artist.

All of the above, true.

But I was soon to become a bona fide teacher, a respected and decent wage-earning member of society.

I wanted to be an M. Mommy.

One day I sat down to tell my Aunt Linda, "If I ever had a little girl, I would name her for my mother, Muriel."

"Why talk of such things? Why talk of things that can't come true? And your mother, she hated her name."

Days later, I called my uncle on the phone. I hadn't got to finish the conversation and tell my aunt about Gabriel. Gabriel had been Uncle Howard's lifelong childhood friend since Ocean Parkway, Brooklyn. My uncle was a great guy, no, the best guy. He and my aunt had taken me in for four years when I was a kid and D. Dad wasn't doing such a bang up job, or actually he was doing a bang up job, bruising me. Even if it was never to be, I wanted my uncle to know I had chosen the name Gabriel. Everyone shares their baby names with their parents — even if they can't have babies.

I stopped going to adoption meetings. S. Scot wanted to marry M. Me.

"Listen, Scot, you can't keep calling me. You live too far away. (Like 3,000 miles away.) You're too young for me. I'm over 40. I can't have kids. Go meet a young woman who can make babies."

"I'll come to New York. I'm coming to New York next month. I was adopted. We can adopt."

"Tell me that in a year. Maybe then I'll believe you."

Scot and I married in A. August.

We moved to Northern California. Redwood trees are lovely. Many a time I had sat by this ocean, this vast magnificent Pacific, and dreamed the city girl's dream of never going back. Now, a full-fledged citizen of the West Coast, I sat in mourning for my maligned city like she was a person who had died. Marriage was okay, but New York, New York, my beloved homeland, how I wept for the concrete I had disabused.

Adopted babies are named anew. If they're new enough, a first. Scot was 18 months old when he came from Korea. He was given a new name. Our child would be a big kid. He or she would already have a name.

Still, I couldn't stop. Driving down the highway (yep, you gotta drive everywhere out here) I had to time to muse. A lot. Boys were back on the table. Boxes had been checked: Gender: any. Age: 3–9. Race: Asian or bi-racial. B. For Scot's grandmother and grandfather. Bekka or Bud. E. Eve or Eli. I. Isadora (as in Duncan or my Great Uncle Ike). V. Veronica (my father's mother) or Vincent (Van Gogh), and my favorite boy M name, Merce. (Merce Cunningham, the great choreographer who had so influenced my artistic sensibility.) Merce could be the M for Muriel.

Meetings. Scot and I went to meetings. Foster care and Foster Adopt and Adopt Adopt and putting up locks and railings and smoke alarms and lying about our sex life and the amount we bickered.

The phone call. There was a boy. L, Lonnie. The "Is love at first sight possible?" quandary answered once and for all. Yes, oh, yes, oh yes yes yes.

Six year old Lonnie, with a very fine name indeed.

All baby names fled my consciousness. What difference does a name make now? This is a whole human being.

Sitting on his foster parents' couch, Lonnie informed me in a businesslike manner the first time we met, "You're going to be my new mom. My old mom told me that you were going to be my new mom." Deep breath. M me M mom. I was mom. There was no breaking in period.

My son was concerned about changing his surname.

"Baby, when I married your Dad, I didn't change my name. I like my name. I understand why you want to keep your name. It's your name."

I was a brilliant parent already. Lonnie didn't have a middle name. We decided he keep his second name as a middle name and use Scot's surname. My son was deeply pleased.

The social worker was not. This wasn't a good idea. The court had not only terminated Lon's birthparents' rights, but prohibited any contact whatsoever. It would not be prudent to encourage any links, especially to a man he could not see and did not remember.

Summer came with lots of trips to that magnificent Pacific with Lonnie and T. Tai, our beloved black dog. Redwoods are lovely. Lonnie proved to be a social being. I overheard him explain to one of my friends: "I'm part Indian and part Korean and part Jewish and part collie, like Tai. He's our dog."

Although he wasn't legally ours yet, Lonnie began using his new last name. Sometimes he even gave my name. Who was he going to be? Slowly the exciting idea of picking a new middle name came into play. He had Scot's last name, maybe we could pick a middle name from my family.

"Well, you know, my mother's name was Muriel, and I always had this idea that I would name a little boy or girl her nickname, Mu. M. Mu. She's been in heaven —"

"I know. She's been there since you were a little girl. And mom, she nice."

"Uncle Howard, the cousins' grandpa (my first cousin's children who visited had affectionately become known as "the cousins"), was my daddy for a while when Muriel died. He had a best friend, since he was little, a long, long time ago, named Gabriel. Gabriel got very sick and died and I think Uncle Howard must miss him very much."

Many a discussion ensued concerning the names Mu and Gabriel. All my life I had dreamed of naming a child for my mother. My young and lovely mother, destined to remain forever lovely and young. Deeper dreams had shone their splendor. Lonnie chose.

"Mommy, I really like Muriel, I like her a lot, but I want the name Gabriel. I think—I—I like dat name."

L Lonnie G Gabriel. Love. Good.

Good Good Love.

Make a Joyful Noise

*Neal Pollack*

# This Is What I've Become:
## Scenes from the Life of an American Parent, 2010

"Daddy," Elijah said in the car, "today I peed blood."

"That's alarming," I replied.

"Well, actually, it was watermelon juice."

"Oh."

"Because I ate watermelon."

"Right."

"And watermelon is red."

"I know that."

"Also, I peed out a seed."

"Oh."

"It was quite painful."

"I'm sure."

"Well, actually it was only part of a seed."

"That's nice, son."

"Maybe half of a seed."

"Can we talk about something else now?"

"No."

"OK."

∾

A couple of Fridays ago, while she was getting her hair cut, I sent a text message to my wife. She'd brought Elijah with her, and, as a semi-bribe, we offered to download "The Simpsons Arcade" for him on my iPhone. He's recently come into knowledge of search functions, and once he discovered the game existed, the pestering didn't stop. I warned him (as I always do) that, Lego Star Wars notwithstanding, games based on beloved pop-culture characters rarely satisfy. But he persisted. Then I noticed the game had gone on sale. I texted:

"Simpsons arcade on sale for 99 cents."

Very shortly thereafter, I received this text:

"Mamas busy ok by. love you."

Mongo discover fire.

A few seconds later, Elijah wrote:

"Ps. I ate all the chees."

Followed by:

"Pleas buy it."

I replied:

"I did buy it! You spelled cheese wrong, ya dope."

Elijah: "Thank you, you ape."

"You're welcome."

Then I got a phone call, and Elijah unleashed several texts in a row:

"Shaq peed on the flor. ok."

Shaq is our old, flatulent Boston Terrier.

"I have a new pug," Elijah wrote, followed by "Fluufy," which is his nickname for the dog, pronounced "Floooooooofeeee," because Shaq, according to Elijah, "has a fluufy chin."

It kept going:

"I get a ice from targit."

"Please respond."

"I mean it."

"Now."

"You lost your brain privleges."

"I like to poo."

"I like to pee."

"ok enough please," I replied.

"I'll stop," he wrote back.

But before he did, he unleashed this doozy:

"Germny marched in to Poland War is deklared by britan France astriea new zeland."

Now that I knew how World War II started, Eljiah could stop texting me. When he got home, he came upstairs excitedly, got my phone, and started playing his game. Within 15 minutes, he was screaming into a pillow on the couch.

"This is the stupidest game ever!" he said. "Stupid! Stupid! Stupid!"

"Never play character-based games," I said, "unless the characters were actually in games first."

"I know," Elijah said. "I KNOOOOOOOOOOOOW! But this game is stupid even though it's The Simpsons!"

And I wept a little inside, for another piece of Elijah's innocence lost.

ᴄ⁄ᴐ

When we announce that it's time for bed, Elijah, like most kids, seeks to prolong the agony of the day by hiding. It's a game for him, but if we play it wrong, we encounter a shrieking, belligerent resistance. Therefore, we need to try out different strategies.

The other night, after I finished reading Elijah his nightly quotient of at least 100 *Calvin & Hobbes* strips, I called through the house to summon mama for bedtime.

"Wait," said Elijah. "Let me hide."

"Whatever," I said.

With that, he moved to the middle of the sofa and covered himself with a blanket. Regina entered the room.

"Well, it's time to brush teeth," I said. "The only problem is that Elijah has disappeared."

"Oh no," Regina said. "That's a tragedy. And just when he was learning how to type."

"I know, tough break, right? Why don't you have a seat here right next to me on the couch, so we can smooch."

"I would," Regina said. "But I really have to fart."

"You know where I like to fart?"

"Where?"

"On top of this lumpy blanket that's next to me on the couch."

The lumpy blanket began to bob up and down, as though something inside it were trying not to laugh. Regina sat down on top of it, puffed up her cheeks, put her hands to them, and blew out a big wet fart sound.

"Oh man, that feels so good," Regina said. "I think I'll do it again!"

And she did, and then she invited me to join her.

"Are you sure?" I said. "I'm dropping some stinkbombs today."

"What else is new?" she said.

So we both sat on the blanket and made farting sounds until we were sick of that, and then we pulled the blanket off, revealing Elijah. From there, he brushed his teeth without protest, went to bed quietly, and was asleep within fifteen minutes.

"Huh," Regina said. "I think we found our formula."

I know the parenting manuals don't tell you to pretend-fart on your kid for behavior-modification purposes. If he tries to pull that stunt at school, he'll get in trouble. But it worked the next night, too, and probably will tonight, and then suddenly it won't work anymore, and we'll have to come up with a new strategy. Innovative solutions to intractable problems: That's why the parenting magazines used to pay me the big bucks.

సౌ

"Elijah, would you help me take out the recycling, please?"

"I'll do it if you give me 50 cents."

"You know, not everything you do earns you money. Am I getting paid to do this?"

"You *could* get paid."

"How?"

"You could write a book called *I Take Out the Recycling Too Much*."

"Oh, yeah, that would sell a *ton* of copies."

"And then you could go on a book tour and tell people that you're a recycling expert. Doo de doo, I'm Neal Pollack and I take out the recycling."

"OK, that's enough."

"Seriously, can I have 50 cents?"

"No."

Sam Apple

# Baby Classes:
## Mommy and Me Yoga, Loneliness, and the Growth of the Infant Brain

*Excerpted from* American Parent: My Strange and Surprising Adventures in Modern Babyland

It's a good time to be a studious baby. American babies today can take a class in just about anything: music and rhythm, dancing, Chinese, yoga, gymnastics, sign language, even cooking.

The classes aren't cheap. In New York, a yearlong music program can cost up to six thousand dollars. But the expense doesn't seem to be slowing demand. Music Together, a franchise of music classes for young children, has expanded to 1,700 communities around the country, and the number of teacher-training sessions has doubled since 2000. Some New York baby classes are so highly sought after that parents add their baby to the waiting lists on the day of their birth. The hottest class of the moment, Little Maestros, a music class for children as young as six months, is so popular that some parents are reportedly trying to bribe instructors for a spot. The brochures for baby classes are usually filled with the same claims about stimulating or developing infant minds that are now found on almost every baby product—in addition to exposing children to music, Little Maestros includes "language development activities." Music Together emphasizes that the classes offer a "research-based, developmentally appropriate early childhood music curriculum." And while many parents no doubt ignore these claims, for some parents the educational benefits of the classes are the main draw. "I want my child to have any edge another child has," one father told *The New York Times* in 2006, explaining why he spends six thousand dollars a year on classes for his three-year-old. In New York, in particular, where preschool enrollment is often a highly competitive process complete with intelligence tests, getting a baby into the right class can feel like a high-stakes proposition. "Fail to provide the right stimulation during early childhood and your child will suffer devastating consequences," Sara Mead wrote in a 2007 Education Sector report on the false claims about infant education. "Pass on baby water aerobics, in other words, and you can say goodbye to college."

The classes and products might be entertaining for babies, but as the Education Sector report makes clear, that doesn't mean that babies gain any developmental benefits from them. In fact, much of the science behind the claims for baby classes and products relies upon the same creative interpretations of brain research that inspired Brent Logan to invent the BabyPlus Prenatal Education System. The enthusiasm for stimulating baby brains can be traced back to the last decades of the twentieth century. Logan was seemingly interested in the growth of neurons—the cells of the brain and nervous system—but the parents, educators, and policy makers hoping to stimulate babies have been more focused on synapses, the chemical junctions that connect one neuron to another.

Neurologists have long known that cognitive development depends upon neurons making connections with one another—but it was only in the 1970s, when a handful of researchers undertook the painstaking task of dissecting animal and human brains and counting the synapses under microscopes, that we began to discover when the networks are formed. And perhaps more so than any other scientists in recent decades, those synapse-counting neurologists changed the way we raise our children today. Before synapse counting began, brain researchers assumed that the adult brain was much more dense in synapses than the infant brain, since adults are capable of much more complicated cognitive tasks. But the opposite now appears to be true. Right around the time of birth, synapses begin to grow at an astonishing rate, trillions of them, and the spectacular growth continues in spurts throughout the first two years of life until the brain has many more synapses than can ever be used. As the brain continues to mature, the active synapses are strengthened and the unused synapses begin to die off—a process known as synaptic pruning, which continues throughout adolescence.

It's easy to see why the findings about the growth and decline of synapses captured the public's imagination as the studies were written up under provocative newspaper and magazine headlines. If synapses in the brain grow rapidly only in the first years of life, and if the synapses that aren't actively used die off, then it takes only a small leap to arrive at the idea that the more our brains are stimulated in the first years of life, the more synapses we will have, and the more powerful our brains will be. And these links—between stimulation and more synapses and between more synapses and more brain power—looked even stronger after a handful of rat studies found that raising young rats in enriched environments could not only make the rats better at solving tasks but could also increase the number of synapses in adult rat brains.

The excitement about synapses also fit together well with another line of research that was generating excitement during the same period. Neurologists at the time knew that if adults developed cataracts and lost the ability to see, their vision would return if the cataracts were removed. But if a child was born with cataracts that were not removed by age five or later, the blinded eye or eyes would remain blind for life.

Because of the ethical problems, it was hard for neurologists to study sensory deprivation in humans. But in the 1960s, attempting to better understand the phenomenon, David Hubel and Torsten Wiesel found that if they placed a patch over a kitten's eye for the first three months of its life, the cat would remain permanently blind in that eye. And when Hubel and Wiesel dissected the cats' brains, they saw that without incoming data from the eyes, the visual cortex failed to develop properly. Eyesight in both cats and humans appeared to be dependent upon a critical period very early in life, and if the critical period passed without proper environmental stimulation, the damage was permanent.

Hubel and Wiesel's famous research—they later won a Nobel Prize—had focused on the visual cortex of cat brains, but the implications were tantalizing for anyone interested in how the human brain develops. Perhaps, the reasoning went, it wasn't just vision that was subject to critical periods. Perhaps if children didn't receive the right stimulation in the first years of life, their brains would forever be as useless as the eyes of those blindfolded kittens.

The move from stimulated rats and blind kittens to the intelligence of babies is one that few scientists have ever been willing to make. But the absence of conclusive research did nothing to stop the flow of popular articles about the new brain studies that began to emerge in the 1980s. In one typical example, a 1986 article in *Parents* magazine titled "Brain Power: You Can Make Babies Smarter," the educational psychologist Jane M. Healy cited the same studies on the stimulation of infant rats that Logan had mentioned to me and argued that the new neuroscientific research implied that if infants were not stimulated from an early age it could affect their lifelong ability to learn.

By the 1990s, the hype about making connections between children's neurons before it was too late had reached a fever pitch. In a 1996 *Newsweek* cover story, "Your Child's Brain," Sharon Begley wrote that a baby's experiences can wire neural circuits just as a programmer uses a keyboard to reconfigure the circuits of a computer. "Which keys are typed—which experiences a child has—determines whether the child grows up to be intelligent or dull, fearful or self-assured, articulate or tongue-tied," Begley declared. ABC, for its part, aired a celebrity-filled prime-time special on the importance of early stimulation. And Hillary Clinton, then the first lady, organized the Conference on Early Childhood Development and Learning in 1997 so that leading scientists and pediatricians could come together to discuss the implications of the latest research on neurons and synapses.

Meanwhile the discussion of brain development in the media was moving beyond claims about intelligence to more dramatic claims about the social implications of failing to stimulate babies. "Unfortunately, for a growing number of children, the period from birth to age three has become a mental wasteland," the Pulitzer Prize–winning science journalist Ronald Kotulak writes in his 1997 book *Inside the Brain*. "Society needs to focus on this period if it is to do something about the increasing rates of violent and criminal acts."

In the face of so much hype, it was easy to forget that none of the studies being touted in the press had shown that babies benefited from early stimulation of their senses. Neurologists and developmental psychologists now believe that, while the early findings about blindfolded cats oversimplified a very complicated process, some fundamental, species-wide human abilities, such as the ability to see and hear and use language properly, are subject to critical periods. But the research had found only that complete sensory deprivation could impede development. There has never been good evidence that extra stimulation—beyond the sights and sounds that all babies hear in the course of daily life—enhances infant development.

The good news for all of us is that, for most of the ways that we learn, critical periods don't appear to exist. The thrust of the most recent brain research points in the opposite direction. Rather than remaining frozen in time after age three, the human brain is amazingly plastic and continues to change—and even grow new neurons—into adulthood. With the notable exception of the ability to perfect foreign accents, the type of learning we do in school or throughout our daily lives has little to do with critical periods, which is why adults can still master complicated cognitive tasks such as reading. As John T. Bruer notes in his book *The Myth of the First Three Years,* "Binocular vision might only develop during a certain period, but we can learn algebra at any point in our lives."

Moreover, as Bruer also makes clear, even if we somehow could stimulate babies and prevent synapses from dying off, we have no idea how additional synapses would affect intelligence, if at all. Some neurologists think that synaptic pruning is the key to intellectual development. Even the rat-stimulation studies turned out to be misleading. Further research found that the synaptic growth in stimulated rats only took place in the visual areas of the rats' brains and, since the same changes would occur when older rats were stimulated, the rat studies said nothing about critical periods.

Perhaps because they don't make for good journalism, the later findings that dimmed the hopes of would-be baby stimulators received almost no attention in the media. Meanwhile, in the early nineties, enthusiasm for critical periods and synapses still on the rise, a single study of thirty-six college students further muddled the public's understanding of infant brain development. The study, published in *Nature,* found that college students did better on tests of spatial imagery if they listened to a Mozart sonata. The effect wore off after a few minutes, and a number of efforts to repeat the results failed, but by then it was too late. The Mozart Effect had been released into the zeitgeist.

In a 1999 review of the most cited studies in the top fifty U.S. newspapers, Stanford researchers found that the Mozart study was cited 8.3 times more than the second most popular paper at that time.

The Mozart Effect generated so much excitement that states across the country drew up legislation to expose children to classical music. Georgia governor Zell Miller asked his state legislature to put aside $100,000 so that every newborn in the state could receive a classical CD or cassette. The state of Florida passed a law that required state-run schools to play classical music to toddlers every day.

And among the people to take note of all of the latest studies about baby brains was a mom in Colorado named Julie Aigner-Clark, who tapped into the baby stimulation craze more successfully than anyone else when she videotaped a handful of toys, set the footage to classical music, and then, in a final brilliant stroke, called her creation Baby Einstein.

Perhaps not surprisingly, there is now a small but zealous backlash against the obsession with infant stimulation. And for any parents hoping to build better baby brains, infant classes and products are probably an enormous waste of money. Even more disturbing, educators and policy makers who believe that the first years of life are the key to intellectual development risk deemphasizing education programs that focus on the following years of childhood, which, the current evidence suggests, have a bigger impact on a child's academic success.

Still, while there is no solid evidence that music classes or Baby Einstein videos help babies develop, there is also no solid evidence that too many products or classes harm babies. And whether or not baby classes have any developmental or educational value, there are plenty of good reasons to sign up for them. I suspect that, like Jennifer and me, a lot of the parents take the classes for a much more practical reason: They have no idea what to do with their time.

As I adjusted to parenthood, my new understanding of time felt almost as profound as when I first pondered the theory of relativity — perhaps even more so, since I actually understood what I was thinking about. Before parenthood, time was elusive. I could get out of bed, have brunch with a friend, and somewhere along the way the day would slip away. But when I was taking care of Isaac during that first year, time was never slippery, no matter how much fun I might be having or how much love I might be feeling. Time was slow and sticky. It clung to the skin like wet paper. When I was a nonparent, I would often start a Sunday at noon. But when I woke up with Isaac at 5:30 in the morning, noon was a million miles away. Noon was like a desert mirage that I could only dream of reaching. Sometimes, to pass the hours and to keep myself awake, I would sing "Ninety-nine Bottles of Beer on the Wall," all the way down. Other times, I would lie on the floor and let Isaac claw at my eyes for sport. (It occurred to me during one of these sessions that this is the real Oedipus complex—*they want to claw our eyes out!*)

The difference in my perspective on time only hit me fully one Sunday while Jennifer and I were shopping at Target. It was around four o'clock. We had already been at the store for several hours and had visited every section at least once.

"I guess we should head home," Jennifer said.

I had spent my entire life trying to avoid shopping trips and yet at that moment, I realized something incredible: I did not want to leave Target. During the winter, when it was too cold to go to the park, leaving Target meant going home, and the one fundamental law of parenting during the first year is that time moves more slowly inside the home than outside.

"Let's just hang around here a little more," I said.

"You want to hang around at Target?"

"Yeah. I think so."

"But we already have everything we need."

I thought for a moment. "Let's look at the DVDs again," I said.

We continued to walk around the store, and as the other shoppers hurried past us, my childhood began to make more sense. I had remembered spending a lot of time at Target while growing up in Houston. But until that afternoon it had never occurred to me that my father couldn't possibly have needed to make that many trips to the store, no matter how wide the selection or reasonable the prices. We had been at Target because Target was a place to be on the weekends. In Houston you went to Target for the air conditioning. In New York you went for the warmth. But the principle was the same.

Jennifer agreed that it was important to get out of the apartment with Isaac, but she wasn't thrilled with the prospect of spending our weekends looking at the same DVDs over and over. Probably we should have just organized a new parents' group or arranged more get-togethers with the new friends Jennifer had made in her moms' group. Instead we decided to spend several hundred dollars on a Music Together class.

The Music Together class was Jennifer's idea, but I was all for it. I liked the idea of sitting and singing as babies crawled around a tambourine-covered carpet and slapped at drums. The problem with Music Together, I soon discovered, is the seriousness with which the company takes this educational mission. Each week the instructors would urge us to practice at home with the CD that we'd been given at the first class—one of the instructors even referred to the CD as homework.

In fairness, it's possible that older children who take the classes get something out of them. Many children who begin playing instruments at a young age do excel. Because musical development is so complicated from a neurological perspective and involves so many different areas of the brain, it's particularly difficult to determine whether a critical period exists. A 2005 review of the literature on critical periods and musical development in the *Journal of Developmental Psychobiology* concluded that "the effects of early enrichment or early deprivation on the emergence of sensitivity to...various aspects of music pitch structure remain largely unknown."

In any case, our Music Together teachers were much more focused on the participation of the parents than the babies. Part of the company's educational philosophy is that babies learn from watching their parents. As one of the founders of Music Together once put it in an interview, "It's an educational tragedy, really, an educational disaster, musically speaking, for one's children, if you just sit on the couch and consume music. They need the model of your musical doing in order to get the disposition to be a music maker."

I had no problem with Music Together's parent-centered educational philosophy, and I was more than happy to sing along. But the instructors' almost militant insistence that parents stay involved even when their children are nowhere to be found led to the same unfortunate scene repeating itself week after week: Isaac would crawl away, or Jennifer would take him into an adjacent room to feed him, and the next thing I knew I would be running in circles and waving chiffon rainbow scarves over my head with a group of strangers.

Music Together was only the beginning of our time-filling activities. We also attended a "Sign and Sing" baby sign language class during which Isaac and the other babies sat and watched as the parents sang about baby kangaroos and learned to sign "I want milk." And one Sunday afternoon, we attended a Baby Loves Disco party at a local rock-and-roll club.

Baby Loves Disco, a series of dance parties for babies and parents that have sprung up around the country, sounded like a great idea to me when I first heard about it. The parties have become part of a larger hipster parenting trend that has swept through New York and across the country in recent years. Critics of the trend have complained that young parents are trying to push back adulthood by dressing their babies in heavy-metal onesies, but, though I've tried, I can't see the downside to ironic onesies. If anything, the right to dress your child in ridiculous outfits struck me as fair payback for all parents do during the first year — or, at least this is what I was thinking when we dressed Isaac as a French painter for his first Halloween and taped a paintbrush and a piece of baguette to him.

Baby Loves Disco lived up to my expectations for a few minutes. I was amused by the scene when I stepped into the dark dance hall. As a DJ spun records onstage, toddlers with juice boxes mingled with beer-guzzling adults.

But the charm of the scene wore off once Jennifer and Isaac and I made it onto the strobe-lit dance floor. At that point Baby Loves Disco became a haunting reminder of my junior-high dances. Jennifer was bopping around and holding Isaac so that he was facing her, and I was left with the unfortunate choice that every awkward twelve-year-old boy knows too well: Either dance by yourself in the vicinity of a female and pretend as though you don't mind dancing alone or hurry to the food table and pretend as though you don't mind drinking twenty consecutive cups of Pepsi. The female sex has ingeniously solved this dilemma by joining together and dancing in groups, but the guys are on their own; like wild apes who have been evicted from the troupe by the high-status males, we can do nothing but lurk and hope — although, unlike wild apes, we can also fantasize about taking over the dance floor with John Travolta's *Saturday Night Fever* routine.

After a minute or so of lumbering awkwardly around my wife and child as "Billie Jean" blasted from the speakers, my inner twelve-year-old returned and I headed to the bar, where I spent the next twenty minutes sucking down juice boxes and feeling sorry for myself. And as I watched the others dance, I realized that the real problem with Baby Loves Disco was the babies. The painful truth is that babies are not that into dark clubs. What parents really need, I thought, is a nightclub with a special soundproofed room in the back full of Pack 'n Plays and nannies. For a moment I imagined how incredible this parenting club would be and how much fun Jennifer and I could have there. Then I remembered that we didn't particularly like clubs and never went to them before Isaac was born.

If I wasn't always at ease during our weekend baby activities, I at least had Jennifer with me. Even though Isaac was becoming better company every month, it was even harder to fill the hours on the two days a week that I took care of him by myself. Because it was closer to our apartment than Target, we spent a lot of time in the supermarket. While the rest of the shoppers rushed by, Isaac and I would fondle the fruits and tip over cereal boxes as though it were a carnival game. Isaac particularly liked looking at the Quaker Oats guy, and, inevitably, from time to time someone I vaguely knew would stroll by and be surprised to find me sitting on the floor of the supermarket with a baby and an armful of oatmeal canisters.

When I would begin to fear that the supermarket management might be taking notice of our prolonged presence, Isaac and I would move on to a café or to Barnes & Noble, where we spent so much time during the winter that I almost felt obliged to begin paying rent.

One particularly lonely day, I had the idea that I would integrate myself into one of the cliques of Caribbean nannies on the playground benches. I had the entire white-liberal fantasy mapped out in my head. I would ask them for advice on some sort of baby issue, and within a few weeks, I would not only be a regular part of the group at the playground but also be good friends with the nannies. Soon the Caribbean nannies and I would be breaking down social barriers right and left with heartfelt cultural exchanges. They would come back to our apartment and teach me how to cook flavorful rice dishes and I would give them thick chunks of store-bought challah and talk to them about forming a union or gaining legal immigration status — that I know nothing about either subject had no bearing on this particular fantasy.

It was a nice, if vaguely offensive, fantasy, but then, I was pretty sure that the nannies didn't like me. Once I got Isaac's foot stuck in a bench at the playground. And as I spent two minutes trying to wrestle it free, I could see the nannies looking at me and shaking their heads. I knew they were thinking, "amateur," but I felt I could do no right in their eyes. Sometimes I would take Isaac out in his fluffy bear suit on a lukewarm day, and as soon as Isaac cried, the nannies would shake their heads and tell me he was hot. Another time, I was wheeling Isaac around in only a T-shirt and diaper, and a nanny stopped and looked at Isaac without even acknowledging me. "Daddy took you out naked?" she said, the disdain visible on her face.

One night, after a particularly lonely day in the supermarket, I complained to Jennifer that Isaac and I needed a new activity. Jennifer suggested Mommy and Me Yoga. She had taken the class before going back to work and had a few passes left.

It didn't seem like a good idea. I'd tried yoga once in high school. I had been going through a bad anxiety spell, and my father thought that yoga might help relieve my stress. When I pointed out to him that I could barely touch my knees, let alone my feet, he said not to worry.

I worried. I knew yoga was wrong for me from the very first *ommm*. The two teachers were a mother and son team, and the son took his yoga seriously. He had a goatee and a ponytail, and I can still see the baffled expression on his face as he tried to wrestle my limbs into places they had no intention of going. I don't think he had ever seen such an inflexible human before.

"Just stretch," the son said.

"That's as far as I go," I said.

I am even stiffer now than I was then, but what really made me nervous about Mommy and Me Yoga was the potential for emasculation. I have always been proud of my stereotypically feminine attributes. When guy friends made fun of my interest in feminist folk music or pointed out that my winter coat was actually a woman's coat—I was aware of this, but it was unusually warm—I always insisted that my womanly ways were really a testament to how profoundly secure I was in my manhood. And yet by attending Mommy and Me Yoga classes, I thought I might be taking it to another level. I wondered if I might be crossing an inviolable line into a realm where no heterosexual man could safely travel.

In the end I decided I would rather be emasculated than lonely. And that is how I found myself walking through Brooklyn with Isaac Björned to my chest, a Starbucks skim latte in one hand and a rolled-up purple yoga mat in the other.

When I arrived at the yoga studio, a dozen or so moms had already unrolled their mats onto the hardwood floor and placed their babies in front of them on blankets. In the center of the room—the mosh pit, I would later hear it called—a few of the more mobile babies were manhandling a small mountain of toys.

As I had expected, no other dads had shown up, and I felt increasingly anxious as the instructor, Trish, stepped in front of the mosh pit and introduced herself. Trish had short red hair and thin muscled arms. She looked tough.

I glanced down at Isaac, lying on his back on a blanket, and suddenly longed to be back at home playing *Claw Daddy's Eyes Out.*

Trish asked us to close our eyes and *ommm.* The sound echoed through the sunlit room, and for a brief moment, I allowed myself to relax, one deep breath at a time.

Then Isaac freaked out.

I felt guilty. The world must have seemed strange and surprising enough without all the people in the room suddenly closing their eyes and humming in unison.

Trish waited for Isaac to calm down and then began to bark out impossibly long Sanskrit words. The moms, to my amazement, seemed to speak Sanskrit. No sooner would Trish say *"Parivrtta Ardha Chandrasana"* than the moms would be balancing on one leg and turning their bodies parallel to the floor. I did my best to keep up, but with each additional *Parivrtta Ardha Chandrasana,* it became increasingly obvious that in a roomful of mothers, many of them still recovering from the physical trauma of labor, I was without question the least physically fit student.

Trish occasionally stopped by to adjust me this way and that, but her efforts were no match for my rigidity. The Tin Man from *The Wizard of Oz* could have made me look bad on a yoga mat. By the fifteen-minute mark, I was drenched in sweat and exhausted. And my desperate situation was only made worse when one of the more mobile babies crawled over to say hello and then—even as I waved my cutesiest wave—took off with my water bottle.

With the exception of this one tiny hooligan, the babies remained mostly calm, including Isaac, who had become otherwise engaged with a crinkly-paper-filled caterpillar. But the tranquility came to an abrupt halt during a grueling round of *Bharadvajasanas*. A baby on the other side of the room began to shriek as if it were he, and not I, who was being asked to rotate his torso 180 degrees. The shriek set off a chain reaction, and soon all of the babies were grunting and crying in unison, a discordant mockery of the *ommming* adults.

I'd like to think that babies cry in response to one another's cries out of empathy, that in their shared tears they reveal something profound about the innate capacity of humans to feel the pain of others. And it might be the case. But I also can't help but wonder if what appears to be empathy is anxiety. Judging by the volume of Isaac's screams, he is either the next Mother Teresa or he was genuinely terrified.

Even as the other babies calmed down, Isaac continued to fuss in my arms. After the colic months, I never thought the time would come when I wouldn't mind Isaac's crying. But the longer he complained, the longer it would be until I had to do another downward dog. So I wasn't thrilled when Trish came by and offered to take him off my hands for a few minutes. I reluctantly handed over my son and then looked on in horror as he began to suck on Trish's bare shoulder.

I knew from experience what was coming next, and I should have stopped it. Instead, I collapsed onto my mat and looked on as Isaac gave Trish a bright red arm hickey.

Trish took the hickey as well as a person can take an unsolicited hickey. "I'd rather get one from him than a lot of other guys," she said. She handed Isaac back to me and then asked us all to lie down with our babies and to position foam bricks under our backs so that they were aligned with our "bra straps."

With those two words, my emasculation was nearly complete, but as I lay down with Isaac and waited for our next instruction, I saw an opportunity for redemption. I began to bench press Isaac up and down, ostensibly to enter-tain him but really to demonstrate that there was at least one physical feat at which I could outdo a mother who was still recovering from giving birth.

To my frustration, no one seemed especially interested in my great show of virility, and after about fifteen Isaac reps, I joined the others in what struck me as the weirdest exercise of the afternoon. Trish asked us to form a circle, hold our babies in front of us, and then swing them right to left so that they came face to face with the babies on either side of them.

I could almost hear the "Check, please!" on Isaac's lips.

After about five minutes of baby-swinging, Trish told us to return to our mats. There was still half an hour left in the class, and I felt as though I was one *Bharadvajasana* away from passing out.

I picked Isaac up and approached Trish at the front of the room. "I should probably go," I said. "He looks like he's getting tired."

*Tonya Northenor*
# Toddler

Sometimes a word grows more significant as it's personally needed.
Think of *hope*—of *cancer, devotion,* or *sleepless.*
*Toddler:* another such word. Not only perfect
in its description of the gait, the wide-legged, hobbling,
determined-for-freedom stance, but
also for the measure it provides in the middle.
Nice as a shopping section at the store—
a mid-ground between over-soft baby pastels
and the vibrant basic reds and blues, like the bruises we're beginning to know.
Positioned between *baby* and *child* it gives parents
the linguistic chance to breathe. To adapt to
the difference between in-your-arms-always care
and let-me-do-it-myself looks.
Between knock-kneed and give-me, give-me.
A word whose definition is a chrysalis, daily morphing
to form its new shape. A meaning with wings.
Something that will, however fragile, soon be able to fly.

*Yi-Mei Tsiang*

# How to Dress a Two-Year-Old

Practice by stuffing jello into pants.
Angry jello.

speakveryquicklywithoutbreathing
untilyoubegintoseeplanets
spinninglike
coinspirouetting
silverflashesof
light
and
balance

Write a blog post against the hegemonic practices of the fully-dressed elite.

Threaten wildly and unpredictably:

D<sub>eL</sub>i̇ve̊r ᴍʀ. P<sub>o</sub>tato H<sub>ead</sub>'s Eₐr i̇̃ₙ an e<sub>nv</sub>e̊<sub>lope</sub>

Froth at the mouth.

Be still.
Hold your words in the palm of your hand,
like birdseed. Let her small bones alight
on you with the hesitant uplift of almost-flight.
Make your hand the earthen weight of gravity.

Promise monkeys

Slice your words into
The.    Anger.    Of.    Pauses.


Quote random passages of Kafka.
It will buy you time.


Forbid her to wear clothes. Dress the dog in her favourite shirt.


Petition city hall to have the by-law officer enforce all non-nudity legislation.


Issa said:

Children imitating cormorants
are even more wonderful
than cormorants.


Here she is, a cormorant, gleaming by the window's lake-light, shirt closing
tight as a snare around her throat.

*Amy Yelin*

# Once Upon a Penis

The boy is obsessed.

"See how big it is, Mama?" he says all the time now.

He sits on the couch watching *Clifford* while fondling it.

When he whips it out in the crowded Lexington Town Common to pee on a tree, I laugh with the strangers and then remind him to keep it our little secret next time. "I'll help you find a special spot," I whisper.

He nods and runs away, one hand down his shorts.

Recently he came up with a theory for its sudden growth.

"Know how it gets big, Mommy?" he says.

'Um, no, how?"

"It's because I eat and then it grows!"

I smile. This is one of those parenting moments when you are faced with a choice: explain the truth to your child, or embellish the lie. I choose to embellish the lie.

"That's right, buddy. And if you eat things like eggs and vegetables it will grow even bigger!"

His eyes light up. Then he leaves to play with a fire truck.

I tell my friend Melissa about Ethan's new preoccupation. "This is normal at this age, right?"

"I think so," she says. Melissa has a little girl. "Sophie always liked to touch herself too. I think it was around that age."

Still, I need further confirmation. So I do a Google search on preschoolers and penises which directs me first to Ask Yahoo. The #1 answer to a question from a concerned mother reads, "Castration is the only cure."

I scroll down in search of other, more serious answers. A response from a JoeJ starts off promising. He writes: *The Phallic stage usually spans from age 3 to 8...since your son has entered it at age 3, it means he has successfully passed the oral and anal phases.* Oh good! I think. Ethan's advanced!

JoeJ continues: *This means he will probably be less likely to drink, smoke or be someone who talks too much. And he will probably be very neat and not procrastinate.*

OK. Maybe not.

Next, I find myself on a site called HealthCentral.com where a woman named Norma cries out for help for her three-year-old son who is "playing the privates game." *Is this OK?* she asks.

A Dr. Dean responds: *Playing the privates game. That's so cute.*

Touching just feels good so at this age both boys and girls will hump and rub themselves.

He goes on: *Even fetuses show sexual activity. I have a wonderful article on female fetuses masturbating to what some researchers propose is the point of orgasm.*

"Gross!" I say out loud.

"What's wrong, Mama?" Ethan asks.

"Oh...Just something I read. Everything's fine."

"Can I watch the trains, Mommy?"

"Yes," I say, relieved. I quickly switch to YouTube while visions of fetuses masturbating dance in my head.

How did I get here? I sometimes wonder. In a house surrounded by boys. A house of testosterone. When I found out I was pregnant for the first time three years ago, I automatically assumed it was a girl. Other sources confirmed this for me, such as an acupuncturist who, upon taking my pulses proclaimed, "Yep, girl."

My boss at work also said girl. "I can just tell," he said. "It's the way you're carrying."

We believe what we need to believe. And so I began coming up with a list of favorite girl names. I began imagining me and my daughter going to Itsy Bitsy Yoga together, and taking knitting classes like Melissa and Sophie.

When I went for an ultrasound at 13 weeks, I had no expectations of finding out the baby's gender. The goal of this early ultrasound was only to assess my risk of having a Down syndrome baby, and, as far as I was concerned, my husband Ben and I still had five more weeks to have the "talk" and decide if we wanted to know the gender ahead of time, or not.

During that 13-week ultrasound I marveled at each image of what I just knew was my baby girl.

"She's beautiful," I even said out loud at one point.

The technician remained quiet, saying only, "The doctor will be in soon," and offering a half-smile as she walked out the door.

The doctor, a balding, spectacle-wearing character resembling Dr. Green from *ER*, soon arrived with the good news that our risk of having a Down syndrome baby was low. The doctor spent a little time examining the images on the monitor and then asked, "So, do you want to know the baby's gender?"

I looked at Ben, then back at the doctor. "You can do that *now?*"

The doctor nodded. "I can tell. So do you want to know?"

"Yes!" I blurted out.

"Wait a minute," Ben said. "I don't want to know. I want to be surprised."

"You do?" I said.

"I want to wait until the baby is born," he said and crossed his arms.

"Well I want to know now," I said. "And I'm the one who has to carry this baby for the next six months!"

There was an uncomfortable silence, when the doctor finally said, "Well, how about this… I'll just type a letter on the screen and whoever doesn't want to know the gender can close his or her eyes."

"Fine!" Ben and I said at the same time.

Ben proceeded to put his head between his legs, like someone about to throw up. The doctor looked at some more images and then said, "Ready?"

I nodded.

He turned the monitor toward me and typed the letter B.

I sat up to take a closer look. "Are you sure?" I asked, trying to sound emotionally neutral.

He nodded and smirked, as though enjoying his power, as though enjoying giving me this life sentence.

That night I had a dream. I was at a party at Ozzy Osbourne's house, and I went into labor. My baby was born smoking a cigar and speaking in tongues. I awoke sticky with sweat.

"Ben?" I whispered. He didn't move. "BEN!" I said louder.

He groaned. "What?"

"Can I tell you now?"

"Tell me what?"

"The sex of our baby?"

"That's what you woke me for?" he said. "I already told you I don't want to know." He placed a pillow over his head and went back to sleep while I remained awake, staring at the ceiling until morning.

To understand my distress about having a boy, one must look at some of my earliest interactions with the gender, or lack thereof. First of all, I grew up in a house of women. There was my mother, my two older sisters, and me. My dad was around, but he wasn't what you would call your "typical" American male. For one, he wasn't even American, but Eastern European. My dad was an intellectual who read voraciously and took daily naps. On Sunday afternoons, while other fathers watched football, my dad watched Holocaust documentaries. He drank one light beer about twice annually. I longed for a brother who would introduce me to the habits and mysteries of boys. But it was not to be. So I went out into the world completely unprepared for the typical American male, while at the same time, I wanted him. Badly.

In kindergarten, I created the Kissing Game. The rules were simple: Girls chase boys and try to kiss them. Boys run as if being chased by vicious Dobermans. We were playing this game on the school playground one morning when a bee stung me on the arm. I screamed and my teacher came running. As she carried me toward a bench, a swarm of boys gathered beneath a tree nearby to watch. I noticed that one of them—a pale, fleshy kid named Joey Steinberg—had both hands down the front of his pants. This image distracted me so much that I missed what I now believe to be the important lesson of that moment—a lesson that might have saved me much future heartache: *Chase Boys. Get Stung.*

Throughout elementary school and high school, I had but one significant boyfriend, Adam, in the fifth grade. We went to Playland, the local amusement park, together and our relationship lasted about ten days. When I broke up with him because my friends didn't think he was cute, he called me a "Goldigger!" and rode away in anger on his banana seat three-speed.

Fifth grade was also the year I saw my first penis.

I was sitting on the front steps of my friend Michelle's house with three other girls when a strange green car drove up.

"Can you help me?" A guy yelled from the driver's seat. "I just need some directions to Korvettes."

Without hesitation—keep in mind, this was the 1970s—the four of us raced to the car. Michelle took a pad and pen from the guy while the rest of us leaned against the outside of the car, giggling about the naked centerfold laid out across his passenger seat.

"OH MY GOD!" My friend Suzie whispered moments later, her finger pointing to the man's right hand as it vigorously played with what I surmised must be his penis. The four of us ran screaming and laughing back to Michelle's house as the guy took off, burning rubber in reverse. I suppose, as first penis memories go, this one did not lay the best foundation.

In college, boys finally pursued me, but they never wanted a commitment. This drawback might have sent some girls running, but not me. I was like a lost puppy, insecure and loyal, waiting until each guy dumped me before moving on. Interestingly, they all claimed innocence; each of them apparently at the mercy of the all-powerful penis. "I can't help it…I'm just horny" was their collective mantra. I didn't buy it. Didn't they need to be in the mood, like me? In their hearts, didn't they really want to snuggle first?

Somehow, I managed to get married and pregnant before resolving the majority of my confusing beliefs and feelings about boys. Hence, the sting of learning my parental fate.

ↄ

Still, for the next three months as my anxieties about our impending baby boy skyrocketed, I managed to keep the baby's gender a secret. Then, over dinner one night, Ben said, "Hypothetically speaking, if we have a boy, I don't want him to be circumcised."

Are you kidding me? I thought. Here my husband wanted me to keep the gender a secret, but at the same time he wanted to lay ground rules about things like circumcision and expect me not to react?

I nodded, trying to remain stone-faced while fighting the urge to chuck a chicken wing at his head.

I Googled "circumcision" first thing the next morning. I had no idea, even from an aesthetic standpoint, what distinguished a circumcised from an uncircumcised penis and after looking at online images of each type, I ruled them equally unattractive. With that criterion out of the way, I considered religion, but only for a moment. I was too disconnected from my Jewish roots to make that my argument. The decision, then, lay solely on which option I thought was best for my child's health and after hours of more research, the result was a tie.

So I would honor Ben's wishes for an uncircumcised child. But only after he first honored *my* wishes and let me tell him the gender.

"Is it really that bad?" Ben asked when I told him how I needed his support, how I needed to be able to talk freely about our baby.

"It's bad," I said, nodding. "I'm a bit of a mess."

We cuddled on the couch and he agreed to let me break the news before dinner that evening. In the afternoon, I rushed to Old Navy and tried not to look at the colorful baby girls section as I grabbed a striped light-blue onesie from the dull selection of boys' items. I put the onesie in a shirt box, wrapped it, and attached a card that read: "Dear Daddy, I can't wait to meet you. Love, your son."

Ben was thrilled.

Ten months after Ethan was born, to my surprise, I was pregnant again.

Again, I hoped for a girl, but not out of fear. I was hoping for a girl because I knew two children was my absolute limit. This was my last chance for a daughter.

At the ultrasound, there was no mistaking the gender of this baby, how-ever, who exposed himself like a drunken office worker sitting naked on a copy machine.

"At least we won't have to buy new clothes," Ben said.

"What if they turn out to be like the Menendez brothers?" I said. We laughed nervously.

∾

These days, I don't have time to let such absurd fears get the best of me. These days, it's all about the obsession. Just yesterday, Ethan came to me with a new dilemma crying, "Mommy, I don't want it to be big!"

I wasn't sure how to respond.

"Well, try not to touch it then," I suggested.

"But it hurts…"

"Ben! Can you come here?" I shouted toward the laundry room. "Ethan doesn't want it to be big!"

Ben sat down next to Ethan as though about to have his first, serious father-son chat. But then Ethan's eyes widened as he heard something from the other room. "Curious George!" he shouted, and just like that, he'd moved on.

This is pretty much how it goes with my boys, who flit like caffeinated but-terflies from one thing to the next, including their emotions. One moment they're wrestling like bear cubs, biting and pinching with an aggression I cannot comprehend, and the next they're comforting each other, giving up the coveted truck or finding the missing pacifier to ease the other's pain. They have taught me so much in such a short time and I am grateful, although I know much more learning awaits. Every now and then, when I see one of them run through the kitchen and come out the other side, I expect to see an adolescent standing before me. What will that be like? I wonder. Then I remind myself: best to stay in the present.

And when my friend Melissa says to me, as she did the other day, "You know, I can't imagine you *without* boys," I have to admit, I can't either. When I try to imagine life without my younger son trying to hump his brother in the bath tub, I grow weepy.

I've come a long way.

*Sydney Brown*
# The Boy with Two Moms

Born into a Kingdom of Breasts, everything makes sense;
he needs no words for their flawlessness, their lawlessness,
these lands answering wholly to his hunger, heart, and hands.

When he launches the placement of one foot in front of the other,
a little linebacker stumbling between mothers, he learns salvation
is a breast clutched and a nipple palmed.

Once the little king can wander and moo-moos are food no more,
he's keen to count them: one, two, three, four. Then one day
from a grocery cart he has his first epiphany in slow-motion:

*countless others have them.* Large herds of breasts in all shapes
and sizes — cookies, rocks, balls and melons — he tries
to count the pairs by twos: 2, 4, 6…11. He learns the words

*wrong* and *chaos.* In elementary school, he fails spelling tests:
*sit* becomes *tit*; *tube* becomes *boob*; memory becomes mammary.
Geometry is not much better; he is hypnotized, ceaselessly doodling

spheres, cylinders, and cones. When Madison Jones brings cupcakes with pillowy-pink frosting to celebrate her birthday,
the boy finds himself in the principal's company for pinching

little nipples into each & every one of them. On beach-day,
he is disciplined and disqualified from the sandcastle contest
for building four humongous towers he deems "Moms' Mounds."

But at night the boy's world is more tolerant —
magical even. He lies in bed and stares at the divine
glow-in-the-dark solar system his moms fixed to the ceiling

and he falls sweetly to sleep in a world of little-star
badoinkees and big-planet baloobas, a celestial
galaxy of a god's everlasting milk bottles.

*Brandon Cesmat*

# Sons

The son I didn't want
waits until I sit on the bank
before running downhill and jumping on my back.
He waits for me to take indefensible positions,
finds me lying on the living room floor,
listening to music, falls on my chest and says,
"My eyes are most like yours, aren't they?"

After his older brothers, I lost time,
stayed awake for two years writing my thesis
and signing student loan checks over to my wife.
I wasn't ready for another son
and told her so. I reasoned that
if my father couldn't raise one child,
I could complain about having three.
She listened, then scheduled a vasectomy
at the Planned Parenthood clinic where she volunteered.

He crawls into our bed every night.
Insecure, I think. Does he know
something his brothers don't?
Mornings, I rise sore from sleeping cramped
on the bed's edge, without covers,
stretch my back and legs to shuffle
down the hall to piss bitterly.

I'd never say I had a favorite
but I have dreamed about him:
we are both five,
running between orange trees.
Women call our names at the edge of the grove,
but they do not come looking among the rows.

I love him because he is like me:
unwanted, hanging around the neck.
Yet I know he'll let go
when he's ready. I pick him up,
throw him high, hold him by the ankles,
then roll him like a sack of apples across my shoulders,
let him climb me like a tree while I pray
the branches don't break for a boy doesn't soon forget
the moment when pressure against the fingertips
releases except for his own squeezing dry wood
in the moment before the ground makes itself known.

He sits in the boughs
as the wind comes up.
I tell him to come down but
he laughs until a gust from the arroyo
takes flakes of bark onto the rushing air.
I climb and straddle the limb beside him,
and we're swaying, scared together.

## Carrien Blue

# Confessions

"Mama. Mama. Mama," she calls, "Just one more thing."

My hand hovers on the doorknob, poised for escape. On the other side of that door are another hundred things that I need to do before I sleep, but also the sweet relief that I made it through another day, quiet, and time to myself to get things done. I am almost free, but no.

I sigh and turn back toward her. "What is it sweetie?" I ask, trying to keep the irritation from leaking through.

"Mama? When all your work is done can you come in and lay down next to me? And if I'm awake can you rub my back and sing me a song. But if I'm NOT awake can you still give me a hug and lay down next to me for a little while?"

Every night it's the same question. Usually I cut her off mid sentence, so great is my desire to escape. "Yes, I'll lay down next to you, but you'll probably be asleep by then and won't know it," I hedge. "Goodnight, I love you, go to sleep."

I slip out quickly, hoping to cut off any more talk. I'm done. I'm tired. Bedtime exhausts me and I long for it to end.

Some nights I completely forget to go back into that room before dragging myself into bed several hours later. More often than I would like to admit.

Some nights I lay down, remember, and get up again to go in and hug her, though she never wakes, so I'll know I kept my promise to her.

I avoid going back in before she's asleep if I can. She takes longer to sleep if I'm in with her, and talks and talks until my mind blanks out entirely and I fall asleep before she does. I can't afford naps like that. They have me up far too late at night, doing work that should have been done earlier. With another toddler who still takes so long to get to sleep I feel I have nothing left for the girl who has finally learned to fall asleep on her own.

Yet every night she falls asleep, happily hoping that I will come in and spend some extra time with her, sing to her, and rub her back.

I'm aware, as I choose not to most nights, that one day I'll wish I had. One day I will regret not taking the opportunity, every night, to spend some more time with my little girl. She will be all grown up and gone and I will wish I could hold her again and spend more time. I even think to myself that if she were to suddenly die tomorrow, the one thing I would regret the most is not going in before she sleeps and laying down with her and singing to her one last time.

I know this is important, and yet, at the end of the day, it feels impossible. Or I just don't want to. Or both. I feel her question like a weight, another burden added to my already full load. Or perhaps it is my own selfishness that burdens me so. I never can tell.

Before I became a mother I thought I'd be really good at it. I imagined myself as this patient and gentle person who would always listen to her children and wisely dole out justice and mercy to her adoring brood. Then I had children. I held on to this imaginary persona for a while, but as more children were added it gradually slipped away and I am faced with the reality of who I am.

I am not a good person, I'm not all that patient, and I'm not very gentle. I get angry. I'm astoundingly selfish. I feel sorry for myself all the time. There are days, weeks even, when I play the perfect mother very well. But when the heat is on and I am at the end of my strength the ugly mommy comes out to play. I feel fury erupting in me because they dared to wet the bed again, through a diaper. I resist the urge to grab their little bodies and shake some sense into them. I feel the edge creep into my voice as I get louder and louder when I talk. I just want them to go away and leave me in peace. In these moments I can feel myself almost hating the ones I love so much. It's a paradox that holds me in its grip; how I can love so fiercely and harbor such violent resentment all at the same time?

I think this is one of the ways in which my children are blessings. They force me into recognition of my own weakness, my failure, which is helpful if I want to grow. At the same time I am humbled, humiliated sometimes, by the way they adore me. They are still at the age when I can make everything better with a hug, a kiss and some of my undivided attention. That of course can drive me to the edge. Undivided attention is difficult to give when everyone wants and needs it at once. I feel the pulling in me, the need to do it right, to get everyone taken care of individually and the desire to retreat to somewhere in my head and snap in irritation when they interrupt by calling me, over and over again.

I find it frustrating and annoying when they ask me to do things for them that they can do for themselves. Perhaps because I suspect it's a way to try and get my attention when they feel that it's lacking, and I feel guilty because of it. Or maybe it's because I'm nursing the baby, she's drifting off to sleep and you don't need me to help you to go potty because you know how to do it yourself. "No, don't stand there in the hallway screaming 'Mommy, I need help' until you pee all over yourself and the carpet, go and use the toilet like you've been doing since you were 18 months old."

It doesn't sound like much of a blessing I know. The thing is, when I surrender, when I give in to this role and allow myself to be moved by their need, their total attachment, I turn into that mommy that I dreamed I could be. All I need to do is deny myself, turn off the "poor me will you give me just one second to myself" speech that runs on autopilot through my brain, and suddenly the answer comes. Somehow, when I let go of my selfish anger, I can see clearly to the end and get through it. It's as though my self-absorption prevents what Anne Lamott calls Spirit from entering and bringing life.

Every time I actually remember to surrender and ask for help, it is forthcoming. It's not what I fantasize about. No one comes and takes my kids for a while so I can have a break. No one gives me a lot of money so I can bring my husband home earlier to be with us more. My children don't suddenly stop wetting the bed or spilling their drinks. But I am more patient, more gentle, more creative, more like the person I want to be, and we get through. And gradually I can feel inside of me a tugging and adjusting, a slow work of transformation that will go on as long as I'm around to renovate.

In the 8 years I've been parenting I have changed a lot. I'm rarely angered by pee on the carpet anymore, though it continues to happen as we add more children. I have gained those reserves of patience that remind me to be gentle when irritated and creative when overwhelmed.

Yet, this daily request of hers for just a few more minutes with me before she drifts off to sleep feels like more than I can give. Can I ever be present as much as my children would like me to, as I would like to be? I wonder if the moments when I do manage to be present will ever be enough.

"Just one more thing Mama, just one more thing," she calls again as I shut the door. "Will you lay down with me for a little while?"

This time I surrender, walk back in and snuggle up close to her on the pillow. I stroke her cheek and run my hands through her hair as I sing to her, our foreheads touching, and I find, once again, that I do have the strength for one more thing after all, and this burden too becomes a blessing.

*Paul Lieber*
# The Unnoticeable Moment of a Cloud

He pinches my chin,
babbles, and it could bloom into Arabic,

Chinese or English. I heard, I live you dada
in elongated porous metallic chirps. Someone

told me all babies sound alike at six months
before they fall into language. Out of the blues

into accuracy. I remember I'd lean into ivory,
play dissonance with all the feeling of something

almost soft and melodious, before piano lessons,
before scales. At one AM I walk the length

of the living room, his head on my heart to remind
him when he curled near a similar beat. I march

back and forth. At fifty-two his legs hang
to my hips and arms are limp. At eighty-five

I crawl back in bed, complete. My wife embraces him
and he sticks to her milk smell. Years ago

an autistic child would say, let's laugh together
and we would, at nothing in particular,

at first forced, and then it would erupt
into the unstoppable gales of hyenas. My son

wakes, kicks his feet in opposite directions,
head leans back, back arches in a stretch

as he chants in nascent Portuguese.

## Chris Baron
# snools

this morning
you called me in
at 5:30
told me
you had found
a "snool,"
your tiny
two-year-old hands
held open
lifted up
before your
smiling, sleepy face.
"what color is it?"
i asked
"it's a blue one."
in this early light
your eyes sleepy
and almond
like your mom
you looked like
someone from a dream
a boy i might hope to know
who'd imagine
"snools," share them
with me when you could.
"i dropped it!" you said,
and looked down
threatened tears
but this is part of the life
of "snools"
they are often dropped
and found again.

*Grace Hwang Lynch*

# An Unlikely Soccer Mom

My son was almost late for his first soccer game, because I had to drag him away from his Legos to get suited up. As we arrived at the field, the other players' jerseys were neatly tucked in as they stretched their hamstrings, while my kid's shirt hung to his knees and his socks were falling down. The whistle blew, but he shied away from the ball, easily distracted by sagging socks or a funny shaped cloud in the sky. My six-year old was big and tall for his age, with a strong kick. But competitiveness and sports strategy did not come naturally to him. Perhaps the coach thought my boy would be better in a defensive role and picked him to be goalie the next quarter. He traded his blue and black striped uniform for a bright yellow jersey and took his place in the box. Seeing the fate of the game dependent on my child filled me with fear. The other team scored one…two…three…four goals on my boy. Our coach threw his cap on the ground and stomped on it. At least that's what I felt like.

That was it. No more sitting in the lawn chair for me. I ran to the end zone with my husband, yelling, "Keep your eye on the ball!"

"Get it!"

"Don't let the ball go by!"

I might as well have been standing in that goal myself. If our team lost, I would somehow feel responsible. But most of all, I was desperate that my little boy did not feel the ire of his coach or teammates. He could only run amok and stare at clouds so long, before he got a reputation amongst the other kids, who had yet to learn how to bite their tongues in the interest of good sportsmanship. When the quarter finally ended, I retreated to my seat to drown my sorrows in copious amounts of Vitamin Water.

Usually it's the dad who encourages his son to play sports. In our family, it's the mom. My husband Steve, a white guy from Orange County, had a childhood full of youth sports: Little League, AYSO Soccer and the like. "Sports leagues are just so competitive," he worried, rattling off stories of quarterbacking dads, some of whom had sons who went on to be college and professional athletes. During our college days at Cal, the football team was headlined by a quarterback whose father was infamous in Orange County youth sports circles.

Despite those warnings, I started our first-born in sports at age four, through a non-competitive tot soccer program at the community center. He was always the kid who kicked the ball in the wrong direction, but laughed and didn't care. I didn't care either—at first. I knew what my motivations were. Unlike other parents, who might have viewed athletic achievements as a way to earn scholarships or to relive their own glory days, I just wanted my kid to have fun, get some exercise, and learn the value of teamwork. I had no glory days on the playing field, and my worst fear was that my child would be like me.

*୧୨*

# 1985

Fourth period gym class, freshman year.

It wasn't like middle school, where all the kids—popular or outcast, coordinated or clumsy—did jumping jacks and push ups together. By high school, any kid with athletic abilities signed up for some sort of junior varsity team. The competitive sports included football, baseball, volleyball, soccer, swimming, tennis, water polo, golf, field hockey, even badminton. Which left only the freaks and geeks in P.E. class. So there I was, a bow legged fourteen-year old Taiwanese girl with a padded Maidenform bra and a frizzy perm, sharing a cold locker room with nineteen-year old seniors who were melting their eyeliner pencils with the same Bics they used to light up their joints.

Lording over us all was Coach Beard. Muscular and sun weathered, she was rumored to have played on the LPGA tour in her younger days. She passed the time in between classes fruitlessly styling her fine white-blond bowl cut with a thin curling iron. At the bell, she jogged down the stairs from her glass office overlooking the changing area, and proceeded to torture me for the next 45 minutes.

We picked teams for most activities. Or rather, other people picked teams, while I stood meekly on the sidelines waiting to see whether I would be the second-to-last or the very last one chosen. "Uh, I guess we'll take *her*," a gangly boy said, to the groans of his teammates. Coach Beard looked annoyed, more by how long team selection was taking than by poor sportsmanship. With a shake of her blond head, she blew the whistle and shooed us off to the basketball courts.

Individual activities—swimming, fencing, golf—were a little better, simply because we did not need to pick sides, and I could just bumble along at my own pace. By June, I realized that another year of state mandated abuse lay ahead unless I did something about it. The ticket out of hell appeared as a mimeographed sheet of mint green paper: a permission slip to play school sports. My only recourse was to jump out of the frying pan and into team tryouts. Badminton seemed reasonably within the grasp of my abilities. Even skinny, bespectacled Asian kids managed to make it on the roster. My parents signed the permission slip. But it required another signature—that of the P.E. teacher.

As I slipped out of my navy gym shorts and into my stirrup pants that day, I grabbed the green paper out of my backpack and marched upstairs to that glass office. Cigarette smoke mingled with the metallic odor of a hot curling iron. Coach Beard jumped up from her seat and met me at the doorway.

"Could you—" I stammered, shoving the paper towards her.

"No," Coach Beard interrupted. She stood there and smiled, her formidable body guarding the entrance to her sanctuary. Perhaps she had misunderstood me, and thought I wanted something else—perhaps to use her phone? Mooch a can of orange soda? Borrow her curling iron?

"Could you sign this form? So I could try out for badminton?" I attempted again. All she did was stare me down with her beady blue eyes and nicotine stained smile. I stood there for a few seconds. Then it finally hit me: she was not going to help. I was being told "No" by a teacher.

That evening, when my mother returned home from work, I tearfully explained the coach's unfairness. "You need to go to the office and talk to the principal," I urged her.

"She's the teacher, she knows best," was my mother's very Chinese explanation. For in Taiwan, questioning a teacher—even one who specialized in jumping jacks and running laps—was unthinkable.

∽

My son's first soccer season had burst my illusions that competitive sports could magically transform an awkward child into a confident athlete surrounded by the camaraderie of buddies. Despite my newfound wariness of team sports, we signed him up for another soccer season. A group of second grade boys from his elementary school was forming a team, which seemed like a good opportunity to get to know some classmates while giving soccer another try. *After all, I wasn't going to raise a quitter.* At the first practice, it became apparent that this team would be much more competitive than the rag tag bunch of the year before. The coach was a former college soccer player who brought a new level of expectations to the field of seven-year olds. "You have to juggle the ball five times before you'll be allowed to practice on Wednesday," he instructed. Juggling, I learned, consists of bouncing the ball from one knee to the other without letting it hit the ground. I wasn't sure that I could even do that.

The practices were painful to watch. My child appeared to be repeating his season of gazing at the clouds and skipping across the field. "Does he like soccer?" the coach asked me one afternoon.

"He enjoys being on the field and running around, but he's not in love with the game," I admitted.

"Not competitive, then?"

"Oh, he's competitive, just not so much at soccer," I bristled. *What was he implying? That my kid was a slacker? And if he was, what did that say about me?* "He's not going to respond well to pressure," I added, noting the way the coach refused to let his own son practice until his homework was completed and how he yelled for the boy to get up every time he fell down on the grass.

"Well, he might not get as much playing time as some of the other kids. Let me know if you think it's too much, or not enough." That seemed fair, but made me uneasy, all the same. Part of me wanted to repeat the coach's words during the ride home. Let my kid know that if he didn't shape up, he was destined to be a benchwarmer. Like his mother.

The season went on, seemingly without much improvement. But my son still wanted to go to the twice-a-week practices and Saturday games. Before one match, I spotted a familiar boy leaving the field. That boy's team — which had dominated the league for two seasons — had just won, and other parents were praising his outstanding performance.

"You owe me two bucks!" the soccer star yelled to his grandfather, who was walking a few steps ahead. Laughter broke out all around, and the old man's face turned red.

"You're not supposed to say that in public!" he barked.

"Well, you *promised.*"

I remembered the soccer star, because he was my son's reading partner in school the previous year. When the end of the marking period drew near, my kid was still a few books away from completing his reading chart. He came home one day excited by what his buddy told him.

"He said he'll give me two bucks if I make my goal. He promised to go home and get two dollars!"

It was all becoming clear to me. Not that I was above such tactics. Each fall, my husband and I drew up a written agreement with our son. *After all, what was any athlete without a contract?* The contract included a clause for the scoring of a goal. In the event that he scored a goal during a game, we would let him choose any Lego set up to a twenty-dollar value. We might as well have promised him a pony, a new car, or a full drum set (what he really wanted), so unlikely it seemed that we would ever have to make good on this deal.

In the meantime, we signed up our younger son for soccer. My job was to take the older one to his games, while Steve went to another field to watch our preschooler score two or three goals each week. Our older son's second soccer season was almost over, and he still had not scored once. But that would all change. During this particular game, the team was already ahead by a few points and the ball was staying at our end of the field, keeping morale high. My first-born was playing offense, and at one point, was standing right near the goal when the ball ended up in front of him. He kicked, but the goalie easily blocked the attempt. *At least he tried.*

A few minutes later, another teammate passed the ball to my son. The scene played itself out in slow motion, as my child trapped the ball with his shoe and carefully set it up. I held my breath, waiting for another player to zoom in and steal the ball right out from under his nose. But no. I saw his leg wind up, and he kicked—the force of all 65 pounds of his body transferred into the black and white leather, which sailed through the air, past the goalie, bowing out the net in the back of the goal.

The crowd erupted. I could feel myself jumping up and down, screaming on the sidelines. Other parents slapped my back, as if I had scored that goal myself. "The look on his face says it all!" gushed another soccer mom. My boy beamed as he skipped over to high-five his teammates. I wiped the tears from my eyes and wished my husband were there to see this. We left the field that afternoon with a hero's fanfare. Never before had I been so happy to fork over twenty dollars for a box of Legos.

At the end-of-season team party, the kids filled up on pizza and cupcakes while the requisite speeches were made and trophies were presented. "He tries as hard as any other player," the coach began, handing him a blue and gold trophy topped with a soccer ball on wings. "He gives it his all at every practice and every game and never complains. He's a model player."

*Is that all?* I wondered. *Is that the standard speech a coach gives when he can't think of anything spectacular to mention about a kid?* Along with the trophy, each team member was issued a sealed envelope. "That's for your parents," the coach added. The envelope held an evaluation form and a full-page typed report of my child's progress.

> He has been consistently improving since the beginning of the season. Once he understands what is being asked of him, he powers through it and tries hard without any complaints… He is one of the best on the team at keeping the ball at the opponents' end of the field.
>
> Sometimes, he loses a bit of focus…he can be distracted by non-game related activities and finds himself wandering a bit out of position.
>
> He should continue with his positive attitude and tireless work ethic.
> —Coach

Reading this letter over, I realized that I may not have imparted the genes for athletic ability. And I may not have provided the environment to groom him into a sports star. But the words on the page rang familiar: *I just want my kid to have fun, get some exercise, and learn the value of teamwork.* Somehow, my son had developed persistence and a positive attitude. And I was happy. My child was like me.

*Joel Peckham*
# My Son, Five, Dancing

Out of empty bags and wrapping paper,
out of the split smile of the overripe
and dripping, out of quickness of lizards
and the long-legged walk of the heron
through fog. Out of hawk-flight, out
of dawn and into the shock of the cold
pond on the groin, and the lightning-
struck tree still thrumming and warm.

Once, on the long drive home from work
I watched an old man dance on the edge
of a bridge above the highway like
some God-stunned snake-charmer,
chin lifted eyes raised and lost beyond
all fearful calls beside and below —

the held-breath of the world caught
on a wobbly pirouette, a heel raised

over absence. There is so much you see
and don't when you spin like a torn leaf
— when you wish to step up into wind
and be lost above rooftops.

Surfaces reflect, refract and seem
to give. Until the window
fractures. And bone. But my son,

turning and flapping the bird-
wing of the body flung
from great heights, will not settle

will not come down until the wind
in his lungs blows singing out
of blood of breath of rhythm of now

and to hell with his old man anyhow.

push me
pull me

*Laurie Zupan*
# puberty

he is caught in the push
and pull of puberty.
the need to stay
in one place grinds against
the feeling of motion
as his blood flows through his body.

he fights
the cells that multiply.
he even declares loudly:
i will not tolerate armpit hair.

he craves the warm
parental embrace, begs
for a kiss
offers his lips, leans against
his mother for comfort
while at the same time
he's repulsed by her
smell and touch and old
person vocabulary.

he trusts innocently in adulthood
forgetting fear
for a moment.
and he dreams tall
bones, developed muscles, strong
body, is proud of his man
feet which will ground him
and support him and take
him far from his mother
some day.

and i, his mother, stand
still and remember. it's not hard
to call back those times
when i too carried all of this
within my own skin
and held love and hate
within me
at the same moment.

*Dorianne Laux*

# Girl in the Doorway

She is twelve now, the door to her room
closed, telephone cord trailing the hallway
in tight curls. I stand at the dryer, listening
through the thin wall between us, her voice
rising and falling as she describes her new life.
Static flies in brief blue stars from her socks,
her hairbrush in the morning. Her silver braces
shine inside the velvet case of her mouth.
Her grades rise and fall, her friends call
or they don't, her dog chews her new shoes
to a canvas pulp. Some days she opens her door
and musk rises from the long crease in her bed,
fills the dim hall. She grabs a denim coat
and drags the floor. Dust swirls in gold eddies
behind her. She walks through the house, a goddess,
each window pulsing with summer. Outside,
the boys wait for her teeth to straighten.
They have a vibrant patience.
When she steps onto the front porch, sun shimmies
through the tips of her hair, the V of her legs,
fans out like wings under her arms
as she raises them and waves. Goodbye, Goodbye.
Then she turns to go, folds up
all that light in her arms like a blanket
and takes it with her.

*Teri Carter*

# The Happy Treatment

For the past few months you've been seeing Ned in the basement of his ex-wife's house. While you've never seen this ex, you often hear her soft-shoed footsteps overhead as you strip to your black bra and black panties then pull up the gauzy white sheet to cover yourself. Today, a December frost bleeds through the basement's concrete so a thermal blanket tops the sheet. You bury your arms deep underneath and draw the covers up to your neck like a shroud.

A white poinsettia, new since your last visit, anchors the edge of a desk. A space heater hums and whirrs in the corner. In the next room, water gushes from a bathroom faucet and you know Ned is there, washing his hands, warming them. You wait. When Ned appears he sits between you and the desk in a black leather chair, manila folder on his lap, pen in hand. He leans back, his chair creaking more like a door than a chair. He props one foot up on your bed-like table. You feel the tug of the sheet.

"How's your back?" he asks.

"Better. Still tight in the shoulder, but my lower back is better."

"And your stomach?" He opens the folder and scans his notes with the pen. When he finds what he's looking for, he taps the nib. "Time before last, your stomach thing was back. I wrote here 'nervous stomach, some diarrhea, nauseous, trouble sleeping'."

"Same, I guess. Sleeping better."

Ned's pen darts back and forth, back and forth, across the page like the needle of a polygraph. "How's Jason?"

"We're fighting over cereal. Cereal. Can you believe it?" Your voice makes light of it, but your once-cold arms feel hot and heavy now. You lift the sheet to free them. It billows. Once the sheet settles your hands clench the hem, you hold it hostage between your breasts.

"Who's doing the fighting?"

"We are. Jason and me."

"Whose fight is it, I mean. Yours, or his? A fight always belongs to somebody."

"Mine, I guess. I don't know. Am I a failure if I pick fights with an eleven year old?"

"Listen to your words. In our first five minutes I've heard 'fight' and 'failure'."

"Come on. December has already been a long month and it's not even Christmas yet. I hate Christmas. All that fake cheer and unrealistic expectation."

"Fake," he repeats. "Expectation."

You decide not to share the rest of the words circling the drain in your head: childish, mean, vindictive, hateful.

Ned stands up, lays the folder and pen on the seat of his chair. He opens a desk drawer where he takes out a packet of acupuncture needles, then looks down at you, hovers, and rips open the rice-paper packet. "How about the happy treatment today?"

The lower rims of your eyes retain a pool of unfallen tears, so you hold your head still and stare straight ahead, unblinking, at the ceiling. Footsteps. Ned's ex-wife, the woman of the house, drifts overhead. It's after three, you think. Her kids must be on their way home from school. You imagine her in the kitchen, baking cookies, pouring tall glasses of milk, perhaps wearing a dainty strand of pearls.

Ned's hand pats your sore shoulder, rests itself there. "The happy treatment it is." He tap-tap-taps in the first needle.

☙

Three years ago you were a single woman living in an ultramodern, downtown apartment, its four square rooms as impeccably coifed as an ad slick. Your dream home. Or at least it might have been your dream home if you'd ever spent time there. You worked too much, traveled too much — you, with your promising career in marketing—until one day you fell in love, got married and came in off the road. You were over thirty by then and your Alabama-raised, belle of the ball, mother was thrilled you'd finally—finally!—found yourself a husband. "Sugar, your time is a-passing you by," she often reminded. She was also thrilled about playing grandmother to the man's eight year-old son, having determined long ago that her only daughter was too driven and too self-centered for the pain, messiness, and general inconvenience of baby-making. "We've got ourselves a little boy to spoil!" she said.

You were more realistic. You had friends with stepchildren—"baggage," they called them—children who lived with their mothers and visited, like unwelcomed guests, every other weekend. It did not work. The kids hated the new wives; the new wives hated the ex-wives; the ex-wives hated the hus-bands. A virtual circle of hate. Still, your situation was different. It was. Jason's mother had, you were told, abandoned him as a toddler. She had disappeared. Your marketing mind spun into gear. Pros: instant family, no need to have a baby of your own, no pain-in-the-ass ex-wife. Cons: instant family, no baby of your own, stepmotherhood. Outcome: unknown, but tenable. So you committed. You sold your white sofa, glass tables and black-lacquered fur-niture—an off-the-showroom-floor ensemble you'd purchased "as is"—and moved to suburbia. You traded the two-seater car for a Volvo. You even broke your "never own a dog" rule and adopted a feisty, black and white cocker spaniel from the local shelter. Family complete. It wasn't long, however, before your new husband's career trumped your own. His law firm was about to take on Big Tobacco in a landmark, class-action lawsuit. He would be spending more time at work, he said, preparing his plaintiffs, his case. He might even get to argue before the Supreme Court. This one case, he insisted, could make his career. Enamored by illusions of his future success you offered to give up your job, for now anyway, and stay home with Jason. You would trade the designer suits and three-inch heels for faded jeans and comfortable shoes.

Your husband was grateful. Ecstatic.

Jason was ecstatic, too. About the dog.

You admired the dog—so elegant in her silky, black and white coat—and imagined how perfect she might have looked in your bygone dream of an apartment.

⌒

In an attempt to become stepmother extraordinaire, you used dinnertime to stake a claim in the household routine. Your first mistake.

"You're in my chair," Jason said, standing next to you at the table.

"Don't you want to sit next to your dad? I can be closer to the stove here, in case you guys need something."

"But this is my chair."

"Okay. I'm happy to sit by Dad."

You stood. Jason sat. "He's not your dad, though."

And so the evenings passed.

Now that you had a family, now that you were home and had the time, you were determined to work on your culinary skills. Your mother mailed her favorite recipe books and you scoured them for hours, aspiring to churn out flawless family meals: chicken francese with wilted spinach; steak tapenade with arugula salad; lamb chops with sweet pea soup and parmesano toast. Most nights, Jason used the tines of his fork to scoot bits of food to the edges of his plate, intent on separating miniscule bits of onions from tomatoes from mushrooms, and asked to be excused. When the dishes were done and the kitchen dark, Jason would reappear, flip on all the lights, and pour himself a bowl of cereal. You protested.

"He's eight," your husband said, too worn down from twelve-hour days of legal briefs and trial prep to have this conversation again. "He eats macaroni and cheese and hamburgers and pancakes."

"I am not making pancakes for dinner."

He shrugged.

You stood firm.

Jason lived on Fruity Pebbles and Frosted Cheerios.

When you asked the advice of friends—the ones with the revolving doors of weekend-only stepchildren—they merely smiled their "I told you so's." Old co-workers mocked your decision to abandon your career to raise someone else's child. "What the hell were you thinking?" they said. When frustration morphed into a persistent stomachache, one of your suburban neighbors—a stay-at-home mother of five—suggested you see Ned.

"What is he exactly?" you asked.

"A healer. Homeopathic stuff. He works in the basement of his house downtown. He does a little bit of everything…body work, acupuncture, Chinese medicine. Appointments last an hour, so you talk a lot. It's like seeing a therapist. With needles."

You weren't so sure about the needles, but you went anyway.

You'd been in Ned's office—the basement—all of a minute when he instructed you to undress to bra and panties and lie down on the table. He left the room. You stripped, embarrassed by your sheer white undergarments, and laid yourself down on the table under a sheet. You wondered what your husband would think—what your mother would think—about your being basically naked in the basement of a strange house in a strange neighborhood with a strange man.

Ned returned, the door latch snapping behind him. "So. Why are you here?"

"Stomachache. It won't seem to go away."

Ned leaned over your prone body and stared you right in the eyes. It felt like a dare. You examined the pores in his face, tiny black dots, and the gray stubble on his chin. "I don't believe you."

"I've had it for months now. I went to the doctor and he said I'm fine, but I'm not fine. I don't feel right." You felt like a specimen under a microscope. You wished he'd sit down. "My neighbor said I should ask for the happy treatment. Whatever that is."

"Sure. You can have that. You can have whatever you want if you can tell me what's bothering you."

"Some stomach thing. Hey, if I knew what it was I wouldn't need to be here, seeing you, now would I."

"Oh, you know. Maybe it's something you can't admit, or can't put into words. But deep down, you know." He pulled the sheet down to your waist, exposing you, and pressed his hand flat against your stomach to the side of your bellybutton. A handprint of fire. "Your anger is here. Not in your stomach, but in your liver. The liver is where we store our anger. It's burning my hand. You can feel that, right?"

Sure, you felt the heat of Ned's hand, but you weren't angry. You had a stomachache. He was way off. And that was when you first heard the footsteps. "Is that your wife?" you said, pointing at the ceiling.

"Ex-wife. She got the house."

"Must have been a good divorce...I mean...if she let you keep your office here." You were glad for the diversion, mindful of his hand, his hovering.

"It works. I get to see my kids every day. I'm here when they have breakfast, before my first appointment, and I'm here when they get home from school. She gets a tax write-off."

"Takes a big person. Big people."

Ned swiped his hand from your stomach and gently lifted the sheet to cover you, as though tucking a child into bed. Next time—if there was a next time, you thought—you would wear a black bra and black panties. Full coverage. Nothing see-through. Ned sat down and opened a file—your file. "I'm going to have you take Milk Weed. It's a liquid herb that repairs the liver. You can find it at any health food store. Ten drops in water, three times a day. And think about the anger, where it's coming from. Otherwise we're just treating the symptom. Come back in two weeks and we'll see where we're at."

You drew the shades down over your eyes and, still feeling the fiery imprint of Ned's hand, listened to the scratch of his pen taking notes.

☙

It had taken you awhile—three years, in fact—to get to Ned.

After your first year as Jason's stepmother, you met with a psychotherapist specializing in women's issues. "We're just not connecting," you told her.

She ran off a list of invasive questions. You answered. She seemed satisfied. "You're a healthy-enough person. He's being a normal kid. Relax. He'll come around."

"I feel like a robot: do your homework, eat your dinner, go to bed. How do you build a relationship with someone out of that?"

"Moms do it all the time."

"But I don't really know what I'm supposed to do. I mean, I never thought I'd be someone's mother."

"It's pretty natural," she insisted. "You'll figure it out."

After two years, you had not figured it out.

"You're being too strict," your mother said. "Take my word: you catch more flies with honey than vinegar!"

"You're not strict enough," your husband said. "Be firm. Kids want boundaries."

"You have too many rules," your mother said. "Learn to have some fun. You always did take things too seriously."

Still, you couldn't make it work.

You used to be proud of yourself, you thought. You used to travel the world; you went to important meetings; you made good money and took care of yourself; you talked mostly-male executives into spending millions of dollars on products they didn't need. Now you couldn't convince a little boy to eat a green bean, to do his math homework, or to wear a jacket with a hood in the pouring rain. Your husband—exasperated and, by now, completely buried in his Big Tobacco case and traveling three weeks out of every month—agreed to find a therapist for Jason. For the next few months, every Monday after school, you drove a brooding boy to his appointment and sat in the waiting room, stomach churning, wondering what the kid was saying about you. You watched fifty minutes tick by, one by one, on the round, white, wall clock. You pretended to read, but were bored by, outdated, well-thumbed magazines. *Family Fun. Fit Pregnancy. Kids' World. Parenting Today.* You smiled often at the receptionist, to prove your innocence. At the end of Jason's last session, his therapist opened his door and invited you inside. "Here she is," the man said, waving a hand in your direction. "Tell her."

Jason stared at his feet. "All she cares about is school. Everyday I get off the bus and all she ever says is 'how was school?'" Then he mocked your voice: "How was school?"

"But I mean 'how are *you?*' It's the same thing." You leaned forward, tried to look him in the eye, but he just looked further away. "It's like when your dad comes home from work and I say 'how was work?' I really mean 'how are you?'"

"Why don't you just say what you mean, then?"

The therapist crossed his arms, raised an eyebrow, nodded in agreement. He seemed to say, "See, that's all there is to it. So simple!" and sent you both on your way.

☙

Now it is the week before Christmas, two weeks since your last appointment, and you are back in Ned's office. There is a small, freshly-cut, Christmas tree in the corner—in lieu of the space heater—and its colored bulbs twinkle and flash with blues and reds and greens. You take off your clothes. You lie down. You pull up the sheet. You wait.

Since the last time you were here you've discovered your eleven year-old surfing hardcore porn on the Internet. You took away his computer. Then a neighbor accused Jason and his friends of bashing their mailbox with a baseball bat. He denied it, but you found the dented bat in the garage. You took away his television and video games. When Ned comes in, when he asks how you are, you imagine saying: "I'm lost! Lost in the land of parental punishments! Save me!"

Last night, with your husband (as usual) out of town, Jason left you a note on the kitchen counter.

> *I hate you. I will always hate you.*
> *You are not my mom.*
> *Stop talking to me.*
> *I hate school and I hate you.*
> *My dad will devorse you anyways.*
> *You love the dog more than me.*

On your way to bed you grabbed a chair from the dining room, dragged it to your bedroom, and lodged it firmly—firmly—under your locked doorknob. You were overreacting. Weren't you? As you were changing into your pajamas your husband called, from some city somewhere, to say good night. What would he say, you wondered, if he could see you now, if you told him the truth: "I think I'm afraid of your son! I'm losing my mind!" But all you said was, "Merry almost Christmas." In bed, once your eyes adjusted to the dark of the room, the silent, white ceiling above seemed to stare right back at you, like a blank mirror.

Today, Ned's usually-white ceiling is flooded with the colors of Christmas. You close your eyes to blot out the blinking lights, and you listen for Ned. The click of a latch. The creak of a chair. The shuffling of paper.

"So how are we today?" he says.

"Better," you lie, picturing the dining room chair lodged under the door-knob. "My neck's a little stiff. I think I slept funny."

"Ahh, a new ailment," he says, nodding, amused. "You know that saying 'Don't lose your head'? Your subconscious is taking it literally. You can't lose your head with a stiff neck." You've come to expect these platitudes, and it occurs to you that maybe what you're really sick of is Ned. Sore throat? Your words are stuck there because you won't say what you think. Stiff back? You're too rigid. Constipated? You can't let shit go.

Ned stands up, lays your file on the desk, positions himself behind the chair. "Come sit down here so I can adjust your neck."

"Are you a chiropractor, now?" You are stalling, not wanting to remove the sheet. "Can't I just get the happy treatment?"

Ned pats back of the chair. Three times. "Sit." You push down the sheet, awkwardly conscious of your standard black bra and black panties. For the first time you wonder what he thinks of your always wearing black. Is it the only color underwear you own? Are you trying to be sexy? In mourning? Does Ned even think about it, or you, at all?

You do as you're told and sit in the chair. From behind, Ned places his hands first on your shoulders, then on either side of your neck. His palms and fingers wriggle up your neck to the sides of your head and, before you can see it coming, he yanks your head to the side. You hear the crack of your spine. "See. That wasn't so bad, was it?"

You feel a bit dizzy.

You lie back down on the table and haul up the sheet, relieved to be under-cover again.

"Brrrrr," you say, exaggerating. "It's cold in here."

"Virginia took the space heater." He takes his seat and lets out a big, irri-tated sigh. "She said I couldn't have the tree *and* the heater. I guess she's afraid I'll burn her house down."

Virginia. You roll the V over and over, like a solved equation, in your mind. Virginia is no longer the phantom in the kitchen, wearing a string of pearls, baking cookies. Virginia is a real person.

"Things any better with Jason?"

"Sure. He wrote me a love letter."

"Really."

"Yes. Really. He left me a note telling me how much he hates me. Made my day."

"You called it a love letter."

"I was joking."

"But you said love. Listen to your words. Love. That's progress." Ned stands up, opens his desk drawer, reaches for today's needles.

"He says I love the dog more than him."

"There's the love again. He's connecting with you. Not the way you want him to, but he's pushing your buttons, trying to figure out who you are. He's asking you an honest question and he's looking for an honest answer."

Ned tears open the new packet of needles, waves them in the air. Overhead, you hear Virginia shuffle across the floor. Ned looks up, rolls his eyes. Across the ceiling, Christmas tree lights spray shocks of color. You close your eyes as he taps in the needles.

☙

Back at home you come in from the garage to find Jason in the kitchen. He's holding an open box of Frosted Cheerios with one hand stuffed inside, rooting around, and he's looking at a giant, white poinsettia on the center counter.

"Hey," you say. "How are you?"

"Aren't they supposed to be red? Like roses?"

"Mostly, they're red. Who's it from?" You drop your purse on a chair and fan through the leaves for a note. You think of red roses and wonder where in the hell your husband has been for these three years. You wonder if Ned's happy treatment is nothing more than some fake panacea, some temporary, feel-good distraction. And then, seemingly out of nowhere, you wonder if maybe—just maybe—what you need is to go back to work. You feel relieved.

"Hellooooo!" Jason says.

"Sorry. Who did you say it was from?"

He sets down his box of cereal. "It's for me!" He holds a tiny card high in the air, like evidence, and pretends to read it. "Merry Christmas, JJ, this says. Love, Mom."

The dog barks. She's sitting next to Jason on the floor, and she mistakes the card he's waving for a treat. She barks again. "Good girl!" he says, and puts it in her mouth.

"Don't let her eat that. It could get stuck in her throat."

Jason shrugs, then wrestles the chewed up card from the dog's mouth. He lays it on the counter, in the same place you found his "love letter" the night before. The dog barks again. Jason reaches down to rub her head, then goes to a cabinet to get her a real treat.

You step back and examine the plant, awed by the enormity of it. It must be three feet tall and wide. What kind of person sends an eleven year old a plant as a gift? "Merry Christmas, son! Here's the poinsettia you've always wanted!" You recall the one time she called on the phone, about a year after you were married, the one time you heard her voice. "Is JJ there?" she'd said. You asked who was calling, and it was as though you'd slapped her. "This is his Mommy!" Her voice was clipped, in staccato, like she was marching against you, pushing you back, staking her place. Such power. For your husband, you think, she most certainly disappeared. But for you and for Jason this mother is ever present, lurking, like invisible Virginia shuffling across the floor above Ned's office. This mother who "disappeared" exists just enough to make you to bristle when you brush up against her, and you can't help but wonder if, when Jason looks at you, he only sees who's missing.

In the corner of the kitchen, Jason is talking to the dog. "Speak!" he is yelling, offering her treats. "Speak!"

"Well, kiddo," you say. "Where do you think we should we put this thing?"

"It looks dead, don't you think? Like all the blood got drained out."

"They *are* poisonous," you add, thinking logically about the dog, pondering where in this house you have a table tall enough and big enough to hold it.

"When Dad calls I'm going to tell him she sent me a poisonous plant for Christmas!"

You laugh. In spite of yourself, you laugh. Jason laughs, too. The missing mother and the missing husband are missing out.

"Seriously. Can we go get a red one instead?" Jason says, picking up his box of cereal and shoving a hand inside. "This one doesn't even look real."

*Susan Webb*
# Wild Sweet William

Wild Sweet William,
also known as woodland phlox,
likes sun to partial shade,
soil moist but not too moist,
and blooms in late Spring.

"I think I'll live with Dad now"
he said, scratching his chin.
In its cleft grew three hairs,
maybe four now.
I touched his cheek.
A slight scratch grazed my palm.
"Will you mind?" he asked.

The woodland phlox
has a deep, blue flower,
grows 12–18 inches tall,
and likes to be planted
a foot apart.

*Carol V. Davis*
# The First Solo Trip Out

The question casually drops in the air
where it drifts undisturbed
in the suddenly vast kitchen.
The space between us stretches
as if a fissure slices the yellowed linoleum,
my son (with a body he has not grown into)
would be swallowed up.
His hand, bigger at 16 than mine,
straightens, then rounds into a cup
with a patience unusual in this squirmy teenager.
*Just the car keys.*
Nothing more.
He does not expect histrionics.
I am, after all, a reasonable mother;
some would say permissive even.
Still I can picture his torso
stretched around my steering wheel,
the radio still blasting, his head cocked,
blood trickling down that baby face.

*Leann W. Lindsey*

# There by Half-Past

On a gray November morning in a town in the north of England, my daughter and I make our way to the station. She has a morning bus to catch. We wait under a shelter made of cast iron and glass. The blustery winter rain slews in sideways. Scarlet-coated transit workers walk up and down checking timetables and directing passengers.

"Do you have your bus fare?" I ask, trying not to sound anxious.

"Yes," she answers. Her blond hair shines under the lights. Her eyes are large and gray.

Another thought occurs to me. "Do you have your student ID?"

"Yes," she says again.

"Do you have your mobile phone? Did you charge it?"

"Yes, I have it. It's charged," she answers calmly.

"Do you remember your address and phone number? Do you have money for lunch?"

"Yes, I remember my address and phone number. I packed my lunch. It's here." She holds her book bag tighter and gathers her purse close. She turns to me, annoyed.

"Mother," she says, "I'll be fine."

She is going off to college in the next town. It is her first public bus ride this far, alone. She is nineteen. God willing, she will be safely home again by dark.

Something catches her attention. Halfway down the enclosure, a girl her age walks our way. My daughter waves awkwardly. The girl doesn't respond.

"Not today," I think, "please, no rejections today." I know how hard my daughter has worked just to be able to speak, to get on a bus to the next town, to make her own way to a supported learning course. Such effort does not deserve to be slighted.

This time, it isn't. A few feet away from us, the girl stops and smiles. I recognize her from my daughter's secondary school. The two seem glad to see each other. I breathe again, and step back to give them room to talk.

As they chat about their new schools, I think of another morning years ago and far away from here. My husband and I sat in a warm, impossibly sunny southern California consulting room. We listened, stricken, as a somber expert explained that our child's life and our own, would certainly be different than we had planned. She was so right.

We had no way to know then that we would move to England, that my daughter would, finally, learn to talk, that she would compete in swim meets, travel to France, perform in amateur musicals. I never saw the autism coming. How could I have anticipated the rest of it? A light touch on my arm brings me back to the present. My daughter's friend has moved on.

"When will I get where I am going?" my daughter asks. Her question pulls me up short.

"I don't know," I say hesitantly, choosing my words carefully. "No one does. You've gone so much farther already than any of us ever hoped or expected, and…"

The look on her face makes me understand that I have mistaken the point of her question. I backtrack quickly.

"…The bus leaves just before the hour and the ride takes about thirty minutes," I say in my best matter-of-fact voice. "You should be there by half-past." I try to sound confident. I want her to believe I am. I hate risk. But over the years of her life, I have had to make my peace with it.

The bus we are waiting for pulls into the bay. My daughter tells me, "Goodbye, Mom," and, "I'll be fine," and, "You worry too much."

She joins the line, waits her turn, buys her ticket, as practiced. She finds a seat in the first row next to the window, facing forward. When the driver pulls away, my daughter does not look back. In a matter of minutes the bus turns a corner out of sight.

The rain pauses as it often does here in winter, providing false hope to tourists and other strangers. All around me people hurry along or wait patiently. Above the iron and glass ceiling of the station, seagulls struggle against a stiff gale. We are all on our way somewhere.

Far above the heavy northern clouds, I know the sky is still blue, and the sun still warms some part of the world. A patch of yellow light winks down through the gloom, momentarily illuminating a direction sign. The rain begins again.

It is time for me to go.

The streets of our adopted town are shiny, dark, and damp. Somewhere between here and the next town, my daughter rides them into her future. A little rain won't make much difference to her now. With any luck at all she'll be there by half-past.

*Susan Cohen*

# Extraction

His wisdom teeth yanked
from their bone cradles,
my son comes home woozy,
hands me four teeth in an envelope
as keepsakes. Their roots curl
like tiny fingers.

I fill the stock pot to the brim
as his friends amble in, unannounced.
They bear sympathy and dinner—
canned tomato soup, a sourdough loaf
too tough for him to chew.

He clutches ice to his stubbled cheek,
tries not to grin around the bloody gauze
in his empty sockets. As I retreat upstairs,
I hear their masculine laughter,
the clumsy clatter of pots and jibes,
how each kitchen chair complains
when six feet of boy sprawls onto it.

I can't ignore the sounds of them
gathered at our table—their separate lives
together—and the sharp beginning
of my own dull ache.

*Marianne S. Johnson*

# Menarche

I thought I covered it all,
the coming of her first period,
those drastic changes in the first months,
an eternity in the life
of a twelve-year old daughter;
the chemical, hormonal, upheaval
moving her from a long rail of a girl
to the curvaceous hint of a woman,
the inconvenient flood of her life's blood
and the equally inconvenient need
to be prepared at all times,
the reshaping of her form the way
a sculptor transforms a lump of clay
into a goddess, a Venus de Milo.
I had it all covered. Except
what I could not anticipate—
                    our beloved dog would turn on her.

Our female Labrador
senses, even hears the hormones
remaking my child's body;
the roar of ovaries, like new factories
churning out those perfect first eggs,
the ordinary waves in deep red,
sprouts of hair, blossoms everywhere.
The dog stares, snarls and cowers,
black ears laid back, a sniff of danger,
a teenager, a stranger in the house,
the sound of a season's change
is a young girl on the cusp of herself.

It took me days to figure out—
why the dog slunk from a room she entered,
growled low in her throat when my girl rumbled by,
and each time I broke inside
fearing the dog would have to go.
My daughter's face became a portrait
of betrayal, her body not her body,
her pet not her pet—
it took them weeks to reach a calm
that nuzzled in between them;
they both learned to abide.
The Lab with her innate patience
sat with her sleepy head in the lap
of my young huntress, a lunar goddess
with another moon's labor ahead.

*Thomas L. Turman*

# The Gang of Eleven

Our front door slammed shut early on a Saturday morning. "Tom? Beebo?" This woke my wife and me just enough for each of us to calculate that, because neither of our daughters were in town at the moment, we were about to get yet another visit from a member of what we've come to call "The Gang of Eleven."

"Tom? Beebo?" again, followed by quick, purposeful thumping up the stairs toward our bedroom at the back of the house.

My wife had just enough time to leap out of bed and wrap herself in a robe before Elle, one of the "Gang," launches herself through the doorway and on to the floor into a puddle of purse, disheveled hair and sobs.

"OH, HE'S SUCH A SHIT," she screams into our carpet. She has just done what all gang members do which is to forget that we may not be up on all the latest details of each of their lives.

I'm sitting up in bed now, still sleepy, and feeling the need for more detail. My wife collects Elle up onto the end of the bed where she tearfully regales us with her latest problems with a boyfriend in that rapid-fire dialogue reserved for close friends and parents. She punctuates her words with tight fisted punches to the bed. Unless you have had daughters lately, you wouldn't understand much of this kind of speech.

Since I don't have anything on, Beebo gently directs Elle downstairs to start breakfast, so I can get dressed. Breakfast is one of things we do best for The Gang of Eleven.

The Gang is made up of our two daughters and nine close friends of our youngest who banded together, back-to-back, like musketeers upon entering Berkeley High School seven years ago. They formed this defensive gaggle through a mutual interest in the strong dance program, but also as an "all-for-one and one-for-all" reaction to the pressures of a large, urban high school.

Early on, our job, other than to attend all performances from ninth grade on, was to host a breakfast for the whole crowd at least once a semester. I love cooking breakfast, so I became the main chef for this occasion, while Beebo made sure I didn't screw things up.

Do you know what it is like to have eleven, active, female musketeers in the same small room? It is a wondrous noise. I designed our kitchen as an open extension of the dining room, so while making crepes, omelets of various composition, fruit salad and coffee/tea/milk/juice, we could hear and see everything. After the first rather formal affair, they treated my wife and me like the parents/servants/buddies we were becoming. One or two called me Mr. Turman at first, but then relaxed to calling me Tom and then Dad.

Their discussions soon revolved around boys, drinking, drugs, boys, periods and then *all* things having to do with boys. For a father, this is often much more than he wants to hear or know. They acted as if we weren't there, or at least as if *I* weren't there. Beebo had presumably been through this herself. I love that they trust us, but the burden of all this inside information made me feel as if we'd bugged their clubhouse castle. It escalated over the years.

One evening, I was in the one place I've always retreated to for silence and calm, our large, deep, claw-foot bathtub. The room was lit by candles only. When our girls were little, I'd try for a little quiet and privacy in the tub, but even then the door would swing open and one or another of my daughters would come in, sit on the toilet facing me and ask things like, "Why are there clouds?" For several days my youngest, Laurel, followed me around, including into the bathroom, trying to get me to adequately explain daylight-savings time. My first, quick descriptions failed and so she followed me around until we worked it out. She told this story to her friends. My solace place was doomed

On a cool winter evening when the gang was in their senior year, the door to the bathroom banged open and Kally, a future stand-up comedian/singer/actress, burst into my candle-lit sanctuary.

"Kally," I blurted, "I'm in the bath." I'd meant to say that I was naked and that it didn't seem appropriate and all that, but I was so stunned it didn't come out so organized as that. As I struggled to move the washcloth into a strategic position, all I could think of was what this was going to sound like in court when her conservative parents found out about this.

Dismissing my discomfort and possible jail time, from her perch on the flat toilet seat, she rattled off in her confident, speedy way, "Oh Tom it's so dark in here I can't see anything and besides we've all seen you running around here with not much on anyway. Besides, I didn't come in here to talk about silly stuff anyway." She leaned forward, her chin in her hands, her elbows on her knees and said, "I need help with my dad. He is being such a jerk. Will you talk to him about dating and stuff?"

My mind was racing as I tried to imagine me counseling an uptight, conservative, psychologist about his daughter's hormonal changes. Before I could formulate what to say to Kally, the door burst open again and Celia, one of the twins in the gang, glided up to the large mirror and began to fix her hair. Squinting in the candle light, she said, "C'mon Kally, we're leaving." And then, "Damn, Tom you need more light in here. I can't see a thing." With that she grabbed Kally by the back of her shirt and they disappeared, leaving the door open for the next confessor. I slipped down until just my eyes were above the water.

Our house was and is one of the gang's bases. After the "bath night," I thought I'd seen it all, but that was before we were chosen for the Senior Prom prep-house, pit-stop and dinner place. I had thought that the breakfast was chaos until I witnessed the gang getting ready for this dance.

First of all, this strong, confident bunch of girls arranged everything. They chose the escorts for the evening. The stammering, gawky males who eventually showed up were just following orders. The boys wanted a date; the gang wanted staff for the evening. The girls rented the limo; bought their clothes; directed their date's clothes; arranged for the flowers and then began the real process; getting dressed. It took all day and every room in our house, both floors. Self-confident as they are, I'd never seen or felt such emotion and panic prior to any of their dance performances. Much money and time was spent on hair, some of which was totally redone at the last minute by our oldest daughter Brenna. There were hours of squeals, shrieks, and melt-down crying jags before they emerged as eleven of the most beautiful young women ever assembled.

The cars arrived to take them to have their group picture taken at the top of the hills with the bay area at their feet. They didn't count on the seagulls forced inland by an approaching storm. When they returned for the catered dinner at tables set up in our large backyard, I spent quite a bit of time cleaning birdshit off tux jackets and delicate shawls.

The most recent breakfast we had was last November when the gang returned from their junior year at colleges all over the country to attend the truly premature funeral of their beloved high-school dance teacher. They were all about to fly all over the world to take their next semester abroad, so the discussions were not those of teenagers anymore.

Looking out over the young women gobbling down the waffles, I realized they were no longer The Gang of Eleven. They had become a room full of swans; some silent, but most honkingly loud, independent, proud, demanding, beautiful and ever graceful. And like swans, they leave us in the Fall, hopefully to return in the Spring.

*George Longenecker*
# 17

You were born with the full moon,
An evening on the cusp of autumn,
When the geese were arcing south.
The maples were aflame; the world was in harvest,
The days were transformed with color and migration.
Geese crossed the moon,
All the night was lucent,
When you were born.

Oh, the summer of your childhood was brief,
Now perched on the edge of womanhood,
You test the wind.
Your days are aflame with plans and schemes.
You preen and long, weep and laugh,
Again testing the winds,
Awaiting the autumn and the day to soar,
Spreading your wings,
Awaiting the full moon.

The fledgling, like the summer, has been transformed,
You are bright and beautiful,
You are watchful and strong,
Knowing your day of migration shall come,
Knowing your moment of birth is near.

TAXI to the DARK side

*Wanda Coleman*
# 'Tis Morning Makes Mother a Killer

mean

day grinds its way slowly into her back/a bad
mattress stiffens her jaw

it is the mindless banalities that pass as conversation
between coworkers

her paycheck spread too thin across the bread of
weeks; too much gristle and bone and not enough

blood

meatless meals of beans and corn bread/nights
in the electronic arms of the tube

mean as a bear

carrying groceries home in the rain in shoes
twice resoled and feverish with flu

it is the early dawn

mocking her unfinished efforts; unpaid bills,
unanswered letters, unironed clothes

tracks

of pain in her face left by time; the fickle high of it
facing the mirror of black flesh

mean as mean can

pushed to the floor but max is not max enough
no power/out of control/anxiety

it is the sun illuminating cobwebs

that strips her of her haunted beauty; reveals
the hag at her desperate hour

children beware

*Meryl Natchez*
# Motherhood

I like it that they give robot babies to teens
to simulate parenthood,
that the robots are programmed to cry
unless they are held. I think
the teen mother has to hold them—no one
else can make them shut off—but maybe
I'm imagining that, maybe that's a level of need
only real babies have. Because
a robot can't prepare you.
even if it cries all the time,
it isn't wired directly
into your nervous system. You can't imagine
the despair and rage snarled
within the besotted adoration
that tiny body wrenches from you
at birth.

This is the blood vow,
the one you cannot break.
You can barely acknowledge
even to yourself, the force
of the urge for escape,
so that you're lying if you say
you don't understand
how anyone
can bash a baby's brains
against a wall.
With luck, you don't do it,
but you understand.

*Jessica Cuello*

# Mastitis

I rise in the middle of night,
milky clouds surround the moon —

the baby is asleep, and I ease
her food from my strange, hard breasts.

An illness from a time before light-
switches: candle-lit rooms, cures

from the mouths of women.
Cohosh and cabbage leaves.

My daughter is curled, a flower
of flesh, skin so perfect I would burn

with fever every night. A beast
down on its side, barely twitching

at the sharp surprise of pain:
I am overflowing.

*Ella Wilson*

# 403 Days Later

It was September 17th, 2007 and I had been in labor for 26 hours. I had been pregnant for almost 10 months, and I had wanted a child since I could remember. I lay on my side, curled my body around my task, and pushed my daughter into the room. When she appeared her face was flattened; we had fought during labor, one of us stretching, the other squashing. She looked like she'd been beaten up. I felt like I had been.

I knew something was wrong as soon as the baby was placed, warm and sticky, on my chest. Something failed to click. I hoped the lack of click was audible only to me. I waited for the rush of love to come, the fierce desire to protect, the animal instincts I had heard all about, but instead I just felt more than tired and less than a mother.

It was one of those moments that made me wish I'd never seen a movie. Other moments like this include: the moment my father told me he was dying, the moment my father actually died, the moment my mother stopped breathing, let go of my hand and started to turn purple. No soft-focus was there. No voice-over telling me how to feel, no cut away to rain running down a windowpane to give me time to digest the scene I had just witnessed. Just one brutally continuous shot, hard light and worst of all, reality. Whoever thought reality was a good idea has clearly never lived.

The birth had gone well, I was told. I could go home the same day, this was offered as a reward, it felt like a punishment. I did not want to go home, I wanted to stay in the hospital. The baby lay on my chest and everyone beamed. She didn't, I didn't.

I did not want to take this baby home. I felt as if I had pushed a watermelon through my vagina and then been given somebody else's baby. I would have felt more connected to a watermelon, at least I would have known what to do with it. But a baby, I did not know what to do with that.

The baby looked like my mother. Not my mother in her prime, it was not in the eyes, nose or mouth that Violet resembled her grandma, it was in her proximity to not-life. They bore a striking resemblance to one another: bald, wrinkled and desperate. And they both looked to me for help.

My husband, the baby and I left the hospital at 9 PM on the same day that I had given birth. I wrapped the baby in blankets and pulled on the blue and pink striped hat that the nurse had put on her right after she was born. I strapped her into the regulation car-seat, she looked like a baby-bird on the sidewalk. I carried her like a shopping bag. I did not look down.

We drove home the same way that we had come less than twenty-four hours earlier, but now the baby was in the back of the car instead of my belly. She cried and I sat next to her as if this would offer her some comfort. It didn't.

Dark and hollow the night reached up above us, the blackness seemed endless in the same way the sea does. Not in an eternal, comforting way, rather in a terrifying, never-ending way. I looked out of the window down to the East River and thought how welcome the smack of its surface meeting my body would be.

We got home and went straight to bed. Four of us: husband, dog, baby, mother. Everyone fell asleep and I awoke to find my dead mother wearing a blue and pink stripy hat and crying. I pulled the covers up towards my face and stuffed the comforter between us. I did not want to touch her, whoever she was.

Somehow the morning came and in the daylight the baby looked like the baby again.

"Shall we go out for breakfast?" my husband said, cheerily. These words meant little to me. Who were we? What was breakfast? So I copied what he did and made it out of the door. I walked with the baby strapped to my front in a carrier. My husband couldn't follow the instructions for the baby or the carrier, so I wore both. As we walked up the street, a happy family, I felt as if I had been sexually assaulted with a cricket bat (the big end). We sat outside a café and ate eggs. I threw up in my mouth.

The next night was not so simple. The baby did not go to sleep when I put her on the bed between us. Every time I lay her down she woke up. She cried. My husband snored. I sat up in the bed and looked at the ceiling, my eyes boring through it and up to the sky. I pictured the world from above, I pictured how small I was, all the better to feel alone. In the end I gave up and took the baby into the living room and put the TV on. As she alternately slept and fed I watched a British detective show involving a drowned teenager. They both looked so peaceful: baby and late-teen. I realized I was becoming maudlin, changed the channel and cried at a commercial for an Elder-Alarm.

In light of my mother's death and my mother-in-law's age I had hired a postpartum doula to help me in the days after the birth. She was a large woman called Shelley Friedman. Her face looked squashed, like a pug's, and she had a tattoo of a flower on her ankle that was stretched and old, it looked dead. I had interviewed her prior to the birth and she had seemed pleasant enough, but she wasn't, I'm not sure anyone would have been.

She came for four hours a day for the first week, in these times my husband went to work, leaving me with two ladies I did not know. Shelley told me about her daughter who had just started her period, Shelley answered her cellphone several times an hour, Shelley talked an awful lot about how she was friends with Rosie O'Donnell, Shelley ate all the cookies, Shelley went home.

I had never needed my mother more, but freshly gone I couldn't think of her without crying, in fact I couldn't think of much without crying, even thinking of crying made me cry, as did thinking of not crying.

Things can be known but not believed—that is why we can watch the news without vomiting. We are good at detaching ourselves from reality while appearing to be actively engaged in it. I had sat with my mother through chemotherapy, I had held her hand in the hospice as the breath rattled from her and she gasped at life. I had had sex with my husband without using contraception, I had moaned and pushed at all the right moments. These things I had done, but what had come of them I did not believe.

The days stretched out ahead of me and I thought about trains and where they go.

The first time the baby had a fever I gave her Tylenol. I was pleased there was something wrong with her, now maybe there would be fixing afoot. She

sucked down the cherry-flavored liquid, her lips red from the artificial color-
ing. There was a picture of a happy baby on the Tylenol box. I gave her a
syringe at bedtime. I gave it to her the next night since she had slept so well.
Then I started giving it to her every night, and before naps—and sometimes
after. She was broken, or I was, either way medicine was sure to help.

After the medication-free birth I had opted for I was in desperate need of
something, but was allowed nothing, as I was breast-feeding. So I developed
a Tylenol habit for the baby. It was the best I could do.

I took her to the doctor's for her two-week check-up with hope in my step.
They would see that this was not right, this baby and me. I looked forward
to the appointment.

The French doctor looked in her eyes and ears and manipulated her hip
joints. She looked in her mouth; as the baby cried, the doctor smiled.

"Is she feeding well?" Yes she was feeding well, but…

"Is she having four or five wet diapers a day?" Yes, but that wasn't the
point.

"Is she having regular bowel movement?" Her French accent made this
sound impossibly chic, and I did not answer.

I stood in the doctor's surgery and sweated.

"Okay, you can pick her up," the doctor told me, but I did not want to.
The doctor was supposed to save me. But she left the room and the baby and
I were alone again.

The weather was warm for September, and the baby and I sweated as I fed
her on the couch. My husband sat at the other end of the sofa with his laptop
computer on his lap. My belly was still swollen from the pregnancy, puffy
with fear. I felt sick. There was a thought I did not dare think. I breathed shal-
lowly those days, afraid to delve below the neck, afraid of the thought that
spun inside me, the thought that I shouldn't have had a baby, that I did not
want this baby. But now I had it and had it forever.

I joined a new mother's group because it was held in the doctor's waiting
room. I liked taking the baby to the doctor's. I thought of leaving it there.
There were worse places for a child to grow up than the reception area of Wil-
liamsburg Pediatrics. There were plentiful medications, lollipops and toys.

At the group new mothers sat in a circle, their babies on their laps. Women
cooed and smiled, I sweated and shook. Smothered in their love I could hardly

breathe. People chatted and shared their stories. I wanted to tell people that I wasn't sure I wanted my baby, but nobody wants to hear that sort of thing, so instead I said I was very tired.

"That's why they make them so delicious," another mother told me, "so you can't help but love them."

I waved my head up and down in desperation and hoped she would mistake it for a nod.

Delicious?

It had been discussed that I might get post-partum depression, having had post-everything else depression and pre-some other things depression. To be depressed when you're a teenager, to be depressed after one or both of your parents have died, made sense, but to be depressed after your baby is born seemed like a whole new level of broken. I decided I could not have post-partum depression, that it was something for Brooke Shields and other women with crazy eyes. So on I went, I smiled at people when I thought I should and I did not want to hurt the baby. This could be my life, I thought: smiling at appropriate times and not hurting anyone.

Whenever I saw young couples walking along, pushing nothing that screamed, carrying nothing that slept, I wanted to run up to them, to warn them—don't do it, don't have a child, stay as you are!

To be clear, I did not hate the baby, I just was not sure I loved her, and that was bad enough.

Thirteen months after she was born I was still hiding in the bathroom so she wouldn't see me. Still smiling uncomfortably when people told me how cute she was, embarrassed that their enthusiasm exceeded mine.

But the effort of pretending I could do this bore down too heavily. The grief of losing my mother, the grief of not being the mother I thought I would be, became too much. There was no way out. I could not leave. Mothers don't leave babies. I began to long for a way out that would not mean me leaving, no trains, no planes, just pills and sleep.

All of this feeling bad and feeling bad about it eventually landed me in a psychiatric ward. Apparently what I was experiencing was not normal. Some mothers really liked their children, hell, they even liked themselves. This I could not imagine.

In the hospital I was labeled as treatment resistant and I had meetings with doctors to discuss electroconvulsive therapy. It seemed I was going to be that crazy mum. The one who spends days in bed and hides things around the house. The one that laughs too loudly at school plays in all the wrong places and then cries in the car. The twitchy one. Shit.

Somewhere far from the baby, in a room painted a purposefully calming color, I was offered a different type of anti-depressant. It was a tetracyclic anti-depressant rather than an SSRI, all of which I had already tried to no effect. Like all psychotropic drugs nobody could really explain how or why it worked; within fifteen minutes of taking the first dose I only had one eye open. Sure it was sedating, but within days my mood began to shift. Maybe shift is too grand a word, but something started to inch. Soon I could lift my eyes from the floor. By the end of the week I was full of all sorts of grand plans like talking to people other than myself.

It was decided that I was ready for a visit from my husband and the baby. Family, the doctor called it.

My husband brought her to the hospital to visit me and I waited by the door hoping I would be pleased to see them. Finally the two of them arrived and I could not believe what I saw. The baby, my baby. I said it over and again — the words I had thought would come 403 days earlier came now.

"My baby!" I nearly laughed with equal parts relief and astonishment.

"I have a child!" I said to my husband, as if he may not have noticed. Violet kicked her legs in excitement and reached her arms up towards me. I picked her up and held her cheek to mine, roundness on roundness.

"I have a child!" I could not get over it. "Why didn't anyone tell me?" I asked. But there are some things that cannot be told.

I held the baby and studied her closely. She was unbelievably three-dimensional, her voice was so life-like it almost confused me. It was as if I had only seen a photo of her before, and rather like the Grand Canyon, she had to be seen to be believed.

We were not naked, she was not wet and warm, she had been out of my body for over a year, but finally the beginnings of joy were there.

"Daddy!" she squealed, which was what she called both of us with equal enthusiasm, and finally I thought maybe I could be a mother.

*Sharon Dornberg-Lee*

# Long Night

Three a.m. You will not sleep,
will not sleep. The clock looms
like a stalker. So many nights
I have held you in cramped arms,
waited for sleep
to find you the way a cat
finds its last errant kitten.
I have watched you until sleep at last
picked you up, gingerly, in its mouth,
carried you off.

Do you dream about warm milk,
the dog downstairs? Do you dream
about the coffee table's sharp corners,
the vacuum cleaner's roar?

Often I dream I have forgotten
you somewhere.
Like a parcel, I leave you
in the backseat of the car
until night falls. Or
like a pocketbook I mislay you
at the store. Once I dreamt
I left you on the edge
of the table while I went
and put my head beneath
the kitchen tap,
let the water run cool
through my hair.
I ran dripping back
to catch you, in time.

Four a.m. You will not sleep, will not
sleep, until at last
your breathing slows, eyes fall closed.
Do you dream of me?
Do you dream I have forgotten you?

*Amanda Pritchard Moore*
# Clementine Asleep

For so long there was only fighting it:
she would cry and cry and we would stand
before this wailing as if before a tremendous
force of nature, a fire,
waving our hands, calling for helicopters,
shifting the weight of the world's sand bags between us
to stack and stack and stack them before her.
She consumed us, and we would sit in the wake
two scrappy pines uncurling amid ash and char,
occasionally disappointed that we hadn't just burned up.

It isn't much better now. She's restless, doesn't want
to turn off this world that so delights
and seems only to exist for her. Still she sleeps eventually
and suddenly, spent like a match, drowsy flames lazily lapping
her toes as she surrenders to a stubborn sleep.

It is then I study her, sweet mouth open,
hands above her head like those first weeks we brought her home
and she would wriggle from her swaddling.
Always the arms above, reaching for something
she left in the other world, something just hers
It isn't fair, this world she makes herself in sleep,
this place we rush her to
but cannot follow.
These are the small lessons, I know. The ones
that marry terror and joy, the great gift of her between us
and an incredible sense of loss.

*Matt Mason*

# Night Terrors

She's started screaming at night,
this baby, gums shredding
with teeth, diaper filled up,
even so, that's old news, this
is bad-Bible-chapter terrified,
slasher-movie-girl terrified,
end-of-the-world kind of alarm, then
as her mom and I run
out of buckets out of rope out
of the thin bone of composure,
she drops back to sleep
like a snowflake sliding to a stop,
our eyes wide, flashlights popping
at every creak in every corner.

*Teresa Stores*
# Psychic

My son trembles, hair fever-glued to forehead, and looks from his dreams
into my eyes. I hold him in his Wooly Worm sleeping bag on the floor, watching
wisps of fog through the dark outside. "Mommy," he says, tears gleaming in the night-
light, "danger is coming. Danger is coming *today.*"

But I hug him close. "No sweetie," I begin, "everything is okay. Everything is fine.
It was just a dream," but we are far from home, and this end of the world is cold
and foggy, and rains, even now in the night, beat on the roof and sodden ground,
a Poe setting to which it seems as if danger might truly come.

But Grandmother is here, and the children have only incubated a contagion
breathed on the transcontinental flight, I tell myself, listening to coughing all night,
a terrible wet rattle as fevers rise. "I want to go home, Mommy," he cries, a weird
intensity focusing his eyes. "I want to go home *now.*" And danger is coming.

But we have reservations. "In a few days," I say. "We'll go home soon." I think
of the plane at 35,000 feet all those hours, held aloft by incomprehensible physics,
some giant hand, some faith, some thing I cannot understand. I want to comfort
my child, who seems now prescient, psychic. Because he is right: danger comes.

But yesterday's news on our vacation here at the end of the world was of war, I comfort
myself, and a deranged man shooting hundreds, and accidents, *no one we know,* I think,
rocking my son. This is just fever, the foreignness of sleep on the floor in an un-familiar
house, the far-ness of illness away from home. I want to say, "No. No danger will come
today."

But we are old parents. I will die before my children reach the age I am now. Death
will visit this grandmother we visit sooner yet. And my own mother lost a son, my ghost-
brother, for whom my boy is named. Have I marked him to remember this pain?
Have I forecast my own pain? I hold him close, fearing the danger coming.

But the night is just the night, I know, fevers will break, coughs ease and fogs and rains clear into Spring, and the plane will rise into blue skies and eastward us home, though traveling with us will be "strangers," we warn, "bad people who hurt small children who don't hold their mommies' hands," and they will cling, worried of danger coming.

"But strangers might be kind," we will say, "just people we don't yet know," but I know some others will be cruel too because you are a son of two mommies, one of a queer little family. Together in the night at this end of the world, I rock and comfort, mystified. How to prepare for the danger that is coming? And will it come today?

But finally, the wheezing eases, medicine soothes dreams, and the children slip into safe sleep again. The rain taps now from trees to roof as if spirits have been raised in séance. And still his words whisper in the dark. They shall be so each day we live—embracing, comforted, despite them, because of them: "Danger is coming. Danger is coming today."

*Frank Haberle*

# Something About Alligators

He wakes up, screaming something about Alligators.

It's 1:45. When I turn on the light he stares at me, cross, not sure he can trust me. Then he puts his arms up. I lift him from the tangled blanket. His head, chest and arms are superheated. But he shudders convulsively; he clings tightly to my torso for warmth.

"Do you want mommy, or daddy?"

When I sit down with him in my lap, he tries to kick his way inside my body.

"I want daddy," he mumbles.

Shit.

I try to doze in the big chair, the blanket draped over both of us. But he can't make himself comfortable. He writhes, lying draped across my lap, shoving his head into my armpit. He sits up, grips the back of my neck with two sweaty palms, wedging his legs between mine.

Finally, when I think he is still, he comes to.

"Want some water," he says.

"Do you want some water?" I ask. I hope he'll say no.

"Want some WATER," he says with force.

With him still attached around my neck, tucked under one forearm, I take him to the kitchen. It's 2:42. I pour him a cup of ice water, but can't find the lid in the dish rack; I take him back to the chair. He takes a sip of water and pours the rest into my lap. It is ice cold.

"Want some MORE water," he says, pressing the empty plastic cup against my chest.

❦

My eyes open. It's 3:34. Someone, one of his well sisters, mumbles in sweet sleep from the darkness, the warm bedroom behind me. A radiator hisses quietly; a siren wails far away. I'm still in the chair. The quilt has fallen to the floor. My legs are cold and my head is bent down in a strained position. Lying limply against my stomach, he is now beyond hot. He burns my bare skin; steam rises from his mouth. The fever has lasted 4 days — 103 degrees, 104 degrees. The clinic won't see him. Mommy has him all day while I work; I have him all night while she sleeps.

❦

Now his head lays against the armrest, mouth wide open, face swollen and blotched, even in the dim light. Trapped beneath his sticky hair, my left arm has gone dead. I pull it out, shake it until the tingling becomes unbearable. Then I look down at him. I lean forward to make sure he's breathing. I cradle him, gently, down to the carpet, and lay down beside him, pulling the blanket over both of us.

A cold draft travels low through the railroad apartment, south to north. I hold him next to me. He wiggles away. Son of a bitch. I really should get up and put him in the bed with me, I think. That would be the right thing to do. I look at the clock again, under the TV. It's 3:51.

❦

Now we're on the train together, and he's sitting in my lap, smiling out the window at the trucks winding their way into Bellows Falls as we click our way out of it, into the notch. It's an antique train with wicker, leather-padded seats. Steam rolls in from the engine; we pass on a trestle over a marsh, under huge green leaves hanging from vines. The horn blasts: Woo-hoo! He looks up at me and laughs, covering his ears. "Woo-hoo!" he yells. The trestle starts rattling, then shuddering. He looks up at me, and stops laughing. "What is that?" He asks me.

❦

I open my eyes. It's 5:45. The little green digital numbers blink on the VCR, like they were waiting for me. Now my neck is bent in the other direction; when I lift it it's like twisting a stick. In the darkness, I reach for him, but he isn't there.

Shit!

I start flailing around for him on the floor.

Shit!

What am I doing? What am I doing now? I have to find him. I have to get his temperature down. I have to put a cold damp cloth on his forehead, I have to get him more ice water to drink. He asked for it hours ago. What the hell am I doing?

I reach into the darkness, stare into the bedroom where the others lie drunk with sleep. Then I see him, just barely. I see the tiny pink sole of his foot. He's climbed back into the big chair, and he's rocking himself gently. He's awake, squinting at me in the dim light that's slowly collecting itself in the windows. I reach for his foot, terrified, and clasp it in my outstretched hand—but it's not too hot, and it's not too cold.

When he sees me crawling toward him, he laughs: "YOU'RE not an alligator."

*Maureen A. Sherbondy*
# Things That Get Lost

It's the little one
I worry about, the fast disappearing
guppy, how his frog green goggles bob
up and down and down
beneath the wet surface,
how the visible becomes invisible.

How for elongated nail-biting seconds
I can't find
the dark mop of soaked hair.

Once I lost him
in a store, aisles and endless aisles
of panic ensued, the floor spun
into a whirlpool of blurred tile.
Circles of loss, small buttons
of me disappearing with each passing second.

Even after I heard his cry,
that tone-specific inflection *mama,*
pieces of me were so far gone,
I could not get them back.

*Nannette Croce*

# Split-Seconds

The mother brushes her teeth, smoothes the thick cream over the creases and lines on her neck and face and around her eyes, slips into her sleeveless, shapeless nightgown, and climbs into bed beside the already sleeping father. Below her, in the family room, the daughter; the during-the-school-year roommate who is visiting from out of town; and the friend-who-is-a-boy but not a boyfriend, sit with their respective laptops, punctuating loud talk with loud laughter.

The mother is not like other mothers she meets and talks to over carts in the supermarket or across the gap between treadmills. She does not strain to hear the secrets rising up from below, in fact, tries to ignore what she can't help but hear. The mother does not expect the boy and the girls to set their sleeping bags in separate rooms. The boy is a friend, after all, not a boyfriend. The mother does not expect the daughter to meet curfews she does not keep when she is away at college, just to call if she will not be in her bed in the morning. Still, the mother's stomach sinks when a phone rings in a handbag, just when she'd assumed they would not indulge that perverse college-kids' habit of going out when everyone else is going to bed.

The daughter flips open the phone, explains that she is hanging out with her during-the-school-year-roommate and her friend-who-is-a-boy, both visiting for the weekend. Club names are exchanged, times and meeting places bandied about the room. The daughter snaps the phone shut, runs upstairs to stroke mascara on her eyelashes in front of her bedroom mirror, calls something through the door of the mother's bedroom, and is out the door before the mother can call, be careful.

So the mother whispers it, three times. Be careful. Be careful. Be careful. Whispers it into the night as she hears the garage door roll up, three car doors slam. She does this so she can sleep, because she knows one cannot wait up until 3:00 AM several nights a week and not turn into a mother-who-does-not-understand.

The daughter slides into the driver's seat of the car she got last year for her birthday, pulls on her seat belt. They all do. They are good-kids. A phone chimes. The during-the-school-year-roommate flips open her phone to check the text message even as she guides the daughter through the garage door and they turn left out of the driveway. The text is from Amanda. She wants to get together.

The daughter knew this would happen, as she drives down Cedar Hill Road—the daughter's road, her family's road—where she focuses on the darkness for the neighbor's black dog that runs loose at night. Why did the during-the-school-year-roommate tell Amanda she'd be visiting? The friend-who-is-a-boy wants to know who Amanda is. A girl who dropped out of their school after freshman year. A weird-girl. A clingy-girl-who-won't-let-go. Pretend you didn't get the message, the daughter says. The during-the-school-year-roommate did this three times already.

As the daughter turns onto Bellevue, the mother is already drifting into sleep. She has emptied the dishwasher three times, gone out to the store twice to buy extra groceries for the visitors, done the wash so clean towels would be available. The day was warm. She is tired but still floats just above deep sleep in a state where she will hear the key in the lock the way she heard the cry in the night twenty-plus years ago.

Bellevue is not part of the daughter's family's development, but is a few houses with driveways-hard-to-back-out-of-on-busy-mornings lining the road on land that was a farm a decade before the daughter was born. The daughter tells the friend-who-is-a-boy how Amanda once barfed in her underpants.

How do you barf in your underpants? Sitting on a toilet when you are drunk, the daughter says.

The friend-who-is-a-boy wants to text Amanda to ask if she still barfs in her underpants. He grabs behind his seat for the during-the-school-year-roommate's phone, but she pulls it away and slaps at his hand. The daughter has stopped at the stop sign then turned right onto Sharpley and is heading toward the intersection-with-the-tough-left-turn the mother warned her to avoid back when the daughter had just started driving to places like the mall and the movies and the mother could still warn her about such things.

The daughter's phone rings. They know it is Amanda calling her now. The phone sits between the daughter's thighs on the seat. She will not answer because she is driving. The friend-who-is-a-boy reaches for the phone. Threatens to question Amanda about her barfy underpants. The daughter laughs, squeezes her thighs tight over the phone, pushes the friend-who-is-a-boy's arm away and takes her eyes off the road for just a second, a split-second, really, but long enough not to see the black car in front of her until the stop lights splash red across her windshield, and she has to squeeze the brake pedal to the floor, and their three heads propel forward then snap back.

The mother awakes to the sound of sirens. What kind of sirens? Police? Fire? Ambulance? How far away? What direction are they coming from? Never good at gauging these things she considers waking the husband—who snores pepperoni breath from the pizza he bought for the kids—but decides against it. The mother wants him to tell her not to worry but she will worry anyway and then two people will lie awake. The mother now hears one siren that is an ambulance. No mistake about that. The mother reaches over, considers calling the daughter's cell phone, then rolls onto her back. The daughter will be 22. She has lived abroad. It is not the daughter's job to reassure the mother. So the mother stares at the ceiling and waits for the call all mother's imagine while knocking on wood before forcing it from their minds, until she cannot separate her thoughts from dreams of sirens and phones ringing and the click of her daughter's key in the lock.

Monday morning the mother sips her coffee out on the patio, enjoying the last bits of summer. Both the during-the-school-year-roommate and the friend-who-is-a-boy left Sunday afternoon, long after the mother had stopped remembering the sirens of the night before. The daughter comes out in the navy blue uniform of her summer job at the coffee shop and sits down. The mother looks up from her newspaper.

The daughter has a confession. She had a slight accident with her car Saturday night. She rear-ended someone near the intersection-with-the-tough-left-turn. No one was hurt. No, the mother won't be hearing from the insurance company or police. There wasn't even a dent. In fact, the driver, a guy-who-was-kind-of-cute, and his friends, met them at the club later. The friend-who-is-a-boy wasn't very nice to them, but the daughter expects the guy-who-was-kind-of-cute to call her anyway. The accident wasn't really the daughter's fault. The guy-who-was-kind-of-cute stopped short because the woman in front of him stopped short. Neither the daughter nor the guy-who-was-kind-of-cute knew why.

The mother tells the daughter she needs to be more careful, shouldn't take her eyes off the road for even a split-second, in a tone that falls between admonishment and prayer and has the effect of neither. If the daughter promises to pay more attention the mother will not tell the father, but she has to remember sometimes life is measured in split-seconds and —

The daughter is late for work, thanks the mother, pecks her on the cheek, relieved to put the secret behind her and remember Saturday as the night she met the guy-who-was-kind-of-cute instead of the night of the accident-her-parents-don't-know-about.

The mother goes back to her paper, wishing she could ask the daughter to call when she arrives at work, but knowing she cannot, wonders if the "be care-fuls" she sent into the night technically worked or technically did not. She flips to the local section of the newspaper, reads the headline — a sixteen-year-old-girl killed in a crash Saturday night. The mother remembers the sirens and searches down the column for the fatal mistake — drunk, speeding — the kind of mistake the daughter who is a good-kid does not make, but finds only a drunk-driver-in-a-pickup-truck who swerved into the wrong lane. A drunk driver who, minutes before, ran the red light at the intersection-with-the-tough-left-turn.

The mother stares beyond the paper to grass and trees she does not see and begins calculating times. The time the daughter left the house with the during-the-school-year-roommate and the friend-who-is-a boy. The time it took to travel the roads from their driveway to the intersection-with-the-tough-left-turn. The time her daughter would have rear-ended the car of the-guy-who-was-kind-of-cute because he stopped short because the woman in front of him stopped short for a reason he did not know. But she stops herself from reading down the column to find again that time she just read in black and white.

Instead, the mother folds the paper in half and half again, leaves it behind her on the chair and goes inside to get ready for work. Life is measured in split-seconds, and sometimes in one split-second a drunk-driver-in-a-pickup runs a red light and kills a sixteen-year-old girl and sometimes in a split-second your daughter rear-ends the car of a-guy-who-is-kind-of-cute who meets her at the bar and will call her for another date.

*W. D. Ehrhart*

# Guns

Again we pass that field
green artillery piece squatting
by the Legion Post on Chelten Avenue,
its ugly little pointed snout
ranged against my daughter's school.

"Did you ever use a gun
like that?" my daughter asks,
and I say, "No, but others did.
I used a smaller gun. A rifle."
She knows I've been to war.

"That's dumb," she says,
and I say, "Yes," and nod
because it was, and nod again
because she doesn't know.
How do you tell a four-year-old

what steel can do to flesh?
How vivid do you dare to get?
How explain a world where men
kill other men deliberately
and call it love of country?

Just eighteen, I killed
a ten-year-old. I didn't know.
he spins across the marketplace
all shattered chest, all eyes and arms.
Do I tell her that? Not yet,

though one day I will have
no choice except to tell her
or to send her into the world
wide-eyed and ignorant.
The boy spins across the years

till he lands in a heap
in another war in another place
where yet another generation
is rudely about to discover
what their fathers never told them.

*Julie L. Moore*

# Lump

Of coal. In your stocking. Solid mass in the toe. Or in your throat if you're a coal miner right before the rush of rock like rain falls on your head. You know you're trapped. The canary's trilling long since silenced. Or, speaking of being underground, the hill by your drive. (The one you're tempted to make into a mountain.) The mole's tunnel leaving the soil soft as a freshly dug grave. Step. Sink. Feel the earth give way. The way it gave and gave and kept on giving when the doctor said, *here, yes, here, I don't want you to be overly concerned but right here* (in your daughter's breast — she's fifteen) *I can feel it.*

*Joe Mills*

# Burning Down the House

My daughter wants to know
if she can have a "baby fire"
to take care of. She promises,
"I won't let it get out, and
I'll call 9-1-1-1-1 if it does."
I'm tempted to say, "I never
got to have a fire at your age,"
but she might not get the joke,
or understand it's not a joke.
Before I was born, my brother
and sister decided to build
a fire in the living room.
They lit paper on the stove,
but only made it to the hall
before dropping the flame.
My parents liked to tell how,
at hearing screaming, they ran
in to find a fire on the stairs;
each time I didn't hear concern,
but laughter and wonder, until
I regretted never having tried
to set the house on fire myself,
never having come so close
to tragedy they loved me more.
I was the youngest, the one
who came along after the family
was already a family, the one
who never destroyed anything,
but who secretly wanted to,
which may be why I ended up
burning so much in my life,

people and opportunities,
money and time and bridges.
Maybe my daughter would be
happier later if I let her play
with fire now? Maybe it would
burn a ring of safety around her.
Maybe for her next birthday,
I will get her a baby fire
instead of Princess Barbie.
It will teach her responsibility,
to be careful with her desires,
how much I love her, how much
I want her to have more than I did.

*Madelyn Rosenberg*

# Blessings

Once they gave lobotomies to unhappy housewives
The most severe cases
A small hole in the frontal lobe
Dreams shrink wrapped in cellophane
Spilt milk no longer a cause for metaphors or tears
After that they gave us little yellow pills
And the Rolling Stones sang about it.
The drugs turned pink
Exotic prescriptions
Advertised by smiling women who chased butterflies.
Then they said "no more drugs.
Count your blessings instead."
We counted them every day.
Obediently
We swallowed them down with a full glass of water
Hoping not to choke.

*Jim Teeters*
# Sackcloth and Ashes

None of us tears our garments any more
when our sins weigh us down
or we are sick with sorrow
like those bible kings of old

They'd rip their clothes
pour ashes on their sorry heads
to let their shame or sadness show

That time I shook my teenage son too hard
when he refused to mow the lawn
might've called for that

It would've done me and him some good
if I'd ripped my tee shirt and jeans
dumped some fireplace
ashes in my hair;
then gone and knocked on his bedroom door
and said I'd been wrong

We could've laughed together
but instead I lay awake
thinking about my misplaced rage
and I waited until he'd grown
into a man to humbly ask
him to forgive me

who are you?
what do you do?

*Kathy Kottaras*

# What We Do

"What do you do?"

Before I became a mom, this question yielded worlds of gooey information from strangers at swanky, low-lit parties who seemed intriguing through my wine goggled haze. The catchall question allowed me to flirt and schmooze — in other words, to be human: to create a Venn Diagram of separate lives, finding commonalities in that short, empty space between you and me.

After giving birth to my daughter, Madeline, in July of 2006, I found that the conversation never got past this point. I met many new moms, at the grocery store, the mall, online, through moms' clubs, but I never made a connection. When I asked, "What do you do?" I received blank stares. You know what I do. You go to bed at 10 p.m., wake up at midnight, 3 a.m., and 6 a.m. You change twelve diapers each day. You spend naptime cruising the internet for a new cure for cradle cap. You coo over the new smiles and dread the five o'clock fussies. You worry about whether they're breathing, why they aren't sleeping or why they've been sleeping for so long today. You are harried and exhausted and exhilarated by this new little being in your life. What do you do? You do everything that I do. Why should it matter what I did before? We're moms now. Shouldn't that be enough?

I started stalking moms at the grocery store, slipping them my email address on the back of receipts, like a teenager in heat. That's what it felt like: that nervous anxiety of finding the perfect boyfriend in high school, wanting to pair up so that the scary new world wouldn't seem so scary anymore. But it never went anywhere; either we'd write a few times, or get together with a larger playgroup for brunch, or neither one of us would follow up. I never could find that special mom.

Until I met Mandy.

Of course, as with all great love affairs, it happened when I least expected it. It was a hot, August afternoon, and for me, a sad one. My mom was in the hospital, her frail body besieged by heart failure and toxic infection. She had been sick, on and off, for years, but her health began a rapid deterioration the month after Madeline was born. When my husband could watch Madeline, I visited her, but on this particular day, I faced a long afternoon, alone, wanting to be with my mom, under a tree in her backyard. Instead, I took Madeline to a park so she could crawl happily under a different tree.

While Madeline rolled from blanket to grass, Mandy and I exchanged the details of our life stories. Mandy, her husband, and daughter, Ruby, had just moved to the neighborhood not one month before. I asked, brazenly, "What do you do?" She was an intelligent, vibrant woman who had chosen to stay at home after a long career in health communications. Mandy admitted that this time at home, particularly in an unfamiliar neighborhood was difficult. She was also searching for company and friendship.

We traded phone numbers and parted ways. I came home buoyant, relishing the details of my encounter to my husband, Matthew. I was happy, but to be honest, I didn't really expect to hear from her.

There was something about our brief meeting in the park that compelled me to Mandy, so I called her, and we set a date to get together. And we did: on Friday, and then on Monday, then every day after that. We started gabbing on the phone like sisters. We just couldn't stop talking and laughing and learning more about one another. It seemed that the most amount of time that went by without a play-date or a conversation was twelve hours, max. (We had to sleep sometime.)

It felt similar to the other moments when I forged other lifelong friendships: middle school's hormonal upheaval and self-doubt brought my trusted confidants Kate and Aimee; the social anxiety and cliquish stresses of high school gave me honest and loving Kara; and college, where a license to be carefree led me to my husband Matthew, who will forever remember my youth. Coming into motherhood is another time of exhilaration, upheaval and change. Particularly for women like Mandy and me who have spent the first decade of our adult lives focused solely on our careers, the decision to stay home to raise our children is a shocking lesson in loneliness. My friends work all day, my husband works all day, and yes, I work all day (besides cleaning bottles and changing diapers, I have the best job of all: cooing at my baby). Yet, the bottom line is, the job description for the stay-at-home in twenty-first century America does not include adult social interaction at the top of its list.

Mandy quickly became my friend, my sister, co-worker, my village. Our meeting was a demonstration of pure simpatico. I tried to support her efforts with sleep training and weaning. She listened to my worries about Madeline's separation anxiety, my decision to return to work part-time, and of course, my mom's failing health.

When my mother died in October, of course, my family and friends checked in on me. But during my day-to-day, hour-to-hour struggle with the loss and emptiness, Mandy was the one who was always there. I could call her at any time of the day, and she would let me cry, invite me over, meet me at a playground, and listen.

Recently, at a summer barbeque, I was introducing Mandy, and I found myself tripping on a fully satisfactory word to describe who she is to me. I started, "This is Mandy, my—." And I stopped, wanting a word, something like *best friend*, something like *sister*, some word to describe the relationship that has evolved so quickly, so beautifully, and so completely. I didn't finish the sentence aloud. But in my head, I uttered a thought, "This is my *Mandy*."

My daughter, Madeline, has given me a joy that I never expected. But along with motherhood came a loneliness that I also never expected. Motherhood was never meant to be a solitary experience. When people now ask, "What do you do?" I say, "Well, I'm a mom, first." And in responding so proudly, I know that I am communicating the significance of this job, most certainly, as the most important job. However, I feel like I am deleting so much: how it can be the most stressful, the most harrowing, and, sadly, for many urban American moms, the most isolating as well. Mandy allowed me to be honest about that. She also filled the emptiness with the most vibrant joy. Every new mom deserves to have her *Mandy*. She shouldn't be afraid to ask not only "What do you do?" but "How do you do it?" And we should be open to answering her—it's what we do.

*Tom C. Hunley*

# Octopus

"I worked hard on that essay. Why did
    I get a 'C'?" the email read.
In reply, I described how hard I worked at tennis
    in my teens, Saturday nights spent
        sweating over my service motion. I could never place
            my shots as well as Andy Roddick, or hit at his pace.
Even if he were drunk, or had a broken leg, I couldn't test him.
                I asked this question:
    why couldn't they just give me
        a Wimbledon trophy
            for my hard work?
        I asked *Couldn't they grade on effort?*
But I deleted it, because this student wouldn't understand.
        Because I don't understand.
I typed *If you've got a grade complaint, take it to the Chair,*
and hit *send.* I never did make my mark as a tennis player,
    and, judging by my classrooms full of whining cheaters,
        I've failed just as spectacularly as a teacher.

This morning, between brewing and sipping my first cup of coffee,
    I changed my two-year-old's diaper, soothed him as he
        suffered the daily trauma of waking up
in a world that's way too big for both of us,
    prepped some rice cereal and a strawberry waffle
        for him and peeled a clementine and toasted a bagel
for my pregnant wife, who is on bed rest,
    wiped our son's mouth at her behest,
        loaded and unloaded the dishwasher,
        and took the garbage to the curb.

Tonight, as I sat, concentrating, in a stolen moment, on a blank page,
   I searched my brain for something to write about, a great
     epic subject to illuminate in a burst of song
     that would be so beautiful and true and strong
   that everyone would say "That Hunley has mastered this art;
                yes, he's really made his mark,"
but my son soon tricycled into my study, crawled
    on my lap, spilled Gatorade all
      over my poem, and cried for my attention.
     I turned, defeated, and almost said to him:
     "You are part of the reason I can't find time to write.
     You are part of the reason I'm not living
     the kind of life that generates poetry.
     You are part of the reason I'm failing
     to make my mark."
But I didn't, because he wouldn't have understood.
   Or maybe because he would have understood.
     Then I remembered this scene from *The Octopus*, by
   Frank Norris: an aspiring poet walks beside a train track, tries
     to think of a subject for his great epic of the American West.
      A flock of sheep charges through a broken fence,
    and the sheep don't stop to look both ways to avoid
the train. Amidst all that bleating and all that blood,
    the poet curses. His concentration has been
   shattered. He can't figure out how his poem will begin,
what it will be about, or how it will end.

*Ben Rogers*

# Electing to Have Kids

Some people will vomit if they see, smell, or merely intuit the vomit of others. My wife, for example. At our house, the cleaning up of mislaid bodily functions falls to me. We have a 2-year-old and a pug, so I keep busy enough.

Our pug has a simple means of determining if something is edible. She eats it, then waits. One might think this flies in the face of self-preservation, even evolution. But one need only look at a pug to clear up any confusion. Natural selection cannot be held accountable for this creature. Like so many dog breeds, the pug's continued existence is an insult to Nature. Hell, bulldogs can barely even mate anymore. The males are too heavy and prone to overheating—making artificial insemination the only realistic means of bringing more bulldogs into this world. And pugs, with their two-dimensional face, are prone to respiratory issues, such as not being able to inhale or exhale. Do you think wolves know about pugs? I wonder if they appreciate that pugs greatly outnumber them.

I was getting on an airplane the other day when I saw a mother and her son waiting near the ticket scanner. She was 20-something and he was 2-something. He was on the floor, dangling from her hand in the way only the very young and the very drunk can. She essentially held the tentacle of a giant squid. This duo ended up sitting across the aisle from me. She buckled herself in and stared into oblivion while her son inventoried the seat pocket. Her face was ashen even before we took off. I went ahead and assumed that she was on some kind of drug(s). Attending to our flight was a graying but fit older man—civil, I'd say, but not affectionate—and a middle-aged woman with blonde highlights. Of the two, hers turned out to be the healthier aversion to human vomit.

Perhaps it was this aversion that prompted her to retrieve the oxygen tank from the overhead bin—an ounce of prevention. The tank was about the size of a deli salami, with a regulator valve and a tube that ran to a soft plastic mask. The flight attendant gave it to the mother, who thanked her. The son watched, fascinated, as his mother fastened the mask to her face and breathed the cool, pure gas. He took her at her word when she assured him all was well. Her face flushed from silver-ish to gunmetal-ish. Her eyes drooped. The mask hissed gently.

I tried to concentrate on my crossword, but I'm no good at them even when conditions are ideal, let alone when seated directly across from the plane's second-most-interesting passenger. The first-most-interesting passenger, for the time being, was actually the guy in the row ahead of us. A Brazilian wearing Nike from head to toe. Literally. As in, not only was every visible piece of clothing and footwear bearing The Swoosh, but a 6-inch version of the logo had been cultivated on the back of his head. The rest of his scalp was shorn save for a cute little mohawk toward the front. I knew he was from Brazil because the flight attendant asked. Because of where he was sitting he couldn't see what the mother and her son were up to without making it obvious. As the situation escalated, he had to cock his ear to listen and look out the corner of his eye toward me, to register *my* reaction to the goings-on as consolation for not being able to witness them firsthand. When our eyes met he'd raise his brow, as if to say, "what's the report?" And I'd make a face that conveyed the tone, if not the specifics, of the situation. In Portuguese.

The mother lay her head back and took shallow breaths. Her son was seated beside her. He wasn't buckled in, but no need: he had become strangely calm. The mother closed her eyes, maybe thinking she could steal a few seconds of sleep. The barf bag she'd been issued sat in her lap like a napkin. The particulars of this scene didn't change really when it happened. The boy was still staring somewhat confusedly up at his mother, his legs straight out in the big-person chair. His mouth agape.

Main difference was, he'd become a fountain of vomit. Not a showy Las Vegas fountain. More the gurgling English garden variety. Dignified and understated. He didn't cry or make a scene. Just sat quite still, gurgling and gurgling and gurgling. His little belly pumped in and out. By the time his mother reacted he'd coated the chair, the seatbelt, the armrests, his clothes, the magazine pouch, the carpet and the straps of the oxygen tank. Finally it stopped and he got a good breath and he began to whimper as tears came to his eyes. I felt sorry for him. I felt sorrier for the mother.

She unbuckled herself and got up. She bent over and told her son through the mask that all was well and she started to undress him. A wizened black gentleman in the window seat beside them set down his newspaper. A moat now separated him from the rest of the plane. The sheer volume of fluid seemed to somehow exceed the volume of its original container. It now seemed quite possible that, in some parallel dimension, this boy actually *was* a giant squid.

The mother worked slowly but diligently. Off came her son's shirt, followed by his shoes and socks, last his pants. She put the clothes in a little pile in the aisle, then used a SkyMall catalogue to scrape off the floor and seat cushions. Through it all she never removed the mask. While the air conditioning system began circulating the acrid fumes throughout the cabin, she chose to breathe cool, fresh $O_2$. And for this I can't say I blame her.

The flight attendants were summoned. The man in the window seat looked up at them imploringly. Something must be done, he said, if only with his eyes. The female attendant turned her back on the mess and whispered something to her colleague. He nodded, snapping on a pair of surgical gloves. While he plucked clothes off the floor and put them in a garbage bag, she made a speedy retreat to the back of the plane — where she was to remain for awhile.

The mother stood next to my seat. She had yet to register a real reaction. Beneath her mask, her pale mouth continued to frown, her eyes to droop. I got the impression she was thinking of falling back to sleep. Her son meanwhile was apparently feeling awesome. He was running up and down the length of the plane in just his diaper, giggling and shrieking, and I was glad for the little guy. May we all at some point know the undiluted joy of cavorting without clothes or self-awareness before seated strangers, high on that unlikely, lightheaded euphoria that follows a good puke.

It was fun to watch people react to the situation. Some found the boy adorable, others not so much. My take was: not *my* 2-year-old. Mine was at home running rampant on my wife. In less than an hour they would pick me up at the airport. Both of them soft and soaped and shampooed and I whiskered and weary. When I landed I would be a functioning dad again.

My mom recently referred to parenting as a painful joy. The more days I spend with my daughter the more it's just joy. I hear it shifts back though, around age 13. Before she was born I loved my wife with all my heart. So, now that she's here, have I reallocated my heart so that some of it loves my wife and some of it my little girl? Could a pie chart help convey the human capacity for love?

Maybe. Charts are wonderful.

Or, there's this house in California. Built by Sarah Winchester, widow of the gun magnate. She broke ground in 1884, but never stopped adding on. For 38 straight years it was under construction. Place has like forty bedrooms. Forty-seven fireplaces. Five or six kitchens, depending on your definition of a kitchen.

You see where I'm going with this.

At some point, a set of absorbent cloth squares were spread out on the floor and across the seats to sop up the mess. When at last the female flight attendant thought it safe to return to the front of the plane she came armed with a little spray can.

Is it okay with you all if I spray some of this? she asked. It's just some lemon essence. It won't bother anyone?

One guy actually said he preferred the smell of sick.

No—of course no one said that. We nodded vigorously. We all but sang in harmony, one voice for change: Yes you can! Yes you can! And spray she did. Her aim might have seemed random. It wasn't. It was all-inclusive. Her spritzing liberal. The aerosol floated across aisles. A refreshing moment in our nation's history.

It just struck me that maybe the reason that the wolves aren't cranking out litters and running rampant is because they see something we pugs don't. A world that doesn't deserve their superior offspring. I read an article the other day about Cass Sunstein and Samantha Power. He's on the shortlist for a Supreme Court seat, works at Harvard, writes books about everything: cloning, Wikipedia, animal rights, pornography, Bob Dylan. She's a journalist who won a Pulitzer about America's responses to recent genocides, helped start the Save Darfur movement. Oh, and she also works at Harvard. They met on the Obama campaign, where they were both working as advisors to Barack. They're soon to be married.

Will they elect to have kids? Should they? Or should the Cass Sunsteins and Samantha Powers of the world go into hiding and wait until we run out of food in our bowls and starve ourselves into extinction? *Then* have kids.

If you just finished reading *Atlas Shrugged*, you might think so. If you read it some time ago, you've likely by now come around to thinking Ayn Rand is an asshole. Or maybe you saw Mike Judge's movie, *Idiocracy*. If you didn't, no biggie — it's not very good. But it should have been: the premise is brilliant. There's this average guy who ends up hibernating for around 500 years and when he wakes up, America has become ridiculously stupid (as in, the Oscar-winning movie that year is 90 minutes of a naked human butt on screen). So this average guy is now the smartest person in the country. The reason for the widespread stupidity is that idiots have far out-bred those who never end up having kids because they're always thinking they need more career stability or more maturity or [insert perfectly rational reason here].

I've veered away from my own poorly executed premise. Let's get back to the sick. The seats at this point looked like a hazmat scene. And the mother was just where we left her, standing like a zombie in the aisle, watching the flight attendant clean up the mess while she breathed oxygen from a tank with puke on the straps and let her little boy have free reign of the plane. The mother, as luck would have it, was the type who can't deal with puke and soon slipped into the lavatory. I could hear her retching in there. The Brazilian could too. He just shook his head.

Such a good boy, I heard a woman behind me say. The little guy had pulled up next to her seat to suck on his fingers. He was probably wondering where his mother went.

The television screens were showing something about a river in China, all chocolate-milky at flood stage. I didn't have my headset on so I didn't know what exactly the show was about. But the images were great. Evidently, there was no bridge in the area and so to get across the river the villagers had rigged up a zip line. They'd snap into a harness and shoot out over the churning river, then pull themselves along hand-over-hand up to the opposite shore. One man tethered not only himself to the line but also his goat. Mothers braved the crossing with children on their chests. The look on their faces placid. This was just how they got across. Then, a little later, the televisions showed some nature program about a troop of monkeys high in a jungle canopy. The mother monkeys were swinging effortlessly from limb to limb with babies clinging to their chests.

By this time, the mother on my flight was out of the lavatory. She and her son now had a whole row to themselves, after a few people volunteered to give up their seats. Out of nowhere, the mother started singing "Yesterday." The pitch not perfect but the lyrics word for word. *Oh I believe, in yesterday…* Nicely and quietly. I dared not turn around to ogle them, so I had to imagine what they looked like, and I imagined the Pieta. Her eyes glazed from exhaustion and stress and whatever else. His eyes unbiased. Her heart getting a new kitchen.

We do the best we can, us parents—at least most of us. It's easy to argue that the best and brightest should breed and breed, but who's to say they'd be good parents? There are no ideal candidates for reproduction. Hell, a dude just gave birth to a baby. Who can say what compels us to bring children into this world? Sure, there's the disproportionate allotment of nerve endings in the groin region, but at a fundamental level, there's a belief in tomorrow. Or at least there should be.

I'll tell you what also sweetens the deal, at least for me: a little lemon essence.

*Catherine Sharpe*

# Somewhat Organic

As usual, we were running late for Circle Time. I was packing my daughter Phoebe's soft-sided jungle animal lunch box, but stopped when I grabbed a four-pack sleeve of "dessert"—my current euphemism for unsweetened applesauce. The individual portion cups were not labeled "organic." At Phoebe's uber-Berkeley pre-school, MonteVerita, organic is expected, sugar is discouraged, politics come in green, and the particulars of Phoebe's birth are hardly cause for comment.

Phoebe is not my genetic daughter. I am the womb donor, her other mother is the egg donor, and #2517 (not his real number) is the sperm donor. Phoebe is my little G.M.O., genetically modified organism. Her genetics were certainly influenced as my unrelated blood coursed through her cute little fetus. If you've stayed up on the latest genetic theories, local conditions can dial genes into the "yes, express me" mode, or "no, keep it to yourself." This keeps us adaptive as individuals and as a species. It is just possible that, like any real parent, my blood supply responded "no" just enough times to keep the "yeses" interesting.

Today I was slotted for my mandatory volunteer hours at MonteVerita, so my excellent parenting could shine without exclusively depending on the lunch I packed. Where I live, organic foods are to good mothering what Hostess Ding Dongs are to Britney Spears.

But I know the fraud that is applesauce—unsweetened, organic applesauce is not dessert.

Applesauce is not a brownie, it is not a Rice Krispies Treat, it is not even a chocolate-chip granola bar. It is roughage masquerading as some kind of thoughtful endnote to nutritious, healthful, unambiguous, boxed love. Phoe-be's lunch must represent all of my parenting aspirations and then some that would never occur to me.

At 9:23, Phoebe was sitting in our front hallway near the front door with her socks on. This did not annoy me. Even if the socks were on her hands. Phoebe in proximity to any pair of shoes and only a yard from the front door was actually impressive, a burst of momentum from my smell-every-fuck-ing-flower-when-we-really-need-to-hustle daughter. I can't tell you how many times I've urged "Quick like a bunny. Quicklikeabunny. Hop! Move! Run! Here comes the hungry hunter with his twelve gauge!" Countless repetitions. But I don't say this in front of my vegetarian friends.

I became annoyed, as I packed Phoebe's lunch, because the foil top on each individually packaged cup of applesauce said merely that—applesauce. Now the outer cardboard sleeve that yoked together this whole team of pureed lunch-sized fruit was clearly labeled *organic*, unsweetened applesauce. And it certainly cost more than the inorganic kind sweetened with high fructose corn syrup.

Goddammit. Anybody could mistake this individual applesauce for just regular applesauce. .

"Okay! Whatever!" I zipped up Phoebe's lunch box. Her socks were still on her hands, talking crazy puppet talk.

"Phoebe, ya have gloves for your feet? Because they're going to be cold without socks. No? Any other ideas?" I said.

Phoebe declined to answer but carefully peeled off one sock, and then the other, like a surgeon finished with his task, but uncertain of the prognosis. I squatted and helped her yank them crookedly on her feet, then rudely intro-duced her feet to her sneakers, then the Velcro to their fasteners.

I didn't mind volunteering at her school. Volunteering was an excellent opportunity to see other kids whine, hit, twist your words, scuttle your plans. A chance to see even the teachers, the Professionals, the Care Providers, the Accredited Ones, flail. It made me feel good, normal.

MonteVerita is all child development blah blah blah, imaginative play blah blah, participation by parents improves child/adult ratio blah, but the truth is that spending a few hours "playing teacher" is the perfect opportunity to spy on my competition. Did other kids come to school with hair viciously matted at the back of the head? How many other kids brought in random bits of twigs, moldy leaves or crushed pinecones to "share" at Circle Time? Why was it that every time I got guilted into staying for Circle Time, some kid shared the weekend family craft project of a paper mâché diorama that depicted Che Guevera's revolutionary lifestyle, or, the cutting from a rare botanical oddity tenderly rooting in a double-throated, hand thrown, Indian-style wedding vase?

For me, the MonteVerita ban on bringing Disney characters, toys, stuffed animals, Tupperware, or partially used cosmetics for Circle Time left little else for Phoebe to share but outdoor things rejected by squirrels.

∽

We were only a teensy bit late for Circle, and my morning of playing teacher went pretty slowly, without any mishap that could be directly blamed on me. Finally, when I got back from the adult bathroom for the seventh or tenth visit, it was time for lunch. I helped unfold and place the oilcloth on the three midget tables, and arranged tiny chairs. I stood sentry as the kids funneled in to the bathroom to "wash" their hands. Each then went to his or her cubby and grabbed a lunch box. Some animal instinct or pheromone or inaudible high-pitched command organized the kids into seating arrangements. I certainly had nothing to do with it.

"Mommy. Now you go around the table with your unzipper," Phoebe instructed me. She had been telling me what to do all morning, and it was really driving me to the banana patch, which is what I say when I am angry, frustrated, resentful, or homicidal. If she knew everything already, why did I need to be here? Couldn't she just put in my hours?

I started with Zach's lunch. Zach didn't have a lunch box. He had a suitcase, a floorplan, a condo village, a planned community of individual plastic compartments nestled into a larger whole—Bento box. He didn't need my feeble help uncovering the cargo of each precious container. Precise coins of carrots. Pre-stripped sugar snap peas. Moist cubes of poached chicken. A sesame-ginger dipping sauce? Hard to be certain. And blueberries spectacularly dark against the carmine hue of the little box where they nestled. Zach's mother clearly loved her son, cherished his body and every bite that went into it. She was a mother goddess, an icon to my mere avatar of parenting.

Meanwhile, across the room, Phoebe settled beside her favorite teacher. She went straight for her applesauce, not at all sucked in by the concept of dessert after protein, starch, vedge — her teacher helped tear off the nondescript foil top, and I felt a momentary sense of loss.

If no one at school could see that the applesauce was organic, if there was no proof, I would not get the credit I so richly deserved.

But around the little tables I went. Kimmy didn't need my help and wouldn't give me a bite of her banana. Greedy monkey. Nathan was sweet and let me smell every one of his eensy tupperwares after I pried off the lids. Ariana had little cubes of tofu and seaweed. Which she actually seemed to be eating, between nibbles of rice cake, but I kept checking back every minute or so to see if she was spitting mouthfuls on the floor. Ina, Sara, and Madeleine had nothing spectacular or peculiar or contraband, pretty much your basic cheese and crackers, a bagel with butter, and a PB&J. They would grow up, pursue carefully considered careers, marry and mate normally.

I then helped Raj — a gorgeous, raven-haired, wood sprite of a kid — unzip his recycled rubber, tie-dye patterned lunch box. He pulled out an apple. Okay. No serious competition there. I sometimes packed actual apples, but considered them practically a main course when not pureed. Next, Raj pulled out some kind of sliced meat — salami. Ho ho! Nitrates!! And what's this? What's this??? A) Plastic. B) Ziplock. C) Full of Cheetos.

I had to love the confident, rugged individualist who packed that lunch.

☙

Most of the time, I try to do the right thing. So when I can buy organic I do. If someone asks me if I do the organic thing, I always say yes. This is not a lie, because I consider myself totally organic. Not to mention fairly natural (except when I'm self-conscious), preservative-free, undyed, and with only natural flavorings. Well, sometimes a modest spritz of Coco by Chanel.

When I can't buy organic, or don't, I perform organic-like behavior. I have crafted a parental identity as organic, layered and believable as any Cold War sleeper spy planted for years in Middle America. I am so convincing, I even believe myself.

I once left a five-pound sack of organic unbleached flour sitting on my counter for two weeks so that anyone who stopped by could admire my organic-ness. I admired it, too, sitting there sturdy and authentic like a Slavic peasant woman. It also blocked the view of all the other inorganic grains and meals and beans and sundry goods that skulked insecurely in the background.

When back from a trip to the Safeway, I peel the incriminating labels off uniformly yellow, unblemished plain ole Dole bananas. Apples, tomatoes, pears, and grapefruit similarly relinquish any identifying stickers. The produce looks just as honest as the Farmer's Market it didn't come from. I ball up the plastic shopping bags and vow to re-use them.

Can it be okay to act like the perfect parent, even when you know, deep inside, you're sometimes a little off the mark?

I once put the exact same sack of uneaten (organic) carrots in Phoebe's lunch three days in a row. I eat Double Stuff Oreos in bed at night after I brush my teeth, and let Phoebe have as much maple syrup as she wants. I even let her lick the drips off the pitcher. I bribe with Pez. I interfere with my daughter's autonomy and creativity daily when I choose clothes for her that match.

I sometimes poke Phoebe when she is perfectly happy because I can't bear not to touch her but know she'll squirm if I keep kissing her, kissing her, hugging her. At some point soon, she'll ask for more information about the exact nature of her heritage, and she'll blow my cover.

Then, I will introduce her to the real me, whom she has known all along—somewhat organic.

## Donna Hilbert
# Domestic Arts

I am a young mother
so bored staying home
I agree to play Bridge
with my neighbors,
who I suspect put up with me
to find a fourth to fill the table.

They are goddesses of domestic arts,
and between games hold forth
on finer points of decoupage, macramé
and the transformation of cans
into casseroles.

Still, I am smug
for I have gifts of my own:
precognitive dreams
and *gift of the phone,*
which I demonstrate by chanting
*Mother Mother Mother Dear*
*call me now while my friends are here,*
and when the phone rings
they are believers.

Because I love an audience,
I tell them my dreams:
how I see trash cans burning
the night before they burst in flame
behind my house,
how Papa's heart attack
awakens me from sleep.
How I knew the night before she labored
Jan's baby boy would be born dead.

Now the neighbors play three-handed games—
Pinochle, Euchre—
keep their children indoors,
cross against the light
when they see me coming.

*Cyn Kitchen*

# It Could Be Worse

When I was the young mother of four children under the age of five I considered starting a support group. I would have called it M.A.P.S., Mothers Against Pre-Schoolers. Any woman who felt she fit could join for free.

I imagined we would hold meetings in a bar, maybe one that featured male dancers. The kids would stay home with dad. The entire evening would be his responsibility. We (me and all the other mothers in my group) would not prepare dinner. Maybe set out a box of Cheerios and a line of sippy cups full of Juicy Juice, but no more. It'd be against the rules. We would leave the house without logging written directions on how to bathe the baby or reminder notes of what to do In Case of Emergency. We wouldn't care if the dog was let out or the cat was fed. Come six o'clock we would simply leave. Walk out the door, no looking back, primed with red lipstick, smelling like a two-dollar whore, wearing spiked heels that'd grown dusty in the detritus at the bottom of the closet. We wouldn't care if we looked trashy in painted on blue jeans or if our dark roots were showing. Meeting night was the night to let it all hang out, become who we fantasized about being every other noisy, sticky, chaotic, smeared, poopy, pukey, dirty, I'm-too-tired-to-have-sex-tonight-night.

Our meetings would be secret, like the Masons. We would meet in a public place, but no one would know our modus operandi. We would call the meeting to order with a round of Jaeger bombs, and thereafter it would be against the rules to make any references to potty-training, lactating, disciplining, cleaning, cooking or compromising. Instead, we would discuss the things that intelligent, vibrant women discussed like literature, music, gardening, exercise, celebrities, sex. We would pretend we were sexy and skinny and single even though we knew were weren't any of those things. We would introduce ourselves by our first names instead of "I'm so-and-so's mommy." We would hold burning cigarettes even if we didn't smoke, and sip martinis even if we didn't like olives. We would pretend we were still young and desirable. We would watch the men dance and drink more shots and laugh and bat eyes at the guy across the bar. And none of us would do anything "Stupid" because we would have signed the Secret Pact that says "We Promise Not to Do Anything Stupid," and if we looked like we're flirting with Stupid our blood-sisters would stop us because the motto of MAPS would be, "Stupidity is What Got You Here."

At the end of the night we'd eventually go back to our homes. Amazingly, it wouldn't look as bad as it had earlier in the day when all four children were crying at the same time, the baby had puked down our bra, the toddler had pooped on the floor and the curious three-year-old had taken a swig of rubbing alcohol. We'd be seeing our lives through Jaeger eyes, and we would weep a little because inside that house was the man we loved, potbelly and all, and the babies we'd made together, in our younger years, during the throes of passion, with the World of Ideals at our fingertips. Each of us would sit in our driveways and think about our Glass of Life being half-full, hell it was flowing over!

And quite unexpectedly a swell of the biggest love we could ever remember feeling (except for the night when the husband, who was still the boyfriend that our parents hated, sneaked us out of our bedroom window so we could go park out behind the community college and let him feel us up), would overcome us and we would fling open the door to our Grand Caravan and, like the wind, rush inside to see our husband and babies sleeping in a pile on the floor, like puppies, and we would stand over the pile and smile at them and think "how precious," and bask in the flow of love that seemed to ooze from our every pore. Since it wouldn't be smart to wake them all sleeping so peacefully like that, we'd get ourselves ready for bed, but when we passed through the kitchen we'd spot a foreign substance dripping off the wall above the stove, and in the sink is every dish we own, dirty. And a foul odor is coming from the trashcan, no, wait, *behind* the trash can. And the table is covered with a sticky substance that has run off onto the floor where we find the cat, all four paws stuck to the linoleum, mewing pitifully.

In the bathroom, cold water stands in the tub and what looks to be a small candy bar is floating on the surface. Every towel we own is in a wet pile in the corner. And the hallway is strewn with every toy that comes in a primary color. We want to muster the energy to blow up, to commit a Mt. Vesuvius, but we're too tired and a little tipsy, so we cry more tears, but these are tears of defeat, surrender, resignation. We want out but there is no way out. We want to change our minds about this life, but it's too late for that. We've made our bed. Figuratively, that is. Our real bed looks like rhinos slept in it, but that's ok. We don't even change our clothes, we just crawl under the covers and put a pillow over our heads. We cry ourselves to sleep with love for the man who is curled on the floor with the love babies piled around him, their little mouths sucking the air. And we console ourselves with the fact that it could be worse, they could be teenagers, and there's no support group for that.

*Tina Traster*

# Love Learned

Everyone said I'd fall in love the minute they laid her in my arms. She was beautiful—a broad alabaster face with slightly-slanted deep brown eyes. She was a flirt: at six months she knew how to flash a dimpled smile, like a come-hither starlet. I was awed by her perfect features as the fleshy woman pressed her into my arms, swaddled in a blanket. A few minutes later she said, "feed baby," and handed me a bottle filled with a brown tea concoction. I took the bottle hesitantly and tipped it toward the baby's pursed lips. How would I know when she was sated or whether she needed to burp? I felt as though someone had lent me an expensive camera I was afraid to fiddle with.

I always thought I'd be a great mother. The love I expressed for my animals reinforced the notion I had great capacity to nurture. At the airport waiting to leave Siberia I had our baby on my lap. Suddenly I heard a pop; then a mountainous ooze of putrid yellow diarrhea exploded from her diaper. I was horrified, unable to stand the smell of the stench. I thrust the baby into my husband's hands. Calmly he changed her diaper and pulled out a clean snowsuit.

Terrified, my first instinct was to push this baby away from me rather than come to her aid I wondered how in the world I would be able to care for her. I was 40 when we went to Russia, in a second marriage, one I trusted would last. Becoming a parent was the next thing to do, like ticking a chore off an errand list. My husband and I had tried basic, non-invasive fertility treatment because we couldn't conceive; when that failed we moved on to adoption without any real aching over the lost hope of having a genetic child. I was secretly relieved because I didn't want to expose my body to more aggressive, hormone-altering fertility treatment like in-vitro fertilization. Maybe I was ambivalent about motherhood and didn't know it.

Like a hiker guided by woodland blazes I moved forward, following what I thought was an obvious path. Never did I sit myself down and think, *I mean really think* about how I felt about motherhood. Six months after the social worker from the adoption agency called and said "we have a baby for you," our daughter was in a make-shift nursery carved from a windowless alcove in our small apartment in New York City. There were no mobiles dangling above her crib or animal-themed borders running along the wall. We'd had just enough time to assemble a borrowed crib, an IKEA bureau of drawers and a changing table. The space was so teeny we couldn't even fit a rocking chair.

No one had thrown me a baby shower. I had not read a single book on preparing for parenthood. In the months leading up to the adoption, my husband lost his job. At times I wondered whether we should go through with it but he convinced me we should. "We're both 40," he had said. "There's a baby who needs parents." I remember the steel-grey November day I got the call from the agency. I heard "Siberia" and "passports" and "arrange flight" but all I could think about were my writing deadlines.

Pregnant women get to arrange the spice rack. Nature slows them down. They come to their baby slowly, symbiotically. When we first brought the baby home she weighed 15 pounds. I had long-term neck and back injuries from sports so I could barely carry her. Putting her in a snuggly was out of the question.

During the first year I fed her and changed her diapers and sang to her before putting her in the crib but I could just have easily been loading a dishwasher, paying bills. I was numb. Ironically I wasn't suffering from sleep deprivation because life at the orphanage had taught the baby to sleep 11 hours a night in a bed by herself. But I had not had a chance to welcome the mother in me. I had not mentally prepared for time to slow down; to be so needed. I hired a part-time nanny but I was terrified to let her leave the apartment with the baby. So through the sounds of my baby squealing with delight at Elmo or crying because she was groggy and resisting a nap, I slogged away at my computer in the next room, teeth clenched, stomach churning.

I didn't believe I had the right to use the term "post-partum" depression. I had not given birth; my hormones were not awry. But I was as blue as I'd ever been and I'm pretty sure I felt what despairing birth mothers feel—isolation, angst, regret. Was I unsuited for motherhood? I'd look down at my gorgeous child sitting on the floor with her little feet out in front of her, surrounded by blocks and other toys, and feel a surge of guilt.

At Mommy and Me groups other babies sat dutifully in mommy's lap. Every time we got to one of these classes my baby's first instinct was to bolt around the room, even when she was still crawling. I'd smile wanly at the neighboring mommy and say, "Oh, my little astronaut." Inside, I was screaming with rejection from this child.

I had gone to the end of the world to get this baby yet we were not bonded.

I began to think I was damaged goods. Or she was. Perhaps I was not bonding to her because she was not bonding to me. There is a syndrome suffered by many adopted children where they do not attach to their new mothers and fathers. Psychologists say the infant is so traumatized at birth she instantly develops an unconscious self-defense mechanism that leaves her unable to trust adults. She is convinced that the only one in the world who she can rely upon is herself.

This clinical explanation made sense. Whenever I tried to hold her, she flexed in the opposite direction. Her instinct was always to flee, rather than cling. She would not look me directly in the eye. When she was 16 months, I hired a young, spirited Polish nanny who took every pain to care for the baby as if she were her own. She could not understand why the baby wouldn't bond with her.

During her toddler years, my daughter adapted to nursery school and later to kindergarten. But her patterns with adult care-takers, particularly women, mimicked what went on at home. She was hyper-active, demanding, even charming but somehow she couldn't be satiated. She spent every ounce of mental energy figuring out how to control her universe.

It was exhausting. I was exhausted. I didn't know what to do. My daughter was an open, pus-oozing emotional sore I couldn't heal. We were both sinking. I had shut down. On the last day of nursery school during a year-end recital I was shaken from my stupor. When I watched my little girl disrupt the concert and the nursery school teacher take her aside and restrain her, I cried hard for the first time. I was wild with anger and grief. Failing as a mother was unacceptable. That evening I went online and researched Reactive Attachment Disorder, the syndrome that prevents adoptees from attaching. I saw parallels with my child's behavior and suggestions about how to bond and raise these children. Many of the parenting skills needed in these cases are counter-intuitive. That's because a child afflicted by this often doesn't mind punishment or isolation. Unconsciously, that's often the result they're courting.

For the next year, my husband and I focused on trying to interrupt our daughter's hard-wired circuit. We'd say the kind of things you'd never imagine saying to a child such as "I know you are afraid for mommy to love you. But I do love you." Last year when my daughter started first grade, we began to find each other. She still had a hard-wired defense system but now she was exercising an intellect that allowed her to ponder behavior and its effects rather than just act reflexively. She could reach for my hand without feeling deep inner ghosts.

Over time, we knit into a unit. We replaced distance and indifference with fierce love and hate. I don't worry when she tells me she hates me because it shows we're tied up, finally, in the tumult of a mother-daughter relationship. I try not to be sad when I think back on lost time. I understand we both needed time to trust primal love.

*Jeffrey Thomas Leong*
# Abacus

To my 88-year old father,
"You were adopted, in China?" I asked,
a boldness made usual in its repeat,
unfilial, except that dementia had spilled his weekly sorrow,
his memory zapped of every happy filigree:
a sister's name, the fading face of my mother.
On a Sunday at the Country Kitchen Café,
suddenly it's 1916 again!
*Adopted? I was sold!* he relates, presses hard against Formica
as if to keep at bay the only story still without fade,
*Six brothers* (really five) *and I was number three,*
a fogged fix, once secreted from the children.
Every slip of a former life, figured
to this pain, freezes him mid-house salad,
dressed in tears, and forking lifts of empty air.

What can a son know of a father's deep feelings,
his erased history of consequence,
transacted to the Lee's and spirited to Gold Mountain?
Of that residual, only fractions remain.
His method: *Tough Guy.* WW II Air Force gunner-mechanic hides all.
And yet, every visit his weak-trickle
of toddler fail, an ache I sense as shadow,
and wishing to know that hulk, its dark cluster,
a step-mother, whose slap so real, her handprint forever planted.
But everything slipped in the memory disease,
sloughed and forever sliding.

I've been told in old *Guangdong*,
the hungry poor sold sons to richer families needing boys.
One birthfather Wong, married to opium, so smoked away his middle child.

But then, under adoptive father Joe Lee's care,
that boy repapered to a "Leong," and on to San Francisco,
a transit he accommodates each week as:
*I'm lucky. I came to America.*
What recompense for such a sale,
as if each sluice of abacus beads can sum a series to even?
Here, in the *Shi Jing* texts, boys inherit property,
fulfill familial deeds, as when my father carried the red funeral candles
for Eldest Sister to Colma, nearly stumbling
on a cemetery's uneven weeds.
In those same tracts, girls written off as unlucky,
carry loom shuttles for toys, cradled on dirt,
where boys slept in beds, clasped new scepters.
Even now, girls drowned like kittens in wells,
never glimpsing light,
at least in 1913, he wasn't born female.

Fingering ancient fumbles, I know not how to carry or solve.
In Chinatown, a boy slaps blackjack under boxwood,
steals gum, and is sent to Ming Kwong Home,
yet later, finds equilibrium selling dry goods to the poor.
*I don't smoke, I don't drink, I don't gamble,* he still chants,
his mantra of clean living.
Can what tips a man start
in the cold imbalance of his own adoption?

In six months, my wife and I fly to *Guangzhou,*
will bus to *White Swan*'s four-star elegance,
where in a matter of hours, we receive an infant girl,
configured to instant family.
Dissolves a childlessness when she comes to us,
absent of orphanages where dozens of unlucky ones
lay evidence to a continued bend towards boys,
the One Child Policy not hers.
When I think of her saucer smile, her gurgling, farting,
insouciance, I wonder, *How did it feel?*
abandoned at 1 month on a police station's steps, *Were you cold?*
But new minds clicking, shifting speed, won't recall,
though hard-wired to a neurological pain.
I ache to shelter her, but some unintendeds must be,

just as a woman pregnant with life,
pushes, birth tunnel stretched to full,
an answer head first to our grasp.

In truth, girls are not boys, daughters not fathers,
some differences plain, without ambiguity,
a Confucian exercise in order.
Perhaps, nothing more to be conveyed on a plane's reroute,
new *xiao xin* sidled against my wife's breasts,
except to fly on cirrus, coursing mid-Pacific faith and duty,
home to California where wired bars gather:
*boy-child, girl-child, siblings* and *sire,*
together snug, so that a son can adopt a father.

*Chris Huntington*

# My Life as a Wrestler

When I was fifteen I was recruited for the wrestling team. I was ninety-eight pounds and there was a weight class with my name on it. "You're not even a ninety-nine pound weakling, Huntington!" said my friend Tim, who was two hundred and twenty and had legs as thick as motorcycles. The coach had mistaken me for competitive because I made straight A's, but the truth was I simply liked to read. By the spring, the trainer used me as a clock because thirty minutes into every practice, I'd come into the training room with a bloody nose. He wondered out loud why I didn't quit, but that wasn't my way. I had grown up in Indiana, where people said that quitting was something pathetic and French. I did win half a dozen meets when my opponents failed to make weight.

After college, I went to Africa in the Peace Corps and was happy there, although I got a terrible scar and dengue fever. On the way home, I fell in love. We were married in France and were very happy until we weren't, which is perhaps the usual story. Still, I would have stayed with her forever, though I've reread my journal from that time and can see she was clearly and coldly a million miles away at the end. When she left me, I spent a year in Paris buried in melancholy, though the city was quite beautiful and the Seine was the color of jade.

Eventually, I met my second wife who was neither five feet tall nor a hundred pounds, but somehow voluptuous. My friend Jim, who is gay, said, "Wow, she's pretty. Makes me wish I was a lesbian." My wife and I both love reading and we have long fantasies about being writers. We can talk about anything together. We used to love having sex until we spent years trying to make a baby, and then it seemed like an exercise in failure. I read a book about evolution and felt alienated by all the mention of genes and passing on traits. And I thought there was really no point to misery. It was just something like the smell of feces: unfortunate, but necessary and kind of beautiful too.

And then I became a father. My son is a little David Copperfield, though he doesn't know it yet. Dagim was handed to us by a stranger in Ethiopia. He can't possibly remember the woman who gave birth to him, though she wept when she saw him last. In the office where we said hello and good-bye to her, this woman could barely look above our knees. She was ashamed of her lack of education and her poverty. My wife and I were ashamed of the opposite—of our luck and our lives of books and our expensive clothes that had only been worn by us. My wife is only four foot ten and Dagim's birth mother was only slightly taller. Dagim clung to my wife though he'd only known her for five days. The girl wept wordlessly. Dagim had been in an orphanage for almost a year. There is no good way to express this happiness, which is so full of pain.

Dagim is twenty months old now and I love him and his big-cheeked way of imitating a dog, licking me on the forehead when I pick him up. He can't talk yet and so my wife has taught him some sign language. He is sometimes a beautiful little Harpo Marx, pinching his fingers together to do the sign for MORE after he eats his mashed potatoes. I love to watch him and my wife play ring-around-the-rosie because as soon as they fall to the ground, he leaps up and flashes his hands together, unblinking, asking for MORE.

I was forty years old when I became a dad. What was I doing with my life before then? I was drinking Diet Coke and trying to write a great novel about Africa and China and myself—but nobody, not even my wife, really wanted to read it. I had fallen in love over and over and it hadn't changed a thing. There were still wars in the world.

But sometimes now I'm holding this little boy in a parking lot and I feel as if I could carry him into the mountains, into the trees, like we could be cavemen and we don't need language or electricity or anything except each other. I feel like a man, like Aeneas fleeing Troy, like Odysseus coming home, and if I were to tell the story of my life, it would probably begin in Addis Ababa, when a stranger handed my wife a fourteen month old Ethiopian boy and I stood there, my hands empty and afraid.

Today, my wife and I talk about what we are going to tell our son when he gets older: why he doesn't look like us, why his birth mother gave him up. One morning my son and I sat together in an empty garden and he carefully imitated me as he ate his animal crackers, watching me after each one, and I wanted to tell him: the reason we endure, the reason we make weak smiles throughout all our suffering, is that any given day, everything can change. Like the morning he was put into our arms and we were all three too stunned and happy to cry, until we weren't.

# NO SORROW LIKE THIS SORROW

*Lisa Williams*

# Miscarriage

You must be
covered now
by moonlight,
and sleeping,
sleeping so peacefully
in starlight
sleeping
in a place where the dead
wait patiently
to become what is alive
once again.

*Oriana*
# David

He meets me at the train station.
A smile dances in his open face,
his elegant lean body.
More than I ever

loved anyone, I love
my son meeting me in my dream—
lost amber of his eyes,
marble cross of shoulders.

How do I know it would have
been a son? A mother knows,
I say, I who have no right
to call myself a mother.

We walk through a quiet town
dripping with lilacs, peonies.
Is it Pomerania where I was born,
Our Lady of the Meadows,

cathedrals of clouds; misty Eden
of the Yvelines, river-rich Hungary—
No, these are the Mourning Fields,
the green

country of that other memory,
rainy mirror of what didn't
happen—
How lonely I've been.

We step on a rain-beaded porch.
As always, he disappears.
And my giving endless birth
in my parched

paradise, what is it if not
the life he has given me.

*John Morgan*
# Sonnet of the Lost Labor

Comes a day at high spring when everything gluts.
The globules of fat within each cell burst
open and the ecstatic heat, seeding the air
with the damp odor of birth, oozes among the grass.

Came a voice like yours, calling me up the stairs
to where you sat in the bathroom, shaken,
leaking the blood our child had nested in.
I hug you again and feel your pain, lost labor:

the ache of birth six months too soon;
but as I approach that moment's stain, my eyes
haze over, my head begins to float.
At the sight of its blood, death red, sight
fails. You catch the little monster in a cup, save
it for the lab. Christ, Nancy, I am not so brave.

*Ella deCastro Baron*

# Entropy

Searching her iPhone, she sees a thread of light at the top of a Google search: "My diagnosed miscarriage is now a six year old girl." All sorts of imaginable misdiagnosed miscarriages that ended in hundreds of viable, full term pregnancies and babies are linked, gazing back at her. It might just be a thread, but she wraps her hands around it and prays it is the tip of a branch of a thousand year old tree that could keep her off the Edge.

Dutifully, desperately, self-consciously, they send out prayer requests, hoping their story will end up a glowing entry on this website.

E-mail replies carry more hope with each click.

*My sister-in-law had the same diagnosis, and they found the heartbeat and baby growing fine at twelve weeks. As a doctor, I hear of this all the time. You just are earlier along in your pregnancy than you thought. Our God is a God of miracles. Thirty-nine is not too old. You are designed to bear life. He planned this child before time began. He knows the baby's name.*

A young man on the church's prayer team writes, *The womb is not a tomb.*

After the third ultrasound and several weeks of faithfully eating for two and taking prenatal vitamins, she opens her squinted, shut eyes first, then uncoils the rest of her limbs from the vanishing lifeline. *There appears to be some trauma at the placenta. We can't say for sure, but our diagnosis remains the same.* She denies a medical intervention. If it is going to happen, she wants to wait for her body to do what it has been designed for. *My body is designed to bear life.* Soon this is all she prays.

Spotting begins.

They drive ten hours north to be with family during winter break. Christmas Day, she collects torn wrapping paper while the kids squeal and show off dolls, transformers, and all things Disney. Her children—an exquisite blend of Jewish and Filipino—are more stunning than she has ever seen. With every wide almond-eyed expression, exaggerated open-mouthed kiss on her cheek, little voice asking for more juice or a few more minutes to play with cousins, she falls deeper in love with them. *How could I lose a child?* She stops herself from thinking.

Soon after the first servings of the holiday banquet, the real miscarriage begins. She recalls standard advice. *Every woman is different,* her OB tries to offer. *Some have what simply feels like a heavy period. Others, on the other hand, feel they are hemorrhaging and have to go to the hospital.* The doctor gives her personal phone extension to bypass the after hours answering service. *Call me anytime. In the middle of the night. For anything. If you need.*

She's soaking through pads and several pairs of pants but doesn't call. Because her sister is a nurse. Because she doesn't want to panic. Because she is counting on having just a "heavy" period. Because it's Christmas and everyone, including her, is happy to be together. Even if it is eleven weeks and the womb hasn't figured it out yet and is growing the environment as if. The placenta, she learns, begins to form almost immediately after the zygote's implantation. An entire creation story is evolving inside her.

Every morning for the next three days, she fakes Okayness. When the family goes to church, she stays out of the sanctuary, crunched in a chair next to the bathroom. The sermon is floating out of circular speakers high on the wood panel walls. She can't listen. The pulsing cramps are relentless. Her family skips In-n-Out for lunch with everyone, goes back to the house early. She sits on the couch taking rhythmic breaths. Hours later, she finally notices she is breathing as if in labor, trying to manage what feels like tearing inside of her uterus. When she has to run to the bathroom again, she looks down to see her two-year-old daughter, oblivious to it all, had crawled into her lap at some point. The toddler is fast asleep, still nursing. She hurriedly pulls her daughter away from her breast, lays her on the couch, and runs to the toilet. Her body expels another mottled, fleshy golf ball. Later, she confesses to her sister that she wished she picked it up and touched it, examined it. She feels like a nonpartisan, outside observer.

They drive the ten hours back home, stopping several times for her to manage the bleeding. The trunk is full of presents.

Her husband starts cleaning and organizing the garage. He sneaks off to whatever store is open at 12:45 a.m. and comes home with more storage bins. He hefts armfuls of the garage soup bubbling up on every square foot of empty space for the last two years, including hand-me-down maternity and baby clothes from church friends. She sits in the family room, and while kids sleep through the night, she sorts anything within her reach. *Costumes. Crafts. Boy clothes. Girl clothes. Donate to Philippines. New Baby.* He takes a break to play World of Warcraft on the computer. She looks online to price sturdy shelving for the garage walls. They agree how excited they are to finally get to the garage. It satisfies them through the night.

The nervous breakdown is subversively ushered in by resettling hormones. Edgy nights carve the rest of the week into a messy, irritable, uncontrollable wash of tears. Everything he does and says aggravates her. They fight about minutia. They fight about their marriage. She can't be a mother to her two kids playing at her feet. She can't be a wife, a friend, or a human being because her skin doesn't fit. She sobs and screams at her husband as she gets her things.

"I CAN'T STAY HERE! I'll be back later today. You're going to have to take care of the kids without me." He's upset but can't be mad at her. He changes his schedule for the day.

She drives and parks, drives and parks but can't be around people. She taps out a plea on her phone for some friends to pray but *please don't come over*—she feels lonely but wants to be alone. Barricaded in the car—the least threatening environment to lock herself in—she cries involuntarily until her head throbs.

She has known depression before. This feels the same—like a drug addict in the nadir of withdrawal—shaky, paranoid, white knuckling sanity. Except this time, nothing fills her thoughts. She has no questions left. No prayers to sow. No energy to hope or dream of this or another pregnancy. A wretched body is held together only by her flimsy skin. The center is not holding. Yet she feels a calm in it. Maybe it's the Numb.

There's a strange harmony to this entropy.

Meanwhile, he plays, cares for, bargains with, feeds, changes, nurtures, and guards the kids from their non-mother even when she is (her physical body at least) finally seated next to them at the dinner table. When she is looking but not seeing, they pick up the backyard, too. Water the citrus trees, harvest a few lemons, store gardening tools—real ones and child-adapted ones (a foam sword, half of a hollow cow, a faded orange plastic bowling pin)—in the tool rack next to the side fence.

She surveys her stomach in the bathroom mirror. Turning to the side, she pats her flat belly. She feels thinner than ever. Her fingers traverse stretch marks on hips, reading the grooves like brail. *Your skin is not frail. It is resilient.* A knock at the door and his quiet, compassionate voice asks if she wants to take a walk at their favorite beach. He arranged for a babysitter to buy them time and a date.

It'll be well into their second mile walking when he asks. *The miscarriage.* "How are you feeling about it?" She opens her mouth and the words are spare, barely lifting off.

"I don't know…I guess okay…I hope it's over soon."

A few steps later, she thinks to ask him how he feels.

He swallows. "I don't think I'm ready to talk about it." She stops walking and looks at his eyes. They are oceans at high tide, full, green. "Every time I start to, it's too much. I'm not ready." It will be later that she finds out he already looked for extra work, that he moved around savings on their budget spreadsheet, even asked their four year old son if he was ready to let his little sister move into his room. So they could have a nursery.

After breakfast, they split up to do errands. She rushes to Costco to buy food for Shabbat dinner. She pushes her cart towards the produce fridge and sees bags of pomegranate seeds. They have a name—the individual seeds—arils. She fingers one of the bags while thinking if they would want these in their salad later.

Checkout lines are eight carts deep, so she pulls out her phone to check messages, e-mails. The free pregnancy update site she subscribes to sends the latest e-mail. *Your pregnancy: 13 weeks.* "Fingerprints have formed…" She scans the rest. "If you're having a girl, she now has more than two million eggs in her ovaries. Your chances of miscarriage drop significantly." She flashes back to the translucent, blood red, flesh-covered pomegranate seeds.

She pulls up her husband's e-mail. The subject line reads: "closure." She types the word "aril" but makes it a name. "*Aril.* The individual seed of a pomegranate is called this. If you look close, it is a small seed—a promise of life—inside of a gestational sac. We can invite some friends and family over for a small ceremony. What do you think?"

Her husband is done at the gym and replies just as she is loading the food into the trunk. "Yes, let's choose a date. I like the name. Our little Aril." It is the next e-mail after the pregnancy updates she no longer needs. She clicks it again and reads on, unsure if she will unsubscribe.

*Barbara Crooker*

# Firstborn

*2-2-1970*

The sun came up, as it always does,
the next morning, its pale gold yolk
bleeding into the white room.
I remember how cold I was,
and how young, so thin,
my wedding ring rattled
on my finger. How the tea
the nurse brought
broke in waves on the rim
of the cup, spilled over
in the saucer; how nothing
could contain my tears.
Three days later, I left
in a wheelchair,
with nothing in my arms.
The center of this gold ring
is a zero. The horizon,
where the sun broke through,
is no longer a straight line,
but a circle. It all comes back
to you.

*Kathryn Lewis*

# A Hair Strand

Curled on the white duvet in her lingerie, Anna hears nothing.

The clock ticks on.

She has not budged since she unsnapped her beige lace bra. She holds her baby's hair strand against her left breast.

Over the day, a circle of sunlight has warmed her. She feels no hunger, no thirst, sees nothing but his chestnut-brown hair that always flew straight up when brushed, shining once more.

The strand appeared this morning, entwined in her baby's nylon comb, when Anna was about to grab a suit for work. The comb, the bone white of his baby teeth peeking through his gums, fell from a summer bag stowed on the top closet shelf, passed right in front of her eyes, and did a two-tap landing by her bare feet on the beige Berber rug. She bent down and, cupping the comb in both hands, brought it to her lips.

Her eyes closed, as she smelled its baby talc scent.

Lying on the bed, she had cuddled the comb.

Around ten in the morning, the phone started ringing. She ignored it at first, then worried someone at the law office where she worked as a paralegal might be checking if she was okay. She dialed her husband's office, told him she felt headachy, nothing serious, and to please let her boss know that she would be in later or tomorrow.

Hours passed before she unraveled the strand. She tried to curl it in her palm. It sprang back the way her baby had resisted his crib.

Had her infant known, Anna had thought afterwards, tried to warn her that his crib would be his deathbed?

She took her baby's hair to her breast.

The clock ticked on.

The whoops and chatter of school kids headed home sounded muffled as though passing through a barrier of her skin, muscle and tissue. She had paid no heed: none of them were hers.

The clock hands move to four.

Her hand against her left breast has gone numb.

She carefully lifts the strand damp with her perspiration.

Barely able to hold it between her thumb and forefinger, she tries to weave it back into the comb for safekeeping.

But the strand keeps slipping out.

She places it back against her breast.

The clock ticks on.

The circle of sunlight fades in the early dusk of December.

Feeling a chill, she presses the strand between her breasts. She fears losing it if she moves to raise the thermostat preset at sixty degrees for when they are at work.

Her eyes burn from straining to see her baby's chestnut hair, inherited from his father along with his cheek dimple.

Barely able to see now, she stretches to switch on the bed lamp.

The strand is gone.

Anna holds in her scream, cannot let it out. She couldn't when her baby died.

People admired her strength. They had no idea that she was like a crackled glass vase on the verge of disintegrating if touched.

The strong were those willing to have another child after losing one.

Anna's hands shake as she skims the duvet. She does not know where to look. The fine strand is so light it defies gravity.

The terror of her child's death is back in full force. This is how she would live if they had another child.

Her husband wants one. She has sensed his impatience with her.

He has reminded her that childhood death was common at the turn of the century. People can go on. He holds out his co-worker as an example. Their third child had died after two years of home bedside care.

The co-worker's wife had told Anna that she visited her child's grave every-day. Then their doctor pushed them to have another child. She had her second third child and two more after.

Anna sees the happy family they are. But for her, five children would mean quintupled fear of death around the corner.

She knows she needs therapy. Her husband has suggested it. But the crackled glass vase she is could not withstand the vibrations of speaking about her dead child.

She spots her baby's hair clinging to her white half-slip. She grabs it into a tight fist. She needs a safe place for it.

She thinks of sealing it in an envelope and goes to the hall desk. She struggles with her one free hand to remove an envelope and spreads it open then thinks how the fine hair could disappear in a corner fold.

She worries it may have already slipped out of her hand. Slowly, her fingers unfold.

Anna looks at the strand.

Her sweat has glued it to the crease of her palm marked with indents where her nails dug in.

Her baby's hair is safe for the moment until the air breathes down and makes it fly away like the seed of a dandelion puff.

She needs something gluey like her sweat to temporarily to retain the hair. Scotch tape might work.

She takes a roll from the desk, bites off a piece and sticks it to the hair and then on the top of her hand.

The strand under the tape on her skin reminds her of the lily of the valley her husband gave her on one of the early dates. She had pressed it between wax paper and considered doing that with her baby's hair.

Her husband would want to see and hold his baby's hair, too.

But his hands are thicker and clumsier than hers. He might lose the strand for good. She cannot take that chance.

She had lost track of her pressed lily of the valley and tells herself the strand should go in with her baby's sterling silver comb from grandma — a place she'll remember.

But she doesn't want her baby's hair sealed in wax and put in a box or worn around her neck in a locket that could break open. She wants it safely with her at all times.

Anna gently lifts the strand from the tape.

She feels again its silkiness as her fingers slide from end to end straightening it to a horizontal before her eyes.

She presses her lips to it as she had pressed her lips to baby's head. She licks it as she licked her baby's cheek.

She curls the strand in the pit of her palm, kisses it then scoops it up with her tongue and swallows.

The strand lodges inside her mouth. She pushes it to the back of her tongue and swallows again.

The strand stays put.

She swallows several more times, wanting her baby back inside of her. She drinks some water. It won't budge like her baby resisting his bed.

Was there a message in this? She might believe so if her next attempt fails.

She breaks off a piece of wheat bread tiny enough to swallow whole and butters it. She fetches the strand from her mouth.

The hair moist with her saliva glimmers in the fluorescent light as Anna pats it to the butter.

She massages her throat, opens her mouth and pushes in the bread bearing the strand.

Then she wonders, is it possible that her baby does not want to go back to his prenatal state? He has lived and has gone on to wherever he is now.

She removes the bread from her mouth, wipes the butter from her baby's hair.

The clock reads six.

Her husband will be home soon. She'll show him their baby's hair strand. And then they'll set it free.

*Daniel A. Olivas*

# Blue

## *One*

All I want is to remember her smell. That's all. It's her smell that I miss most. I can't forget anything else, though. The labor pains, the nurse wiping my forehead with a damp cloth and calling me sweetie and reminding me to breathe. And then the doctor saying she saw her head peeking out. And then almost like magic, the sight of her wet, squirming, new body. But I can't remember her smell. That smell from the next day. After her first bath. She had trouble feeding. Didn't want to take my milk. They'd give it a while before giving up. The nurse said, sweetie, that happens some times. But she knew it didn't matter. So I tried to coax her. I directed her little mouth to my nipple, cooing to her: drink baby girl. You gotta drink to get strong and meet the world. And I'd put my lips on her hair and breathe in her freshly-washed smell. Baby smell. My baby's smell. But it's been too long since that time. And all I want is to remember her smell.

## *Two*

My old man said it was for the best. She'd have a better chance with a family that could feed her, give her a good home, a proper upbringing. My old man said that when he and mom got married, they were out of high school. And he had a good job. That's the way you're supposed to do it, said my old man. Finish school. Then get married. To a man with a good job. Why couldn't you wait, mija? I never could answer my old man. I was in love, though. That's something. Right? That's something, all right. No one can tell me different.

## Three

Little Green. That's what Richard called me. Because when he first saw me sitting in Mr. Bruno's biology class, I was wearing this green T-shirt and a green skirt. All green. And it wasn't even St. Patrick's Day. So I was Little Green to Richard from then on.

## Four

Carey. That's what I would have named her. There's no Careys in my family. One of the reasons I like the name. And it's a strong name, too. Because a girl needs to be strong. Right? Stronger than a guy. That's what I think. I wonder what they called her? Wouldn't it be amazing like a movie if they named her Carey? And I used to think that one day we'd meet and I'd tell her I would've called her Carey, too. And she'd know that we always had a connection, like magic, like we always were together. But I don't think that anymore. No reason to.

## Five

Blue is what they call people who get sad. It's weird, though. Blue makes me happy. And there are all kinds of blue. The sky in the morning. The sky in the afternoon. Richard's eyes. How he got blue eyes no one ever figured out. Those eyes made me fall for him. A blue so clear they made you blink and wonder if they were contacts or something. But no. They were real. Blue like you've never seen. Blue that can't be described. Blue that isn't sad at all.

## Six

California became home for my family. In San Diego, L.A., Bakersfield, even Sacramento. Up and down the state. Mom's family came from Mexico and settled in L.A. about forty years ago. But Pop's family. When they crossed the border, they scattered. They're the ones in those other cities. Pop jokes that the Moreno blood must be in my veins because I'm not afraid to wander.

Nine cities in seven years. But I always call home. They always know where I am. I'm not running away. I'm just seeing California. That's all.

## Seven

This flight tonight to Vegas wasn't too expensive. Mom and Pop helped me with it, anyway. I just couldn't drive. Too tired. But I had to go. Wouldn't you? I got the call last week. They had tried my parents first. And then Pop called me where I'm living now. Oakland. He was gentle. With the news. I don't know why they wanted me to know. Maybe they knew that I've been trying to remember what she smelled like. Maybe they knew I always thought of her. I don't know. It doesn't matter. At least they called.

## Eight

River? That's a river? That's what I said to Pop when he first pointed out the L.A. River to me. I guess I was fourteen. A year before the baby. We were on the freeway driving to tía Rachel's house in Canoga Park and he pointed and said that's the L.A. River. But it looked like a big V of cement with bushes and some trees growing in it. Not too much water, too. Nothing like the rivers I've seen in my geography books. You know, like the Amazon. River? I said. That's a river?

## Nine

A case of you is like a case of the flu. That's what Mom liked to say. But she hasn't said it a lot recently. Now she just says how much she wished I'd stay put. Near home. I look down from the plane and see only clouds. Mom is down there someplace. And soon I'll be near my baby. But she's not a baby anymore. She's a girl. Or was. But at least I'll be able to see her. And her parents. And I'll thank them for giving her a good home. That's what I'll say. Because it's true. I'm sure.

## Ten

The last time I saw Richard was at high school graduation. He didn't come to my house for the party. But he came up to me right after the ceremony while I was trying to find my parents in the crowd. It was so hot and all I wanted to do was get out of the robe and stupid cap and drink something cold. But he came up to me and said, happy graduation, Little Green. And I said, happy graduation. He touched my arm and gave me his blue eyes. Said he was leaving the next day. For Tulsa. I said, there's no Mexicans in Tulsa. He laughed and his eyes got bluer. But I guess he's a wanderer, too. Don't know if he's still in Tulsa. I wish I could tell him, though. About my trip to Vegas. To see my girl. Our girl. They told Pop about it. About the pool gate opening when it shouldn't. How it happened during the party and no one noticed until hours later when people were beginning to leave. But it was a night party so it was kind of dark. And they told Pop about how they tried to make her breathe again. But I know she had a good home. With lots of love. Lots of toys. Thank you, I'll say. Thank you for taking care of my baby.

*Richard Krawiec*
# don't worry

when she says she's afraid
she might kill
her baby
when she says she's worried
she could kill
her baby
when she says she thinks
about giving him
an overdose
when she imagines the headline
mom murders sitter
and child
when she says the reason why
this year is significant
is this is the year
he dies

don't remember
how she shook a toddler
so hard its head whipped
back and forth
or punched bruises
on your arms
or told stories
of her own mother
        slap-slapping her face
        smashing her brother's head
        driving her car into the son
            who misbehaved

it's organic
this illness
not the result
of environment
thoughts are random
illusions she surely
wouldn't act upon

they have drugs
amazing drugs
surely don't worry for
your
child

when she says
she knows
the secret she will
kill him
when she tells you
the jump rope
would make an excellent weapon

*Sylvia Levinson*
# I Watch You Breathe

For days now, your chest,
under the thin, blue gown, responds
to each cycling of the ventilator.
Your mouth encircles the corrugated tubing
threaded down your throat, taped to your face.

A nostril tube drains who knows what.
IV stands and strands of tubing,
feed their solutions into your arms.
Central line in your neck,
aortic line in your wrist,
catheter in your penis.
I look away when they bathe you,
change your sheets and you are exposed.

After this morning's visit,
after a week of gray wind and rain,
the sun is bright when I leave the hospital.
I feel the need for ocean. Spring Break.
The boardwalk and sand are crowded
with tourists, bicycles, skateboards,
bikinied young women, full-breasted and tan.

At a café, in view of curling surf,
mellowed by a Bloody Mary and warm air,
I watch bare-chested young men
dive and leap for a volleyball.
Five older women at a nearby table
laugh loudly, celebrating a birthday.

When I return to your bedside,
I ask the nurses what has changed—
new tests, new meds, fever or none,
outputs more or less.
I watch you breathe
like I did when you were a baby,
stroke the part of your arm that is
needle-free.

*Regina Murray Brault*
# Just Below Her Heart
*The grave hides all things beautiful and good...*
— Percy Bysshe Shelley 1792 – 1822

In a story on page four of Monday's paper,
the teeth of a back-hoe ripped open
an unmarked grave, exposing a pioneer mother
(the victim of childbirth)
and her baby's bones,
which had slipped from her
skeletal arms
into her egg-basket shaped
rib cage.

Tuesday morning while witnessing sunrise
from my own fetal attitude, I thought
about that mother, long deceased,
and of her pioneer-child whose fingers
had never stroked the earth
that holds her, and I felt content
despite the fact that daughter never lived

or else because of it.
she knew what she was doing —
returning to the only place
remembered safe,
inside that mother
who had left herself wide open,
affirming from graveyard dust
that her child
could always come home.

# turning the tables

*Steve Kowit*
# Poem for My Parents

## 1.

One night, back home in Brooklyn after 15 years,
I sat around with Mary & the folks
going thru the books of their old photos:
pictures of my dad in knickers
in his late teens looking rakish
in a t-shirt & sailor cap,
holding the center pole of a pup tent —
in his early 20s, hitchhiking
to Montreal & drinking from a flask
at the side of a road.
Next to that, a piece of birch bark
that he sent my mother
from that escapade — postmarked Maine,
Sep. 27 a.m. 1926. My mother
with a tennis racket, '27,
& smiling from a swimming pool in '28.
They are sitting on the railing of a ship;
my father in a bowtie & knit sweater,
she beside him, a lovely girl of 16,
their arms & feet touching.
They're just kids. They look beautiful,
both of them, the picture's dated
July 4, 1923.
& there's my mother with the Guild Players
in Disraeli & there they are
at Camp Allegro
surrounded half a century ago by friends
who have remained beloved to this day.
& then they're on their honeymoon
skating on a frozen lake

out in the woods of Pennsylvania
in the faded sepia gold of old snapshots —
a series of them
skating on the ice, holding hands,
my father with a pipe by a pine tree,
my mother leaning on the pillar of the house
where they were honeymooning,
hands sunk in her pockets,
her face gleaming, in the last
of that series Mickey, my father,
has his arms around her,
they stand on the frozen lake
the woods behind them
in their black skates & leather jackets,
he holds her to him,
they are radiantly happy
they have just been married; it is December, 1928,
the ancient, black paper edges
of the photo album
as I turn the pages, crumble
like confetti,
& fall like tears.
Beyond the joy & tenderness & passion
of these early snapshots,
that are dated in the upper corners,
but which time has partially erased,
& against the zeitgeist: all fashion,
the grief of history
& the drift of the age,
I honor them for the steady burning of their devotion.
May all of us be blessed by love
as faithful & unswerving.
They have been married 50 years.


## 2

Dad, one day over 30 years ago
you rigged a small sail
to an old rowboat
& we set off across a lake
high in the Berkshires.

It was the end of summer,
a day in August bathed in stillness.
I was a small boy, you
a strong, quiet man in your 40s.
Now & then small waves
slapped the thick sides under the oarlocks.
Then a wind came up so fast & quietly
we hardly noticed it until it seized us;
the small boat tossed about
bobbing like a cork. I
grabbed the sides, you worked the sail loose
quickly & unleashed it
& we drifted, oarless, far out,
waving our arms & fruitlessly calling out
to the few oblivious
figures on the dock, the sun
glinting ominously off those high waves.
Had it come to that we might have swum
for the other shore. Summers before
you had taught me: one hand
lifting my belly the other pressing
my back — I would kick & kick
holding the rope with both hands
squinting my eyes from the splashing.
Quiet, gentle, efficient, infinitely patient,
I think you are more
healer than teacher.
In those childhood illnesses,
I would wait hours for your figure
to appear out of the shadows of the hallway;
you would enter the room & say "hi, Butch,"
& sit quietly at the edge of the bed,
& it was the same quiet reassurance of your presence
beside me that summer day, bathed in light,
when we were tossed about on the waters together,
which turned what might have become a small boy's panic
into a kind of bliss
that we were stranded
together,
alone, drifting…

& 30 years later felt the same bliss
when we swam together in the warm waters
off the coast of Miami. Alone
with you again I had the same experience
of your gentleness,
your quiet grace & strength.
Dad, I think your tolerance
& patience for the world
has been my strength for 40 years.
Odd, how little we have ever spoken to each other
& how absolute the love that has bound us.
The distance of a continent means nothing.
We are still together,
tho older,
a man & his small son
drifting thru a void
that is turbulent & calm by turns —
marvelous beyond words, ineffable
& exquisite: silent
in a world of absolute stillness
on a lake that is infinite.

## 3

Ma, you stand at the dining room table & unfold
a paper napkin & place it, a white, translucent shawl
over your dark hair. Then you light two candles.
It is Friday evening. Outside the light is fading
from the world over Brooklyn, over East 14th Street,
with the darkness of early winter. As the room surrenders
to that darkness your white hands circle the small flames
of the two candles: they thin & flicker
under your fingers. Then you close your eyes
& recite the brocha. I can barely hear you.
An elevated Brighton Local rumbles thru the darkness
over Kelley Park. The shadow of your body
sways almost imperceptibly against the stairs:
How red your cheeks are in the light
of those two candles. Then the sound of the train
disappears & I hear you sobbing — tears
run down your cheeks.

You cover your face with your hands (perhaps
because I am there at your side in the dark room),
but your grief cannot be contained.
Your body trembles.
The candles, that are for the sabbath,
& honor the creation, are also, like the *yertzite*
candle burning in the glass in the kitchen,
for the dead. For your mother, Bertha,
my grandmother, who has recently died.
& as your grieving shadow sways & sobs
the brocha, you have become again
that small girl dancing down Second Avenue
more than half a century ago.
You are in a yellow dress, with ruffles,
you are carrying something home, some fish
or fruit wrapped in newspaper a page
from the *Daily Forvitz*, you are dancing
among the pushcarts of Delancey Street,
you are dancing thru the door of the settlement house
& under the impoverished tenement stairways
of the east side.
In this family portrait your father's image
is dissolving as you & your brothers & sisters
blossom into your own lives.
Now you are married, now the chaos
of the great depression, now Mickey graduates
from law school, you give birth to a daughter,
& a son. The pitiless war like an evil wind:
your brothers disappear
for 4 years. They write from the battlefields
of France. There are tormented, desperate phonecalls
in Yiddish. The Jews of Europe are slaughtered.
The screendoor of the apartment in Bensonhurst slams shut.
Roosevelt dies. We move in with your mother in the Bronx;
Rosemont catches fire; you buy the house
on 14th Street; Camp Tamarack & the Pines,
& the black Plymouth & college for the kids
& Carol's wedding. Your son
kisses you goodbye & flies off to California.
It flickers, all of it, on the wall by the stairs
with your weeping shadow twenty years ago.

As I watch you there, in silence, helpless,
not just my mother now, but a woman, swaying
over the sabbath candles in the most ancient grief,
how my heart embraces you,
tho I say nothing. Not a word. How dark it is
& how quiet. We are alone. Dad is dozing in the dark
in the other room. Carol is upstairs with her homework;
the last gray light of the day seeps thru the curtain.
A loaf of challah catches the light. It stands on
a silver tray on a white cloth. The tissue paper shawl
on your dark hair shivers in the flame
& glows with its own light.
& then it is done.
Your hands withdraw from your face.
The *brocha* ends. & the sobbing.
& when you take off that shawl all the past
disappears into those two, small yellow flames.
I wake Dad up, & standing at the foot of the stairs
yell for Carol to come down to dinner
& now you are taking the roast out of the oven & dad
does his funny cakewalk into the dining room,
that mischievous grin on his face & you say,
"Mick, don't be such a wise-guy, please"
& I laugh, & Carol sets the table & I
grab a piece of challah & dad grabs a piece of challah too,
& ma, you tell us to hold our horses & you
complain about having to put the roast back three times
but your face is beaming — your complaint full of joy
& I squeal I have to have gravy, I can't eat
anything without gravy, Carol brings in the potatoes
& we're all talking at once, the mindless
yammer of delight about the feast you have prepared
for us so lovingly-with such devotion —
that you have always prepared for us —
& it's great, ma…
it's absolutely delicious — all these years,
the feast you have made for us all. Ma, it's wonderful
it's absolutely wonderful.

*—For Michael & Billie Kowit on the occasion of their 50th*
*wedding anniversary*

*Wanda Coleman*

# Strapping

Daddyboy squeezed the joy into us when he tossed
us within a hand's tap of our cool peach-toned ceiling
then caught us by the waist as we dropped,
but gitty-up-horsey was our favorite daddy game,
fighting each other for first mount across
his broad glistening honeybrown back, kicking
heels as he'd break his workout routine
to gallop hands-and-knees across the living room
floor to the dining room. Mommygirl would take a beat, peek
out from the kitchen-way, smiling, hands to hip and apron,
then she'd go back to dinner duty. our biggest thrill
was when he lifted his right foot, massive torso,
and began to rise from the floor, grasping the childrider
firmly by leg, easing into a canter out the front door,
across the porch, off at a clip down 89th Street to the envy
of neighbor kids who wished their dads were boxer strong
so they could fly piggyback under the evergreens,
hands to his neck and jaw, hanging on for dear love

*Dorianne Laux*
# Augusta
*for my mother,*
*Frances Margarette Comeau*


She is born in a white room
in winter in the short
light to a shout of birds, the sky
locked in ice. Found on a convent
doorstep, nuns' black hoods dip
like coal scuttles to her cry.
Fed potato milk, she thins
into adolescence, grows beans up poles
in a patch behind the chapel.
Piano practice. The oldest nun breaks
a switch from a branch, holds it
over the keys, rings
the twig off her knuckles until
the right note sounds.
Summer cracks the dirt road.
She sits on the rotting end
of the porch, smokes cigarettes
stolen from a visitor's purse.
Draws nipples on the sculpted cherubs.
Is beaten for this.
Is beaten for most things.
Night rolls her body over, thin cot
smells of piss and moldy ticking, the moon
peeling as she leaves, elbows sharp,
her new heels spike through the snow.
Italian, he says, her dark hair
wasted in his hands. No, she whispers,
Algonquin, works with him to make
a single shape.

This is where I begin, as a fist
pounds the wall for quiet. As snow
breaks loose from the eaves.
I am not old enough to remember
the broom handle in his hands, her teeth
skipping kitchen tiles, blood
that spattered the bassinet to dotted swiss.
Winter can't hold her in. Her tracks
leave blue chains on the snow, a path
from his open door of yellow light.
In California she speaks French, sips
amber tea, ice chipping in a sweaty glass.
She meets the sailor who will become
my new father. He holds me to his chest.
She smiles. Her hand covers her mouth.

*Sydney Brown*

# The Truth of the Blue Vein

*[A] true pilot must of necessity pay attention to the*
*seasons, the heavens, the stars, the winds, and everything*
*proper to the craft if he is really to rule a ship.*
                    — Plato, *The Republic*

Last night in the half-light
a vein in my right breast
seemed especially blue

& I thought of my mother's words:
"The day I knew I was pregnant
a vein ripened on my breast."

Besides the blue
and my mother's words
I knew nothing

but the statement a kind Rilke
scholar once made at a dinner party:
"Not having children

is the greatest
political statement
an individual can make,"

but then I considered the rumors
that he had a son to whom
he did not speak,

and I was reminded
of my own father
on Sundays

working in the yard
in the same stained T-shirt;
I followed him with the afternoon sun

listening, listening, listening
to my own philosopher king
who no longer speaks to me.

And besides the truth of the blue vein
and my mother's words
I know nothing

except that 11 Amish schoolgirls
were shot by Charles Carl Roberts IV,
a milk truck driver and father of three.

And I know nothing
except that maybe 600,000
have died in Iraq

and that some of them
are children.

*Ravinder Sangha*

# Stone-words

I see my father in the mirror
fixing his turban,
dark maroon, medium starched,
when through a crack
in the window,
*anger* flies in,
invisible,
but I know her scent.

She takes my father's words,
*befikar, buddhu, khamosh*
grinds them into bits,
then using her spit
kneads them
into balls
hard and odd
heavy
like stones.

She decorates
the stone-words
with a poisonous moss,
the kind that pollutes
a lake or pond
and turns the waters
chalky and rancid
so no fish or frogs or lilies
grow in dark
air-less waters
only strange

microbes
that feed on filth.

When she is done
she flies back
through that crack,
leaving words
too heavy to lift.

*Iain Macdonald*

# Inheritance

There was never any honeyed glow
bathing both of us
as we worked together,
never any Hollywood moment
of knowledge being passed on
father to son.
Instead, his impatience
would transmit itself to me
and the spanner would slip
again and again
until he'd seize it
from my nervous grasp
and finish the job alone.

Tonight, *his* hands
are the ones that tremble
on a pair of pliers
as he attempts to help me
while I crouch before him
repairing his wheelchair.

Finally done,
we put the tools away.
"That screwdriver cost me sixpence
sixty years ago," he says,
"at Woolworths in Stornoway."

Silently, I heft its weight,
feeling the warm, brown wood
of its well-worn grip
familiar and solid
in the palm of my hand.

*Leah Browning*

# I Go Back in Time and Rescue My Mother

I know just where to find her, standing at the stove,
frying potato latkes in a cast-iron skillet. Her apron
is spattered with dark spots of grease, and waves
of heat rise up from the stove, pasting her dark hair
against the dampness of her neck and temples.

"Can't you make them any faster?" I am asking,
ten years old, at the table with my brother and sister.
The little pancakes are made of raw potato, grated
into a bowl and mixed with egg and salt and pepper.

It is dark outside, early winter. I arrive as a gust
of cold air, blowing in under the front door, hovering
in the space over the table, over the serving plate
with its bed of paper towels to absorb the excess oil.

There have been so many times that she's said,
"I just want to run away," spoken in anger
and in desperation, that I expect her to come
willingly, to take the ghostly fingers I offer
and allow herself to be pulled away

from all of us, from that life—the whining,
bickering children, the unfulfilled ambitions,
the husband who works long hours and listens
from a distance. The loneliness. The emptiness.

Everything that I know now she must have felt.
"I can save you," I whisper, pulling at her hand,

but she slips away, turning instead toward the table,
squandering what feels like her only chance for escape,

though the door is unlocked and she's chosen a million
times to stay. So I seep out of my childhood
home and go back to my own life. To the whining,
bickering children, the unfulfilled ambitions,
the husband who works long hours and listens

from a distance. The loneliness. The emptiness.
My mother calls on weekends after going
to bookstores or concerts, after sleeping until ten.
I stand at the stove, cooking hot foods over cast iron.

When my daughter arrives from her future life
to save us both, I find that I scarcely feel the hint
of air on my hand. But I am ready. I've been waiting
years now for someone to come and rescue me.

She pulls my arm away from the clothes I am folding,
from the dirty dishes and the trash that needs to go out.
And we get all the way to the front door before I hear
her voice—nine and a half years old, siren sweet rising
up the stairs—and find that I, too, am unable to leave.

Diane Raptosh

# Elations

Here is my sister, steady as a table, and this woman with whom she shares
a meal of eggplant and snow peas is my mom. For years, they have dined
nightly like this. When my sister goes quiet, as she does tonight, green eyes
staring like grapes, she is my father, and I become the youngest in the house,
never mind the presence of my teen-aged nephew and my tiny daughter
building towers of quarters together on the floor. In such times, my sister's
son turns into my brother, and thereby, my children's uncle. My own brother,
by his own admission, not to mention my mother's, insists he and my sister
should long ago have traded flesh. For a few years in the seventies, after our
father died, he and I were, respectively, our mother's mom and dad. Because
time is one fierce wheel sprung from the trunk of a single bristlecone pine,
back then, I was simultaneously my mother's dad, my sister's child, and my
nephew's sibling, even though he was decades from having been born, while
my full-grown father was from what was basically day one the not-quite-son
I never had. My smallest daughter behaves in a manner *grandmotherly*. My
oldest daughter, taller than I, wants to have a family bash honoring the hunch
she is more or less a happily gay man swathed in an almost-woman's body. On
her eighteenth birthday—with only her boyfriend as witness—she wants to
change her first name to *Merganser*.

# About the Authors

**Malaika King Albrecht**'s poems have been or are forthcoming in many literary magazines and anthologies, such as *Kakalak: An Anthology of Carolina Poets, Pebble Lake Review, The Pedestal Magazine, Boston Literary Review, New Orleans Review*, and *Letters to the World Anthology*. Her poems have recently won awards at Salem College and Press 53. She has taught creative writing to sexual abuse/assault survivors and to addicts and alcoholics in therapy groups and also is a volunteer poet in local schools. She is the founding editor of Redheaded Stepchild, an online magazine that only accepts poems that have been rejected elsewhere.

**Sam Apple** is a graduate of the creative non-fiction MFA program at Columbia University. He is the author of *Schlepping Through Alps: My Search for Austria's Jewish Past with Its Last Wandering Shepherd*, which was a finalist for the PEN/Martha Almond Award for First Nonfiction as well as *American Parent: My Strange and Surprising Adventures in Modern Babyland*. Apple's writing has appeared in a variety of publications, including *The New York Times, Financial Times*, and *ESPN The Magazine*. He lives with his wife and family in Brooklyn, New York.

**Kristy Athens** writes nonfiction and short fiction that has been published in a number of magazines, newspapers and literary journals, most recently *Babel Fruit, Greenbeard, Tonopah Review*, and *Stone's Throw Magazine*, and forthcoming from *High Desert Journal*. She coordinates the Columbia Center for the Arts Plein Air Writing Exhibition, and is a guest blogger for New Oregon Arts & Letters. She has served on the boards of the Hood River County Cultural Trust, Independent Publishing Resource Center, and Northwest Writers. She edited *Columbia Gorge Magazine*, and ran the Oregon Book Awards and Oregon Literary Fellowships programs of Literary Arts from 1999 to 2006.

**Chris Baron** holds an MFA in poetry from San Diego State University. He holds it tightly (so he can remember to write) because he is also a professor in the English Department at San Diego City College, where he is the director of the Writing Center. Chris has been published widely in poetry, fiction, and creative non-fiction, in literary journals, magazines, and anthologies. He lives with his wife and children somewhere in East County San Diego where there is no surf, and is the opposite of New York City where he grew up.

**Ella deCastro Baron** is a first-generation Filipina American living in San Diego. She teaches English and creative writing at San Diego City College and is a lifelong student on how to be a wife and mother. Ella hopes to be a witness to her interracial family, her faith, and how it may (or may not) fit together. Her debut book, *Itchy Brown Girl Seeks Employment* was published in 2009 by CityWorks Press.

**Lori Miller Barrett** is a freelance writer living in Chicago. She has written for *Time Out Chicago*, a weekly magazine there, and the *Wall Street Journal*'s "Personal Journal" and "Weekend" sections. She also contributes to a local food blog called *Drive Thru*. Her daughter is now in fourth grade and proud to name a foreign country when her classmates talk about where they were born.

**Carrien Blue** is the mother of four children. She is the administrator/co-founder of a non-profit organization that supports orphanages caring for Burmese refugee children in northern Thailand and combats child trafficking by strengthening the communities where at-risk children are born. She also writes about her journey as a parent and non-profit worker, as well as books for children.

**Regina Murray Brault** has twice been nominated for the Pushcart Prize. She was also honored to receive the 2009 Angels Without Wings Foundation, Vermont Senior Poet Laureate Award for her poem, "Mother Tongue." Over 200 of her poems have appeared in more than 90 different magazines, anthologies, chapbooks and newspapers in such publications as: *The Comstock Review, Midwest Poetry Review, Poet Magazine, Karamu, The State Street Review, Sacred Stones Anthology*, Random House Anthology *Mothers and Daughters*, and *The Mennonite*. Regina has also been the recipient of numerous poetry awards including the Clark College Award, the Tennessee Literary Award for Poetry, and the 2009 Euphoria and Creekwalker Awards. She leads a monthly poetry workshop called The Cherry Lane Poets in Burlington, Vermont, and is the proud mother of three and grandmother of six.

**Teresa Breeden** is a member of the Ash Canyon Poets, has an unrequited love for the words of Tony Hoagland, and adores garden tomatoes. She was a recipient of the 2007 NV Arts Council Fellowship for Literature, and has poetry published in 13 states. Teresa's best two poems are her children.

**Sydney Brown** is the Creative Writing Program Co-Coordinator at Grossmont College in El Cajon, where she also teaches poetry and composition. Her fiction and poetry have appeared in *Sonoma Review, Southern Anthology, two girls review, Hawaii Pacific Review, red, Sunshine/Noir, HOW2: Contemporary Innovative Writing Practices by Women*, and *Hunger and Thirst* (City Works Press, 2008). Thankful (and quite frankly, a little surprised) for the inspiration domesticity provides, Sydney lives in La Mesa with her husband, Steve, and two schnauzers: Vladimir and Lolita.

**Leah Browning** is the author of three nonfiction books for teens and pre-teens. Her first chapbook, *Making Love to the Same Man for Fifteen Years*, was released by Big Table Publishing in 2009. Her second chapbook, *Picking Cherries in the Española Valley*, is forthcoming from Dancing Girl Press. Browning's fiction, poetry, essays, and articles have appeared in a variety of publications including *Queen's Quarterly, Queen's Feminist Review, Mothering Magazine, The Saint Ann's Review, Tipton Poetry Journal, Literary Mama, Blood Orange Review, Salome Magazine, Mamaphonic, and Fertile Ground*, on a broadside from Broadsided Press, on postcards from the program Poetry Jumps Off the Shelf, and in several anthologies. In addition to writing, Browning serves as editor of the Apple Valley Review.

**Teri Carter**'s work can be found in *Columbia, The MacGuffin, Superstition Review*, and other journals. She is working on her first book, *A Heartland Education*, a memoir about growing up in Missouri. She lives in northern California.

**Brandon Cesmat**'s most recent book of poems is *Light in All Directions* (Poetic Matrix Press, 2009). His book *When Pigs Fall in Love* is forthcoming. He teaches literature and writing in Southern California.

**Susan Cohen** is the author of *Backstroking* (2005), which won the Acorn-Rukeyser Chapbook Award, and *Finding the Sweet Spot* (Finishing Line Press, 2009). Her poems have appeared in *Atlanta Review, Poet Lore, Poetry International, Seattle Review, Southern Poetry Review, Tar River Poetry, Verse Daily* and elsewhere. She's a journalist in Berkeley, and co-author of the non-fiction book *Normal at Any Cost* (Tarcher/Penguin 2009). Her two children are no longer children.

**Wanda Coleman** is featured in *Writing Los Angeles* (Library of America, 2002), in *Poet's Market* (2003), and *Quercus Review* VI (2006), she has been an Emmy-winning scriptwriter, former columnist for *Los Angeles Times* magazine; a nominee for poet laureate, California 2005 and for a USA Artist Fellowship, 2007. Coleman's books include *Ostinato Vamps* (Pitt Poetry Series, 2003-2004); *Bathwater Wine*, winner of the 1999 Lenore Marshall Poetry Prize — the first African-American woman to receive the award; and *Mercurochrome* (poems), bronze-metal finalist, National Book Awards 2001. Her honors include fellowships from the John Simon Guggenheim Foundation, the National Endowment for the Arts and the California Arts Council. *Jazz and Twelve O'Clock Tales* (Black Sparrow Books, 2008) exemplifies her fine fiction.

**Nannette Croce** is a writer and editor. Her work has appeared in various online and print publications including *The Philadelphia Inquirer, The Rose & Thorn Journal* and *The Bare Root Review*.

**Barbara Crooker** has published poems in magazines such as *Yankee, The Christian Science Monitor*, and *The Denver Quarterly*; anthologies, including *The Bedford Introduction to Literature* and *The Bedford Introduction to Poetry, Worlds in their Words: An Anthology of Contemporary American Women Writers* (Prentice Hall) *Good Poems for Hard Times* (ed. by Garrison Keillor)(Viking Penguin) and *Boomer Girls* (University of Iowa Press); ten chapbooks, and three full length books, *Radiance*, which won the Word Press First Book Award and was a finalist for The Paterson Poetry Prize, *Line Dance* (Word Press, 2008), winner of The Paterson Prize for Literary Excellence, and *More*, which is forthcoming in 2010 from C&R Press. She has received three Pennsylvania Council on the Arts Fellowships in Literature, and the Thomas Merton Poetry of the Sacred Award, and is the mother of four, including one who was "born asleep."

**Jessica Cuello** is a poet who teaches French in Central New York. Recent poems have appeared or are forthcoming in *Copper Nickel, RHINO, Harpur Palate, Melusine, The Dos Passos Review*, and *Literary Mama*.

**Carol V. Davis** is the author of a bilingual poetry collection, *It's Time to Talk About...* and two chapbooks, *Letters from Prague* and *The Violin Teacher*. She won the 2007 T.S. Eliot Prize for Poetry for *Into the Arms of Pushkin: Poems of St. Petersburg.* Twice a Fulbright scholar in Russia, she teaches at Santa Monica College, California and was 2008 Poet-in-Residence at Olivet College, Michigan.

**Lucille Lang Day** is the author of eight poetry collections and chapbooks, most recently *The Curvature of Blue* (Cervena Barva, 2009). She has also published a children's book, *Chain Letter*, and her poetry and prose have appeared widely in such magazines and anthologies as *The Hudson Review, The Threepenny Review*, and *California Poetry: From the Gold Rush to the Present* (Heyday).

**Mary Christine Delea** is the author of *The Skeleton Holding Up the Sky*, two chapbooks, and numerous published and prize-winning poems. Her publishing credits include a poem in the City Works Press anthology *Lavandería: A Mixed Load of Women, Wash, and Words* ("Brigit Sullivan, Maid at the Borden House in Fall River, Massachusetts, 1892, Writes What She's Learned about Justice"), *NOR, North Dakota Quarterly, Zone 3, Spoon River Poetry Review*, as well as many other journals and anthologies. Christine has lived all over the U.S. and now, a recovering academic, she lives in Oregon with her husband and their cats and is the President of the Oregon State Poetry Association.

**Sharon Dornberg-Lee** is a geriatric social worker at CJE SeniorLife and an adjunct instructor at the University of Chicago School of Social Service Adminatration. She lives in Chicago with her husband and nine-year-old daguther, Sophie. Her poem "Winter Bath" recently appeared in *Literary Mama*, an online journal. Her work has also appeared in *Earth's Daughters* ("The Subject is Dreams"), in the collection *They Would Smile: Images of an Inclusive Community*, a publication of the Connecticut Council on Developmental Disabilities (in the Israeli Holocaust Museum) and in *The Red Shoes Review* ("Death of the Family Dog, There's a Drawing on My Classroom Desk"). Her essay "Cold Turkey on Big Bird" was featured on the Chicago Public Radio program *Eight Forty-Eight*.

**Juliet Eastland** has written for magazines, newspapers, websites, and anthologies. She lives in Brookline, Massachusetts with her husband and two lovely daughters.

**W. D. Ehrhart**, who fought in Vietnam as a U.S. Marine, teaches English and history at the Haverford School in suburban Philadelphia. His most recent collection of poems is *The Bodies Beneath the Table* (Adastra Press, 2010). His daughter Leela, who was four years old when "Guns" was written, recently graduated from Drexel University; she will not be joining the Marines.

**Carol Gremli** received a BA in Speech and Theatre/English Education from Montclair State College in New Jersey. After a professional career as a performer, she transitioned into her next life and became a teacher of theatre arts and dance. She subsequently received her MAW degree from Manhattanville College in Purchase, N.Y where her thesis, *Bach Family Fugue* (a screenplay), received the Dean's Distinction Award. Collaborating with her husband Jack, she has written articles in arts education and learning styles that have appeared in *Our Children*, the national PTA magazine, and other education publications. She lives outside New York City and has two children: Jordan (all grown) and Ana (almost grown).

Stories by **Frank Haberle** have appeared recently in magazines including *Cantaraville, Necessary Fiction, Birmingham Arts Journal, GUD, 34 Parallel, Taj Mahal Review, Broken Bridge Review, Adirondack Review, Hot Metal Press, Melic Review, Johnny America, East Hampton Star, Smokelong Quarterly,* and *21 Stars Review.* Frank is on the Board of Directors of the NY Writers Coalition, a community writing program for disenfranchised New Yorkers.

**Donna Hilbert**'s latest poetry collection is *The Green Season,* World Parade Books, 2009. Earlier books include *Traveler in Paradise: New and Selected Poems,* Pearl Editions 2004, as well as *Transforming Matter, Deep Red* and *Women Who Make Money and the Men Who Love Them* (short stories), winner of England's Staple First Edition biennial prize. Ms. Hilbert appears in and her poetry is the text of the just completed documentary *Grief Becomes Me: A Love Story* by award-winning filmmaker Christine Fugate. She teaches the master class in poetry for PEN USA's Emerging Voice's program as well as an on-going private workshop.

**Tom C. Hunley** is an associate professor of creative writing at Western Kentucky University and the director of Steel Toe Books. Three of his poems have been featured on The Writer's Almanac with Garrison Keillor. Others have been published in *Triquarterly, New York Quarterly, North American Review, New Orleans Review,* and *River Styx.* He has won two book contests, one for a full-length poetry manuscript (Logan House Press) and another for a chapbook (Pecan Grove Press). He is also the author of *Teaching Poetry Writing: A Five-Canon Approach* (Multilingual Matters Ltd., 2007).

**Chris Huntington** became a father in 2008. His writing about adoption was featured on National Public Radio's *This I Believe* (and is found in the second anthology of that series, published by Henry Holt). For ten years, he worked in Indiana prisons, and his prison fiction has appeared in *Natural Bridge* and *The Tampa Review.* His novel, *Mike Tyson Slept Here,* will be published in the spring of 2011. He currently lives in China with his wife and child.

**Marianne S. Johnson** holds a BA from Cal Poly, San Luis Obispo, and a law degree from the UC Hastings College of the Law. She is married with two children, and a practicing attorney in San Diego. Her poetry is published in *Calyx; Lavanderia: A Mixed Load of Women, Wash and Word; San Diego Writers, Ink: A Year in Ink, Vol. 3;* and *Sport Literate.*

**Cyn Kitchen** teaches creative writing at Knox College in Galesburg, IL. Her writing has appeared such places as *The Louisville Review, Menda City Review, Minnetonka Review, Carve* and *Ars Medica.* Cyn gave birth to four children in five years, a plan she didn't think out too well, but nearly has all of them raised, though she's not certain what that actually means. Despite the travails of motherhood, she is glad these people are in her life, and she looks forward, some day, to all of the schemes she'll get away with as a grandmother.

**Kathy Kottaras** taught high school English for seven years before becoming a mom. She also holds an MA in English from the University of California, Irvine and teaches

English at Pasadena City College. She has work published or forthcoming in *The Edith Wharton Review*, *edible Los Angeles* and *ReadWriteThink.org*. She was also the 2004 recipient of the Music Center's Bravo Award in Los Angeles.

**Steve Kowit** was an animal rights activist for several years. His latest books are *The Gods of Rapture* (City Works Press, 2005), *The First Noble Truth* (U Tampa Press) and *Crossing Borders*, a collaboration with the painter Lenny Silverberg, *(Spuyten Duyvil Press)*. He lives with his wife Mary, six cats and two dogs in the backcountry hills near the Mexican border.

**Richard Krawiec**'s first book of free verse poems, *Breakdown*, was a Finalist for the 2009 Indy Awards for Poetry. His poems and stories appear in some of the top literary magazines in the U.S. — *Sou'wester, many mountains moving, Shenandoah, Witness, Cream City Review*, and others. He has also published two novels, a story collection, and four plays. He's been fortunate to have received fellowships from the National Endowment for the Arts, the NC Arts Council, and the Pennsylvania Council on the Arts. He teaches online Fiction Writing for UNC Chapel Hill, and won their Excellence in Teaching Award for 2009. Krawiec has worked extensively with people in homeless shelters, women's shelters, prisons, literacy classes, and community sites, teaching writing.

**Jenny Kurzweil** is a writer and editor for a nonprofit organization that works to advance Chicanos/Hispanics and Native Americans in science. Prior to becoming a writer, she spent ten years as a professional cook with a passion for organics and seasonally based menus. Her first book, *Fields that Dream: A Journey to the Roots of Our Food* (Fulcrum Publishing) was released in 2005. Her articles have been published in *Science Careers, Science, Winds of Change Magazine, Hispanic Outlook on Higher Education, Journal for Minority Medical Students, HopeDance, California Certified Organic Newsletter*, and *Bricolage*. Jenny lives in Santa Cruz, California, with her partner and their two sons.

**Dorianne Laux**'s fourth book of poems, *Facts about the Moon* (W.W. Norton), is the recipient of the Oregon Book Award. Laux is also author of *Awake, What We Carry*, and *Smoke* from BOA Editions, as well as *Superman: The Chapbook* and *Dark Charms*, both from Red Dragonfly Press. Her fifth collection of poetry, *The Book of Men*, will be published by W.W. Norton in 2011. Laux teaches in the MFA Program at North Carolina State University.

**Jeffrey Thomas Leong**'s poems have appeared in *Crab Orchard, Cimarron Review, Flyway, Bamboo Ridge, Manzanita, Asian Pacific American Journal*, and other publications. He and his wife are parents of a rambunctious eight-year old girl adopted from Jiangsu, China. In his poetry, Jeffrey examines the mysteries of gender and race. He lives in the San Francisco Bay Area.

**Sylvia Levinson**'s two children managed to survive her single parenting and are now productive and, hopefully, well-adjusted adults. Sylvia has been published in: *Snowy Egret, Blue Arc West, City Works, Hunger and Thirst, San Diego Writers Ink Magee Park, Christian Science Monitor*. Awards: *City Works*, 2007, National Winner. Her book, *Gateways: Poems of Nature, Meditation and Renewal*, is available at: www.sylvia-levinson.com.

**Bethellen Levitan** is an interdisciplinary artist working with words, paint, and clay, to explore creativity and Being. She is the author of two chapbooks: *Scenic Route* (1996), and *Through the Glass* (2001). Her writing appears in many small press publications. She lives and works in San Francisco and Willits, California.

**Karen K. Lewis** teaches with California Poets in the Schools and has work in journals and anthologies including *Hip Mama, Drumvoices, Iron Horse Literary Review* and the anthology *Sunshine Noir* (City Works Press, 2005). She earned an MFA from Antioch-Los Angeles and co-parents four young adult children with her sculptor husband, Will Lewis.

**Kathryn Lewis** has published a novel and is working on another. Her work has appeared in *Fodderwing* and *New York Stories.*

**Paul Lieber** produces and hosts "Why Poetry," a radio show on Pacifica Radio in L.A., KPFK. The intention of the show is to de-mystify poetry and then perhaps to mystify it again. His poems have been published in *Summerset Review, Askew, Eclipse* and *Spot Lit., Poemeleon, Solo, Beyond the Valley of the Contemporary Poets, New York Quarterly, Santa Barbara Review*, among many other journals and anthologies. He has worked as the facilitator for the poetry workshop at Beyond Baroque, the oldest literary institute in Los Angeles. He holds an MFA in poetry from Antioch. He also works as an actor and lives with his wife and son in Venice California.

**Leann Wise Lindsey** currently lives in England with her husband, an unfledged child or two, and a left-over dog and cat. Her roots are in the deep south of the United States and most of her stories derive from family history and her experiences raising children, including one with autism. Her poetry and fiction has appeared in *Southern Hum, storySouth, Literary Mama*, and *Doorways* magazines.

**Sara Lippmann** received her MFA from the New School. Her work has appeared in or is forthcoming from the *Mississippi Review, Word Riot, Slice, Carve, Fourth Genre, All Things Girl, Fiction Circus, NANO Fiction, Fiction at Work, LITnIMAGE* and elsewhere. She lives in Brooklyn.

**George Longenecker** teaches in the Department of English, Humanities and Social Sciences at Vermont Technical College. His most recent publications are in *The Dos Passos Review* and the *Rockhurst Review*. His poem "Edsel" was a winner in The 2009 Allen Ginsberg Poetry Awards and is forthcoming in *The Paterson Review.*

**Grace Hwang Lynch** graduated from the University of California at Berkeley with a BA in Rhetoric. She has reported for television stations around California and Idaho. Her work has also been published in *Lavanderia: A Mixed Load of Women, Wash and Word* (City Works Press, 2009). When not busy raising her two sons, she blogs about Asian mixed-race families on HapaMama.com.

Born and raised in Glasgow, Scotland, **Iain Macdonald** has earned his bread and beer in a variety of ways, from factoryhand to merchant marine officer. He currently lives in Arcata, California, where he works as a high school English teacher. His chapbook *Plotting the Course* is available from March Street Press.

**Mary Anne Maier**, a Wyoming native, is coeditor with Joan Shaddox Isom of the creative nonfiction anthology *The Leap Years: Women Reflect on Change, Loss, and Love* (Beacon Press, 1999). Her essays and articles have appeared in such varied settings as National Public Radio, *Southern Living, Christian Science Monitor, Journal of the American Medical Association,* the online journal *Terrain,* and creative nonfiction anthologies. Maier taught college English for several years and was a writer and publications editor for the University of Texas at El Paso. She has presented at numerous conferences, including the Poynter Institute's National Writers' Workshop, and was writer-in-residence for nonfiction at the Oklahoma Fall Arts Institute. Maier works as a writing coach and editor for individuals and trade and academic publishers.

**Matt Mason** has won two Nebraska Book Awards (for Poetry in 2007 and Anthology in 2006) and read and organized poetry programming with the U.S. Department of State's Bureau of International Information Programs Speaker/Specialist exchange program in Minsk, Belarus in 2008. He edits PoetryMenu.com, a listing of every Nebraska poetry event, and founded Morpo Press, which, since 1997, has published 30 chapbooks by up-and-coming local writers. The Backwaters Press released his award-winning first full-length collection, *Things We Don't Know We Don't Know*, in April, 2006 where it was listed on best seller lists for contemporary poetry. He also has 9 chapbooks of poetry, including *Mistranslating Neruda* (New Michigan Press, 2003) and *When The Bough Breaks* (Lone Willow Press, 2005). His poems have been published in *Prairie Schooner, The Laurel Review, Poet Lore, Green Mountain Review, Mid-American Review, Rhino, Chiron Review, South Dakota Review,* and over 100 others.

**Jim Miller** is the author of the novels *Flash* (AK Press, 2010) and *Drift* (University of Oklahoma Press, 2007). He is also co-author of the radical history of San Diego *Under the Perfect Sun: The San Diego Tourists Never See* (with Mike Davis and Kelly Mayhew on The New Press, 2003) and a cultural studies book on working class sports fandom, *Better to Reign in Hell: Inside the Raiders Fan Empire* (with Kelly Mayhew on The New Press, 2005). Miller is also the editor of *Sunshine/Noir: Writing from San Diego and Tijuana* (City Works Press, 2005) and *Democracy in Education; Education for Democracy: An Oral History of the American Federation of Teachers, Local 1931* (AFT 1931, 2007). He has published poetry, fiction, and non-fiction in a wide range of journals and other publications.

A faculty member at the University of North Carolina School of the Arts, **Joe Mills** has published two volumes of poetry — *Somewhere During the Spin Cycle* and *Angels, Thieves, and Winemakers* — and numerous works of fiction, non-fiction and criticism. For many years he wrote a parenting column called "Crib Notes," and he has published work on parenting in several forums, including *Adoptive Parents, Austin Parent, Latitude Magazine,* and *The Truth About the Fact.*

**Amanda Pritchard Moore** just relocated to the San Francisco Bay Area from Detroit, trading the artistic confines of Cranbrook for a new adventure. She received her MFA in poetry from Cornell University in 2001 and retreated into a life of an all-consuming job before having her daughter Clementine and returning to both teaching and poetry. Her work has been published in *Best New Poets 2009, 5AM, Third Coast, Cream City Review,* and *Green Mountains Review,* among others.

**Julie L. Moore** is the author of *Slipping Out of Bloom,* forthcoming from WordTech Editions, and the chapbook *Election Day* (Finishing Line Press). Moore is a Pushcart Prize nominee and recent recipient of the Rosine Offen Memorial Award from the Free Lunch Arts Alliance in Illinois, the Janet B. McCabe Poetry Prize from Ruminate: Faith in Literature and Art, and the Judson Jerome Poetry Scholarship from the Antioch Writers' Workshop. Moore has contributed poetry to *Alaska Quarterly Review, Atlanta Review, CALYX, Chautauqua Literary Review, Cimarron Review, Dogwood, The MacGuffin, Sou'Wester, Valparaiso Poetry Review,* and others.

**John Morgan**'s latest book, *Spear-Fishing on the Chatanika: New and Selected Poems,* was published recently by Salmon Poetry. In 2009, he served as the first writer-in-residence at Denali National Park. He and his wife Nancy live in Fairbanks, Alaska.

**Meryl Natchez**'s poetry has been published in *The Healing Muse, Lyric, BloodLotus* and won third place in the Pinch Literary Contest. She is the founder and director of TechProse, a placement service for technical writers, and she lives in Berkeley, California with her husband.

A doctoral student in English at Texas Tech University, **Brent Newsom** lives with his wife and infant son in Lubbock, Texas. His work has appeared in *The Southern Review, America, New Texas,* and *New Delta Review.* New poems are forthcoming in *Cave Wall* and *Subtropics.* He received the 2009 Foley Poetry Prize from *America* magazine and a Fulbright grant to work on a novel in China.

**Tonya Northenor** is an Assistant Professor of English at Owensboro Community and Technical College. She earned an MFA from the University of Memphis. Her poetry has been published in literary journals including *Appalachian Heritage, Calyx, Earth's Daughters,* and the anthologies *From the Other World: Poems in Memory of James Wright* and *Imagination & Place: Ownership.* She lives with her husband and young son in north-central Kentucky.

**Daniel A. Olivas** is the author of five books including *Anywhere But L.A.: Stories* (Bilingual Press, 2009). His first full-length novel, *The Book of Want,* will be published in 2011 by the University of Arizona Press. Olivas is the editor of *Latinos in Lotusland: An Anthology of Contemporary Southern California Literature* (Bilingual Press, 2008), and his writing has been widely anthologized including in *Sudden Fiction Latino* (W. W. Norton, 2010). His fiction, poetry, essays and book reviews have appeared in many publications including the *Los Angeles Times, Exquisite Corpse, Jewish Journal, California Lawyer,* the *El Paso Times,* and *La Bloga.*

**Oriana** was born in Poland, and came to this country when she was 17. Her publications include *Poetry, Ploughshares, Best American Poetry 1992, The Iowa Review,* and many others. She lives in San Diego and works as a private instructor.

**Joel Peckham** is an assistant professor of creative writing at the University of Cincinnati—Clermont. He has published two books of poetry, most recently *The Heat of What Comes* from Pecan Grove Press and has had individual poems published in many journals, including *The Southern Review, Prairie Schooner,* and *Black Warrior Review.* His essays have appeared in *River Teeth, Under The Sun, Brevity,* and *The North American Review.* In 2004 he was in a car accident that took the lives of his wife and oldest son, leaving him a single parent and widower as well as a chronic pain sufferer. He is now remarried and has rebuilt his life and his body. Still, each day is a struggle and his writing has reflected that hard work.

**Rosalie Sanara Petrouske** currently teaches writing classes at Lansing Community College in Lansing, Michigan. Her poetry has appeared in several literary magazines such as *Passages North,* Southern *Poetry* Review, *The Red Rock Review,* and *Driftwood.* Finishing Line Press published a chapbook of her poetry, *A Postcard from my Mother,* in 2004. Her most recent publication includes a series of journal entries about her daughter, Senara Rose, included in *Keeping Time: 150 Years of Journal Writing* published in 2009 by Passager Books. Her daughter, who is now seventeen years old, continues to be the inspiration for many of her poems and essays.

**Neal Pollack** is the author of *Stretch: The Unlikely Making of a Yoga Dude,* published in August 2010 by HarperPerennial, as well as several other books, including the best-selling memoir *Alternadad,* the cult classic *Neal Pollack Anthology of American Literature,* and the rock novel *Never Mind the Pollacks.* A contributor to many magazines and websites, Pollack lives in Los Angeles with his wife and son.

The Eyck-Berringer Endowed Chair in English, **Diane Raptosh** has taught literature and creative writing at the College of Idaho for 18 years. She has published three collections of poems, *Just West of Now* (Guernica Editions, 1992), *Labor Songs* (Guernica, 1999), and *Parents from a Different Alphabet: Prose Poems* (Guernica, 2008). She has published widely in journals as *The Los Angeles Review, Michigan Quarterly Review,* and *Women's Studies Quarterly.* Her poetry, fiction, and nonfiction have appeared in numerous anthologies in the U.S. and Canada. Through the Idaho Commission on the Arts, she has won three fellowships in creative writing.

**Ben Rogers** is a writer living in Reno, Nevada with his wife and two daughters. An excerpt from his novel *The Flamer* garnered a 2007 Nevada Arts Council Fellowship. His fiction has been published by *McSweeney's* online as well as in Nevada's literary magazine, *Brushfire.* In 2005 he earned a Sierra Arts Foundation Literary Artist Endowment Grant. He studied journalism and mechanical engineering at the University of Nevada and has worked as a newspaper and magazine writer and currently as a research scientist. He is the lead author of *Nanotechnology: Understanding Small Systems* (CRC Press), the first-ever comprehensive textbook on nanotechnology, published last year.

**Madelyn Rosenberg** is a freelance writer living in Arlington, Virginia. Her nonfiction work has appeared in *Parenting, eMusic, The Rough Guides Book of Playlists,* and more. Her poems have appeared in *Literary Mama* and on buses in Arlington and Fairfax, VA. Her first picture book will be published soon with Hyperion.

**Charlie Rossiter**, NEA Fellowship recipient and three-time Pushcart Prize nominee, hosts the audio website poetrypoetry.com. He is the author of four books of poetry and numerous chapbooks. His work has been featured on NPR, and at the Geraldine R. Dodge Poetry Festival in NJ. He was among a handful of poets chosen to perform at the Chicago Blues Festival in 2005. His latest book, *All Over America: Road Poems* (2009) is based on 60,000 miles of road trip experiences around the United States and Canada.

**Judith Sanders** teaches English at Shady Side Academy in Pittsburgh, where she lives with her husband and son. She has a BA in literature from Yale, an MA in writing from Boston University, and a PhD in English from Tufts. She has taught literature and writing at Bowdoin, Tufts, MIT, and Boston University, as well as in France on a Fulbright fellowship. She has also worked as a freelance editor, writer, and writing coach. She has published articles in *The American Scholar, Journal of Popular Film and Television, Modern Jewish Studies*, and *Film Quarterly*, and in the anthologies *Mama, Ph.D.* from Rutgers University Press and *From Wollstonecraft to Stoker: Essays on Gothic and Victorian Sensation Fiction*, forthcoming from McFarland. Her poems have appeared in *Poetica*, anthologies, and the *Pittsburgh Post-Gazette*.

**Ravinder Sangha** was born in India, immigrated to Canada and settled in USA. She has a PhD in Microbiology but her passion is for writing poetry about travels, dreams and daily living. She lives in San Diego, California with her husband, two teen-aged sons and a black Labrador.

**Greg Schreur** has three children and lives in Grand Rapids, Michigan. He currently teaches high school English and history and has had work published in *Rock & Sling, The Broken Plate, Eclectica*, and *Brain, Child*.

**Catherine Sharpe**, middle-aged "divorced" lesbian mother of one miracle IVF baby, lives and writes in Oakland, California. She almost won a prize once when she was nominated as a finalist in the Penelope Niven 2009 Nonfiction Award. Her first book, a collection of interlocking essays and short fictions, *Ambition Towards Love*, has not yet been published, although look for excerpts in *Opium Magazine, The Battered Suitcase*, Offsprung's *Reproduciness, Errant Parent*, and upcoming in *The Decameron Annual* anthology, and other fine entities yet to be confirmed.

**Maureen A. Sherbondy**'s two chapbooks are *After the Fairy Tale* and *Praying at Coffee Shops*. She lives in Raleigh, NC with her husband and three sons.

**Stephanie Silvia** was born in New York City where she taught public school and directed a modern dance company. Her poetry and articles have been published in the *Northcoast Journal, College of the Redwoods Writers and Poets, Women.Period* (Spinsters Ink Press), *The Cherry Blossom Review*, hotmetalpress.net, *elephant*, and chapbooks compiled by the poets attending Diane di Prima's annual workshops at the Center for Visionary Women. She currently lives on the Redwood coast of Northern California with her fisherman husband Scot and their adopted son, Lonnie, and is attending Diane di Prima'a Foundations of Poetics I class in San Francisco.

**Curtis Smith**'s stories and essays have appeared in over fifty literary journals and have been cited by *The Best American Short Stories, The Best American Mystery Stories*, and *the Best American Spiritual Writing*. March Street Press published two collections of his short-short stories, and Press 53 has published two other story collections (the most recent one was *Bad Monkey*, put out last month). Last year, Casperian Books published his second novel, *Sound and Noise*, and this spring, they released his next novel.

**Jyotsna Sreenivasan**'s short stories have appeared or are forthcoming in: *American Literary Review, Catamaran, Green Hills Literary Lantern, India Currents, Iron Horse Literary Review, Nassau Review, Phantasmagoria, Tampa Review,* and *Tiferet.* One story was anthologized in *Living in America: South Asian American Writers.* She is also the author of books and stories for children, as well as a new reference book, *Utopias in American History,* published by ABC-CLIO. She has also received two grants from the Washington, D.C. Commission on the Arts and Humanities.

**Teresa Stores** is the author of three novels, *Getting to the Point* (Naiad, 1995), *Side-Tracks* (Naiad, 1996), and *Backslide* (Spinsters Ink, 2008). Her fiction, poetry and essays have appeared in numerous literary magazines, including *Sinister Wisdom, Rock & Sling, Cicada, Out Magazine, MotherVerse, Blithe House Quarterly, Oregon Literary Review, Bloom Magazine, Earth's Daughters, Blueline, Damselfly Press, SawPalm,* and *Kudzu.* Her work has been supported by grants from the Vermont Arts Council and the Barbara Deming Fund, and she was a resident at Bread Loaf and a scholar at The Community of Writers at Squaw Valley. She is the winner of the 2009 Kore Press Short Fiction Award for "Frost Heaves," the title piece of her collection of twelve linked stories set in southern Vermont. A graduate of the MFA program at Emerson College, she is an associate professor of English at the University of Hartford. She is also the "other" (non-biological) mother of twins, now six years old. This year her partner, artist Susan Jarvis, and the children and she are living in a small village in the south of France, chronicled on their blog.

**Thea Sullivan**, MFA, MAT is a creative writing instructor and writing coach. Her poems and essays have appeared in many publications including *The Sun* magazine, *Barrow Street,* and *The Cortland Review.* She lives in the San Francisco Bay Area with her husband and their long-awaited son, now 3 years old.

**Jim Teeters** has published poetry in *Hiram Poetry Review, Beginnings, Arnazella,* and *Northwest Renaissance Poets* among others. He is active in poetry readings in the Seattle area through the Striped Water Poets. He is the author of the book *Teach with Style* (Redleaf Press). He produced a traveling book called "My Goldfish Stole the Moon — Poetry Fun" that inspires kids to write poetry. Teeters is a retired social worker living in Kent, Washington.

**Tina Traster** writes the bi-weekly "Burb Appeal" column for *The New York Post.* It chronicles her life in suburbia and references her former life on the Upper West Side. She also writes "The Great Divide," a biweekly blog for *The Huffington Post.* Traster has been a published writer since 1987. Her essays, articles and columns have appeared in more than 40 publications including *The New York Post, The New York Times, The Bergen Record, The Journal News, The Asbury Park Press, Time Out New York, Crains New York Business, Inside Magazine* and *New Jersey Monthly.*

**Yi-Mei Tsiang**'s poetry has been previously published in literary journals such as *CV2, Arc Magazine, Vallum Magazine, The Antigonish Review,* and many others. She has two books forthcoming in 2010, *Flock of Shoes* on Annick Press and *The Mermaid and Other Fairy Tales* on Leaf Press. She also has another full-length manuscript *Sweet Devilry,* which has won the Ontario Arts Council Works-in-progress grant. She is currently studying in the University of British Columbia's MFA program.

**Tom Turman** is an architect in Berkeley, California whose two daughters inspired "The Gang of Eleven." He has written two books: *WAWA — West Africa Wins Again* and *Teacher-Stories to be Read and Graded by Friday*. He has published stories and articles in *The Denver Post, San Francisco Chronicle, Nevada Magazine, Martha's Vineyard Magazine* and Laney College's award winning literary magazine *Good News*.

**Davi Walders'** poetry and prose have appeared in more than 200 anthologies and journals, including *The American Scholar, JAMA, Washington Woman, Seneca Review, Potomac Review, Travelers' Tales*, and elsewhere. She developed and directs the Vital Signs Writing Project at NIH in Bethesda, Maryland, which was funded by The Witter Bynner Foundation for Poetry. *Gifts*, her third collection of poetry, was commissioned by the Milton Murray Foundation for Philanthropy. She has received a National Endowment for the Humanities Grant, a Puffin Foundation Grant, a Maryland State Artist Grant in Poetry, a Luce Foundation Grant, and fellowships to Ragdale Foundation, Blue Mountain Center, Virginia Center for the Creative Arts for her writing. Her work has been choreographed and performed in NYC and elsewhere, read by Garrison Keillor on Writer's Almanac, and nominated for Pushcart Prizes.

**Tracy Wall** lives with her husband and twin daughters in Somerset, UK. She has had poetry and plays published and produced and she regularly performs her poetry across England at various festivals and venues — the most memorable being on a red double-decker bus. Having just completed an MA in creative writing, she is working as a poetry tutor and freelance writer.

Originally from New York City, **Susan Webb** currently lives in Houston, Texas where she practices and teaches adolescent psychiatry. She is at work on her first collection of poetry. "Wild Sweet William" was written for her son, now a college student, as is his sister.

**Lisa Williams** is the author of *Letters to Virginia Woolf*, published by Hamilton Books (June 2005). She also wrote *The Artist as Outsider in the Novels of Toni Morrison and Virginia Woolf* (Greenwood Press, 2000). Lisa has published her writing in *Washington Square Review, The Mom Egg, The Women's Studies Quarterly, The Southern Humanities Review, The Tusculum Review*, and *For She Is the Tree of Life: Grandmothers Through the Eyes of Women Writers*. She teaches writing and literature at Ramapo College of New Jersey.

**Ella Wilson** is a writer and creative director of an advertising agency in Brooklyn, NY. She received her MFA from The New School in May 2009. She has been writing nonfiction for the past seven years and has given readings in both Manhattan and Brooklyn.

**Wendy Wisner's** first book of poems, *Epicenter*, was published by CW Books in 2004. Her poems have appeared in *The Spoon River Review, Rhino, Natural Bridge, The Bellevue Literary Review*, online at *Verse Daily*, and elsewhere. In 2007, Wendy quit her teaching job at Hunter College to be a full-time mom.

**Amy Yelin** is a Boston-based writer and mom with an MFA from Lesley University. Other work has appeared in the Gettysburg Review, the Baltimore Review, on WEKU (an NPR radio station), and in the Boston Globe and Globe Magazine. She also had a notable essay mention for 2006 in the *Best American Essays 2007* anthology.

**Laurie Zupan** has had work published in *Writer's Digest*, Downtownster.com, *Lost and Found*, Plymouth Writers Group, and elsewhere. She earned an MFA in Creative Writing from Antioch University in 2001. Laurie currently writes and teaches in Southern California.

# Acknowledgements

First and foremost, I (Alys) would like to thank my mother Marion Frances Masek. Her grace, creativity and ability to be an amazing mother to eight children while not losing sight of herself are a continual source of inspiration to me. Next I'd like to thank my husband Alan whose quiet strength and wicked, sly sense of humor sustains me day in and day out. What can I say? Barging into your dorm room twenty plus years ago to introduce myself was the smartest thing I've ever done! I'd also like to thank my co-editor and friend Kelly Mayhew and her husband Jim Miller. It is rare indeed to meet such kindred souls and I treasure all my memories of Dead shows, epics walks up and down the hills of San Francisco, and bleary Sundays passing each other parts of the paper. And I must thank my dear friend Beth. I would not be a writer without her and to this day, she is always my first and best editor. And to my posse (you know who you are!) who got me through the difficult years of infertility and who sustained me and cheered me on throughout my pregnancy, you have my everlasting love and gratitude. Lastly, I'd like to thank City Works Press and all the amazing and dedicated individuals who keep it alive for the opportunity to work on a project so near and dear to my heart.

*—Alys Masek*

For a project this personal, the acknowledgements have a range from the structural to the heart (with lots of overlap of course). So I (Kelly) would like to thank a universe of folks who've made the birth of *Mamas and Papas* possible. First off, my co-editor and co-conspirator, Alys Masek, who has been a dream to work with and who has been such an incredible friend through these many years. I can't imagine having a better *companera* to do this project with. Secondly, my deep and abiding regard goes to our crew at City Works

Press: Will Dalrymple, our production editor/guru, Rondi Vasquez, queen of the covers, and Carrie Gordh, editorial triage nurse, literally make our books possible. Thanks also go to the San Diego Writers Collective, which helps fund our books and gives the green light to worthy projects and to Sunbelt Publications, which aids us immeasurably in releasing our books into the universe. On a personal note, my extended family of friends and allies has made my personal, parenting and writing lives possible. I am blessed to have such a loving circle of allies to go to for help, support, sustenance, baby-sitting, a shoulder, a beer, and everything else that makes life worth living. For over twenty years, Jennifer Cost has provided me ballast as well—thank you, dearie! Without the parenting I got from my mom, Bonnie Sawyer, my dad, Donald Mayhew, and my stepmom, Carol Mayhew, I doubt I would have been able to negotiate these waters as I've done. Walt has the added benefit of having incredibly attentive grandparents, who most likely, given my "advanced maternal age," wondered if they'd ever get the opportunity to dote on my progeny as they've been able to. Thanks also to my brother Scott, sister-in-law Deeann, and nephews Miles and Maddox. My mother-in-law, Marion Miller, has been a steady presence in our lives as have my brother-in-laws, John and Scott, sister-in-laws Lynn, Marianne, and Trees, and delicious niece, Sarah. Finally, the person who more than anyone else in my life has influenced and encircled me is my husband and pal, Jim Miller. It was his idea to found City Works Press, his urging that helped me see myself as a writer and scholar, and his good will and partnership that enabled me to become a mother. I can't even say how much his presence in my life has meant. So I won't even try. I don't want to jinx myself.

—*Kelly Mayhew*

# credits

"On Your Birthday" by Malaika King Albrecht was originally published in *Best Poem Journal*.

"Baby Classes" by Sam Apple is an excerpt from *American Parent: My Strange and Surprising Adventures in Modern Babyland*, © 2009 by Sam Apple. Reprinted with permission of the publisher Ballantine Books.

"I Go Back in Time and Rescue My Mother" by Leah Browning was originally published in *Salome Magazine*, 2007.

"The Happy Treatment" by Teri Carter was originally published in *Buzzard Picnic*, an online magazine.

"Sons" by Brandon Cesmat was originally published in *Driven into the Shade* (Poetic Matrix Press, Madera, CA, 2003).

"Extraction" by Susan Cohen originally appeared in the online journal mamazine.com.

"Strapping" by Wanda Coleman was originally published in *Bathwater Wine* on Black Sparrow Press, © 1998 for the author.

" 'Tis Morning Makes Mother a Killer" by Wanda Coleman was originally published in *Imagoes* on Black Sparrow Press, © 1983 for the author.

"Firstborn" by Barbara Crooker was originally published in *Calyx* and in *More* on C&R Press, 2010.

"Birth Mothers" from *Wild One* (Scarlet Tanager Books, 2000) by Lucille Lang Day was originally published in *The Chattahoochee Review*.

"Night and Day" by Juliet Eastland originally appeared on hotmetalpress.net.

"Guns" by W.D. Ehrhart is reprinted from *Beautiful Wreckage: New & Selected Poems* on Adastra Press, 1999, by permission of the author.

"Octopus" by Tom C. Hunley is the title poem of his collection *Octopus* on Logan House Press, 2008.

"Menarche" by Marianne Johnson was originally published in *CALYX, A Journal of Art and Literature by Women*, Vol. 25, no. 3, Winter 2010.

"I Watch You Breathe" by Sylvia Levinson was originally published in *City Works*, 2007, *San Diego Poetry Annual 2006* and was awarded First Place in Poetry by San Diego African-American Writers and Artists, Inc. in 2006.

"Girl" by Sara Lippmann was originally published in *All Things Girl* and anthologized in *View from the Bed: View from the Bedside* on Wising Up Press.

"17" by George Longenecker was originally published in *Sahara: A Journal of New England Poetry*, Winter 2006–07.

"Moloki" by Jim Miller was originally published in *City Works*, 2007.

"Burning Down the House" by Joe Mills is also published in his collection *Love and Other Collisions* on Press 53, 2010.

"Lump" by Julie L. Moore was originally published in *Alaska Quarterly Review*.

"Sonnet of Lost Labor" by John Morgan was originally published in *Spear-Fishing on the Chatanika: New and Selected Poems* on Salmon Poetry.

"Blue" by Daniel Olivas, was originally published in *Anywhere But L.A.* by Daniel Olivas (Bilingual Press/Editorial Bilingüe, Tempe, Arizona, 2009).

"My Son, Five, Dancing" by Joel Peckham has also been published in *Movers and Shakers* (Pudding House Press, 2010) and the *Valpairoso Poetry Review*.

"This is What I've Become: Scenes from the Life of an American Parent" by Neal Pollack was originally published on nealpollack.com, © 2010 Neal Pollack.

"Elations" by Diane Raptosh was originally published in *Best Poem Journal* April, 2008.

"Comforting Jack When He Wakes Coughing and Crying with a Cold" by Charlie Rossiter was originally published in *No I Didn't Steal This Baby I'm the Daddy* on A.P.D. Press, 1995.

"Somewhat Organic" by Catherine Sharpe was originally published on *Errant Parent*, October, 2009.

"Things That Get Lost" by Maureen A. Sherbondy was originally published in *The Independent Weekly*.

"Vision" by Curtis Smith was originally published in *The Bellingham Review*.

"The Mirror" by Jyotsna Sreenivasan was originally published in *Green Hills Literary Lantern*, Missouri.

"Sackcloth and Ashes" by Jim Teeters was originally published in *If I Awake Before I Die*, 2008.

"Love Learned" by Tina Traster was originally published in *Mamazina Magazine*, an online literary journal.

"Miscarriage" is an excerpt from *Letters to Virginia Woolf* by Lisa Williams, reprinted with permission of Hamilton Books, 2005.

"His First Week" by Wendy Wisner was originally published in the online journal *No Tell Motel* (www.notellmotel.org), March, 2010.

# about the editors

## Kelly Mayhew

## Alys Masek

ALYS MASEK is an attorney and poet. Most recently she has been working with Pacific Islanders whose land was severely contaminated as the result of atmospheric nuclear tests conducted in that region by the United States. She has previously published in the *Noe Valley Review, City Works* and *Hunger and Thirst*. She lives in San Diego, California with her husband and daughter. When not working, she spends her time running after her daughter and dreaming of a good night's sleep.

KELLY MAYHEW is co-author with Jim Miller of *Better to Reign in Hell: Inside the Raiders Fan Empire* (The New Press, 2005) and co-author with Jim Miller and Mike Davis of *Under the Perfect Sun: The San Diego Tourists Never See* (The New Press, 2003). She has also had work published in *Fiction International, American Book Review, Rattle,* the *San Diego Union-Tribune, A Community of Readers,* and elsewhere. Kelly is a founding member of San Diego City Works Press, for which she serves as Managing Editor. Currently, she is a Professor of English at San Diego City College. She lives in downtown San Diego with her husband and son.